Teaching
Literary Theory
Using Film Adaptations

KATHLEEN L. BROWN

Foreword by Peter Lev

McFarland & Company, Inc., Publishers
Jefferson, North Carolina, and London

LIBRARY OF CONGRESS CATALOGUING-IN-PUBLICATION DATA

Brown, Kathleen L., 1947–
    Teaching literary theory using film adaptations / Kathleen
L. Brown ; foreword by Peter Lev.
      p.   cm.
    Includes bibliographical references and index.

    ISBN 978-0-7864-3933-1
    softcover : 50# alkaline paper ∞

    1. Film adaptations — History and criticism.   2. Motion pictures
and literature.   3. Literature — History and criticism — Theory, etc.
I. Title.
PN1997.85B76   2009
801'.95 — dc22   2009000160

British Library cataloguing data are available

Cover photograph: Warren Beatty and Natalie Wood in *Splendor in
the Grass*, 1961 (Warner Bros./Photofest).

Manufactured in the United States of America

McFarland & Company, Inc., Publishers
  Box 611, Jefferson, North Carolina 28640
  www.mcfarlandpub.com

Table of Contents

With thanks to my colleagues
at Stevenson University and
to Alma, Linda, Doug,
and especially Tom

Foreword
by Peter Lev

Writers, filmmakers, critics, and scholars have had a long conversation about the merits, purposes, and qualities of films adapted from works written for other media. Around 1950, the majority opinion was that film was interesting insofar as it was different from other art forms, and therefore a writer-director-producer-performer such as Charlie Chaplin was admired for his specifically cinematic creativity. A few years later the *auteur* theory, championed by the French critic (and soon to be director) François Truffaut, proposed two somewhat contradictory ideas about cinema's uniqueness: first, that adaptations emphasizing the contributions of screenwriters were a bad idea; and second, that it didn't matter where the story came from if a strong director was on hand to make a film unique through the wonders of *mise-en-scène.* Cinematic specificity received an interesting twist in the 1960s from American experimental filmmakers such as Stan Brakhage and Paul Sharits, who thought that physical qualities of the medium — e.g., the grain of the film, or the flicker of light — could be central to motion picture creativity.

Despite this thirst for the specific and unique, most feature films are adapted from other media, primarily novels and plays. Critics and scholars have analyzed and theorized about this work, struggling at times with a double sense of inferiority — for an adaptation is not cinematically specific, nor is it an original work of literature. Many of the scholars who wrote about adaptation came from literature departments, and their strongest allegiance was to the literary canon. Thus began the doctrine of fidelity, which declares that adaptations are good to the extent that they are "faithful" to the original work. This sets an impossible standard (if you want fidelity, read the original), but in practice fidelity critics have been surprisingly flexible — they look for what the film does to present or interpret the original work, and many fidelity critics write intelligently about filmic additions and omissions. Still, the term "fidelity" is badly chosen; David Kranz proposes "comparative" criticism as a useful alternative (85).

The great critic André Bazin, Truffaut's mentor, had a different approach to adaptation study: he didn't care if films were "pure" (cinematically specific) or "impure" or "mixed." Although Bazin did at times write about fidelity to a book or play, his main interest was exploring the many possibilities of cinematic expression. One extraordinary potential of cinema was the ability to rework a story or subject from another medium; this could be done in any number of creative ways, so there was no point in narrowly defining correct and incorrect methods of adaptation. Bazin loved literature and theater as well, and so one focus of his criticism — he was a critic more than a theorist — was to show how a brilliant literary idea or trope could be translated and transformed by the film medium (53–153). This kind of thinking is actually quite traditional; it is the equivalent of studying how Shakespeare used his sources.

What has changed in adaptation study since Bazin was defending mixed cinema almost sixty years ago? Well, for decades this area was rather quiet, although *Literature/Film Quarterly*, edited for many years by James M. Welsh, provided a forum for adaptation scholars, and notable books were written by George Bluestone, Joy Gould Boyum, and Bruce Kawin, to cite only a few examples. Then, within the last ten years, the field has exploded. Australian scholar Brian McFarlane anticipated the current period with *Novel to Film: An Introduction to the Theory of Adaptation* (1996). More recently, James Naremore, Robert Stam, Alessandra Raengo, Thomas Leitch, Sarah Cardwell, James M. Welsh, John Tibbetts, Deborah Cartmell, Imelda Whelehan, and Linda Cahir have written or edited works of substance, and my list is by no means complete. New journals have appeared to challenge the still-essential *Literature/Film Quarterly*; one of them is simply called *Adaptation*. Two studies of the screenwriter's role in adaptation, a much-neglected area, were published in 2008: *The Screenplay in America* by Kevin Alexander Boon and an anthology, *Authorship in Film Adaptation*, edited by Jack Boozer. It seems that the hybridity of film adaptations and the hybridity of adaptation scholars (whose work does not fit neatly into an academic discipline) are no longer disadvantages, as the current climate favors an exploration of what happens between disciplines. Indeed, adaptation study is on the way to becoming Adaptation Studies, a formally named discipline (or at least subdiscipline) in its own right. The prospect is encouraging but also scary, for most of us don't want to see the birth of an Adaptation Studies orthodoxy.

Kathleen Brown's contribution to the growth of adaptation study lies first of all in her emphasis on pedagogy. Thousands of instructors teach film adaptations of literature at various levels — university, high school, and perhaps younger grades — and their numbers seem to be expanding. For example, film adaptation is now part of the curriculum in many university foreign language departments, in both the United States and the United Kingdom. Yet there are few resources designed for adaptation teachers — instead, almost all of the field's energy goes to scholarly books, articles and conference papers. Occasionally a textbook is published, for example Linda Cahir's *Literature into Film: Theory and Practical Approaches* (2006). Kathleen Brown's book is not exactly a textbook; it is a discussion and demonstration of how one might teach film adaptations of literature, drama, and poetry. She presents adaptation study as a way to revitalize the teaching of literature. With a notable work of fiction, for example Kate Chopin's *The Awakening*, plus two film adaptations and a scholarly article or two, she demonstrates how much insight and depth adaptation study can generate. Not limited by incremental lesson plans, she gives *The Awakening* its due with a long and excellent chapter.

Pedagogy is certainly a neglected and justified subject within adaptation study, and yet I am tempted to see Kathleen's focus on her fellow teachers as part of a more complex rhetorical strategy. Address to one's colleagues means that a level of education and competence can be assumed, so a pedagogical study can go faster and further than a standard university textbook. But the readers of Kathleen's pedagogy will not be graduate school-trained experts in adaptation, and so clarity is essential throughout. An unwritten maxim of this book might be "If a theory is useful and important, you should be able to explain it to a colleague." Kathleen Brown meets that standard beautifully; she is even able to bring clarity and simplicity to the ideas of Jacques Lacan, a master of the abstruse. This book also pursues clarity and simplicity in its second section, which analyzes the many metaphors attached to literary and adaptation theory. By limiting theorists to their metaphors, Kathleen is able to concisely and sometimes amusingly survey the landscape of theory.

Another part of the book's rhetoric is that though it addresses colleagues it could work perfectly well as a college text, and students might appreciate a behind-the-scenes glimpse at what their teacher is thinking. Also, a colleague-to-colleague discourse might push students to work harder and achieve more, especially since the author has been so careful to stress clarity. This book does not cover a great deal of ground, but why should it? If, in the course of a semester, a student can delve into the psychological dimensions of *The Awakening* and the dynamics of social power in *A Streetcar Named Desire* and the poetic meditation of Wordsworth's "Ode: Intimations of Immortality from Recollections of Early Childhood" as a source for the film *Splendor in the Grass*, then the semester has been well-spent.

British scholar Sarah Cardwell has perceptively focused on the "purposes" or "aims" of adaptation study as a way of understanding the field (2002, 3; 2007, 59–60). Cardwell proposes that critical and scholarly work on adaptation should and will vary widely according to what the critic is trying to achieve. Then she carves out a rather shocking purpose for herself by suggesting that British miniseries based on "Heritage" novels — e.g., *Brideshead Revisited* and *Pride and Prejudice*— can be analyzed as a televisual genre rather than as interpretations or popularizations of the novels (2002, 105–106). Kathleen Brown's purposes in analyzing literature and film are, at least on the surface, more conservative: she wants to add to the tools available for classroom literary study and thereby to passionately involve students in the analysis of literature. She tells us that "the teacher must begin where the student is," though she is not considering a study of video games or instant messaging. "Where the student is" becomes an extended study of film adaptation but with the explicit aim of helping students to understand and appreciate literature.

Yet there is more to the study of film adaptation than this, even within a very traditional English curriculum. The added value is suggested by Thomas Leitch's discussion of a "writerly" rather than "readerly" approach to culture (12–13); the terms come originally from Roland Barthes. When we teach, write, study, read, and view, we are rewriting cultural history, in however modest a way. When we introduce films into the English or History or Modern Languages curriculum, we are changing the intertextual grid of what an educated person should know. The interplay of influence between literature and film can be analyzed via the term "palimpsest," a delightful word that Kathleen Brown discusses in her section on theory and metaphor. An adaptation rewrites its literary source, sometimes extensively, while leaving a trace of the original. Some viewers may see only the surface layer of the parchment, whereas others will have the education and habits of mind to find one or more layers underneath. Another useful metaphor would be "ghost" or "ghost image." The source text would be integrally connected to the adaptation but would be visible only to some viewers at some times.

But what if the palimpsestic order could be reversed and if the adaptation were haunting its source as well as being haunted by it? An example from the New York stage suggests that this is a reasonable description of how source and adaptation intertwine. In the fall of 2007 a Wooster Group production of *Hamlet* presented a live performance of the play in front of a screen projecting Richard Burton's 1964 film version of *Hamlet*. According to the *New York Times* review, the 2007 live performance tried to mimic the Burton film — itself based on a Broadway stage production — in sets, costumes, and acting, but the film image appeared and disappeared, perhaps indicating the difficulty of drawing inspiration from the earlier version (Brantley). The film performance became part, albeit a ghostly part, of a current interpretation of Shakespeare's play. The palimpsest had three layers, but the order was open to question: was Shakespeare the ghost behind both performances, or were the performances ghosts of Shakespeare's text? Was the Wooster Group's version a mere shadow of Burton's *Hamlet*, or vice versa? The answer, clearly, is "all of the above." So, not only does Wordsworth's "Ode" haunt *Splendor in the Grass*, as Kathleen Brown demonstrates, but the film's creators — William Inge, Elia Kazan, Natalie Wood, Warren Beatty, et al. — are also haunting Wordsworth. Kathleen's students discover Wordsworth via their affection for the film, and we can assume that the poem-film relationship sticks in their minds. Therefore, it seems that the study of adaptation enhances literary analysis but also leads to a new, cross-media form of cultural knowledge. As teachers and writers, we cannot reach back to an essentialist understanding of Shakespeare or Wordsworth or Kate Chopin. We must strive to understand these authors within the intertextual and critical/theoretical resources of today.

Peter Lev is professor of electronic media and film at Towson University in Maryland. He is the author, editor or co-editor of five books of film history and criticism, most recently *The Literature/Film Reader: Issues of Adaptation* (2007), co-edited with James M. Welsh, and *The Fifties: Transforming the Screen, 1950–1959*, volume seven of the *History of the American Cinema* series (2003).

Preface

My interest in film studies began when I learned that my grandmother, grandfather, and great aunt had all worked in the Baltimore silent movie theaters before World War I. My grandmother read the subtitles, her sister played the piano, and my grandfather painted the sidewalk placards. At about the time that my grandmother told me the story of her early life, I was allowed to walk to the neighborhood theater, which was the large, deco-style Senator built in 1939, still in operation today and whose picture graces the cover of Robert Headley's *Motion Picture Exhibition in Baltimore*. I fell in love with the experience of going there, usually alone, and happily spent my babysitting income on the admission fee of a quarter, with a bit of money left over for candy.

Years passed, and in college I took several film courses offered by the Art Department at Towson University and worked for a summer on a crew (I was in charge of continuity), but mainly my time was committed to the English Department. Even though my time was not equally spent between English and Art, it was while I was an undergraduate that the work of these two departments merged, and I became enchanted with film adaptations.

Part I focuses on what I discovered when I began to teach: that certain adaptations could, in fact, function much like critical essays and, further, that they were not only interpretations in their own right but could also be paired with essays that took a similar, or even identical, stance toward the primary source. Although nearly all of the film critics speak of adaptations as interpretations, there is no instance of the kind of pairing that Part I relies upon — a twinning, as it were, that is fairly easy to construct with a bit of ingenuity and with more than a superficial knowledge of the primary source, its major critics, and its existing film adaptations. By looking at the critical essays in light of the films, students can see the same ideas expressed through two different media and thus, through the delight that the film affords, become more comfortable with the written text, indeed finding in it too a delightful expression of what might otherwise have been a murky, distressing reading assignment.

Part II casts a wider net, moving away from specific critical schools and specific films and focusing instead on the rhetorical technique of classification. Although many studies speak of adaptations in similar terms (they closely follow the primary source or diverge from it in different ways and to different extents) there has heretofore been no attempt to use imagery as a way to categorize them. Because, as Victor Shklovsky emphasizes, imagery is "a practical means of thinking, ... a means of placing objects within categories" (23), it can help us to not only make sense of adaptation theories but also connect them to the "parent" literary theories that inform and inspire them.

It is my hope that other teachers and even some students might use this book as a guide to a new way of studying literature, theory, and film and then explore for themselves the intertextual webs that suit their own courses and their own interests.

Introduction

> Yet this only is reading, in a high sense, not that which lulls us as
> a luxury and suffers the nobler faculties to sleep the while, but what
> we have to stand on tiptoe to read and devote our most alert and
> wakeful hours to. — "Reading," *Walden*

This study arises from the English teacher's perennial desire to help students become more willing and better readers, to inspire them to read "on tiptoe." Although occasionally a few latter-day Thoreaus may come one's way — those who keep a rich and challenging book by their bedsides — the general rule seems to be quite different. As Sandra Gilbert and Susan Gubar observe, "What was once a powerful culture of print seems to be disintegrating as one-time readers — including most of our students (and even many of our colleagues) — increasingly put aside their books and turn on their TVs, VCRs, CDs, and PCs" (xxii). Even this assessment seems too optimistic: most of my students have never been "one-time readers" in any serious sense. They do read school assignments, some best-sellers (usually romances or thrillers), or informational texts connected to particular hobbies or interests. But by and large, they experience "stories" through film and television, through role-playing games like *Dungeons & Dragons*, as well as through numerous video games, some of which bear a relationship to film. As Janet Murray points out, "[S]ome game designers are making good use of film techniques in enhancing the dramatic power of their games. For instance, the CD-ROM game *Myst* (1993) achieves most of its immersive power through its sophisticated sound design" (53). She notes that *Doom* is played "from a situated first-person viewpoint ... where we see the landscape of the game and our opponents coming toward us as if we are really present in space. These gaming conventions orient the interactor and make the action coherent. They are equivalent to a novelist's care with point of view or a director's attention to staging" (145–46). Five years after Murray's work, the 2002 *ScreenPlay: cinema / videogames / interfaces* asks important questions:

9

But what happens in the interface between cinema and video games? Is there a merging of languages as games influence movies and movies influence games? *ScreenPlay* explores the extent to which the tools of film analysis can be applied to games, in particular, [and] how the pleasures (and frustrations) of computer games can be compared with those of cinema [*Film Studies* 6].

What have come to be called "postmodern hypertext" novels can also be related to film and to adaptations. For instance, *Patchwork Girl*, by Shelley Jackson, is an interactive adaptation of *Frankenstein*, written by "Mary/Shelley & herself." Christiane Paul's *Unreal City* is "a hypertext guide to T.S. Eliot's *The Waste Land.*" Linda Hutcheon expands her definition of adaptation to include "theme park rides, Web sites, graphic novels, song covers, operas, musicals, ballets, and radio and stage plays" (xiv). Song covers is a particularly interesting topic since music plays a large part in our students' lives. Leonard Cohen's "Who By Fire," released in 1974, is believed to be an adaptation of an eleventh-century poem by Kelonymus ben Mechullam, several lines of which read "Who shall perish by fire and who by water / Who by sword and who by beast / Who by hunger and who by thirst / Who by strangling and who by stoning" ("Origin"). Cohen's song has been covered by Coil, a band with which many of today's students are familiar. A classic adaptation occurred when "Ball and Chain" was turned over to Janis Joplin by Big Mama Thornton. Thornton's "Hound Dog" was covered by Elvis Presley (strangely so, since its words clearly point to a woman singing to a man, a "dog.") Nonetheless, Elvis's rendition was immensely popular and brought black music into the mainstream. This cover had an additional life in that Alice Walker wrote "Nineteen Fifty-Five," a story about the relationship between a black composer and a white boy who made good. If the story were made into a film, the cycle would be complete. But all this aside, it is mostly the video games that are the media with which these students grew up and through which they receive, in Gerald Mast's words, their "primary cultural pleasure" (279). Little wonder that they become impatient with the serious literature they are asked to read in college, especially when the language is too difficult or the book too long. Further problems arise when they are required to write about such literature and incorporate secondary sources into their papers. Although the Internet and such tools as the MLA Bibliography on CD-ROM now make locating criticism a relatively painless procedure, students often become confused and beleaguered when it comes to comprehending what they have retrieved.

Perhaps the only indisputable premise of the art of teaching is that the teacher must begin where the student is. The accessibility of current technology in even the most old-fashioned of classrooms makes it possible for teachers to meet students on familiar terrain and to easily use film and television adaptations of literary texts to help them not only to become more deeply engaged with the literature itself but also to cope with secondary sources — analyses written by their classmates, by students and faculty members at other institutions who have established Web sites, and, most especially, by the traditionally published critics, still the pillars of the research paper.

Joseph Moxley concludes that some students "avoid writing (and literature) courses because they perceive English and writing to be an esoteric discipline, an artistic (or even magical) activity depending solely on divine inspiration" (qtd. in Bizzaro 16). This avoidance is magnified when a literary research paper is required. Similarly, Joy Boyum identifies an attitude towards what she perceives as the "authority of literature," an attitude, however, that does not arise when the text is a movie: "Joyce and Dostoyevsky, Lawrence and Virginia Woolf, intimidate us: we may even tremble before them, assured that there is something we are supposed to get from their work, some implicit set of meanings, some carefully predetermined understandings. Not so in the case of movies" (47–48). Connecting "early views about the mission of adaptation"— to deliver classic stories to the masses — with what she sees today, Boyum wonders if we have "come full circle ... only now, not with the great unwashed mass as target audience, but with just about everyone" (77). This interesting prophecy is chilling if one allows oneself to speculate that the movie-house "readers" of old, those who, like my grandmother, stood on the side of the stage (at the back of which hung the screen) and to serve those in the audience who were illiterate, read the titles or other words (on maps, signs, documents, etc.) that appeared as part of the *mise-en-scène*. This old-time practice might experience a renaissance, albeit in a different context, if Sven Birkerts is right in predicting that we have reached a "critical mass." For example, even if we still subscribe to and read newspapers, we also listen to the news being read on television. And too many of us have given up our subscriptions altogether:

> Over the past few decades, in the blink of the eye of history, our culture has begun to go through what promises to be a total metamorphosis. The influx of electronic communications and information processing technologies, abetted by the steady improvement of the microprocessor, has rapidly brought on a condition of critical mass. Suddenly it feels like everything is poised for change; the slower world that many of us grew up with dwindles in the rearview mirror [Birkerts 3].

The fact is that many students can be intimidated by their reading and writing assignments. At the heart of this intimidation is often the seemingly inaccessible primary source. However, when this text is presented as part of an intertextual web that includes its film adaptations and when students can begin to compare and contrast what they have read with what they have seen and heard, classroom frustration does markedly dissipate. Further, the rhythm of comparison, the mental swing back and forth from one medium to the other, embodies Geoffrey Hartman's definition of reading: "the methodical willingness to scrutinize texts again and again, for their open as well as resistant character" ("Fate" 385), a "conceptual flipping back and forth" (Hutcheon 139).

At the most simple level, students watching an adaptation unwittingly and automatically mimic George Bluestone's methods in his 1957 *Novels into Film: The Metamorphosis of Fiction into Cinema*, the first book to propose a theory of adaptation, when they "assess the key additions, deletions, and alterations revealed in the film." With some prompting, they can go further to "center on certain significant implications which [seem] to follow from the remnants of, and deviations from, the novel" (x). Because film "allows us a greater critical freedom and personalization of response" than literature (Boyum 48), even the most reticent students are likely to join this kind of classroom exploration.

However, because a good adaptation is one which has interpreted the literature on which it is based and thus functions, in Neil Sinyard's words, as "an activity of literary criticism" (117), it has the potential to teach more than this. Although what Boyum has to say about film adaptation largely rings true, her assessment that "a reading of a literary work embedded in a film will ... be of a different order entirely than one contained in a critical essay and will certainly be less complete" (73) shortchanges the more fundamental similarity: both screenwriter and literary essayist perceive the primary source through a critical lens. This close connection between source, critical essay, and adaptation is illustrated by Horton Foote's anecdote:

> I remember after agreeing to dramatize *To Kill a Mockingbird* feeling very depressed. I read it over and over searching for a way to begin my share of the work. Then I happened to read a review by R. P. Blackmuir called, I believe, "Scout in the Wilderness," comparing the book in a very imaginative and profound way to *Huckleberry Finn*, a great favorite of mine, and suddenly I began to feel at home in the material [7].

It would be over-generalizing, however, to suggest that all adaptations are interpretations. Sinyard maintains that only "the best adaptations of books for film can ... be approached as an activity of literary criticism" (117). Adaptations that do not take a stance towards their material — much like expository essays that do not have a thesis — are not very thought-provoking. We instinctively judge them as being slight.

Because good adaptations are themselves interpretations, they can be used to demystify written criticism and theory. The same students who find themselves at a loss for words when faced with, for example, Cynthia Griffin

Wolff's "Thanatos and Eros: Kate Chopin's *The Awakening*" become more articulate when they are shown *Grand Isle*, the most recent adaptation of *The Awakening* and the one which employs the same sort of critical apparatus as does this essay. The same students who at first actually do "tremble" at what they perceive as Wolff's sophisticated and foreign ideas and organizational strategies can more confidently return to the essay after the film has broken the ground that the written interpretation covers.

In his foreword to *The Johns Hopkins Guide to Literary Theory and Criticism*, Richard Macksey succinctly identifies two relationships: one between theory and the world, the other between theory and interpretation. "[L]iterary theory always bears the impress of larger political and cultural debates but also aspires, from Aristotle to Hans-Georg Gadamer or Jacques Derrida, toward a systematic statement of the principles and methods governing interpretation and evaluation" (v.) In terms of the relationship between theory and interpretation, when students know something about what "governs" what they are reading, they have a better chance of comprehending and working with critical essays in more sophisticated ways than merely excising direct quotes from this one or that, without having understood the whole, and then splicing these quotes inappropriately into their own work. In terms of theory and the world, it might be argued that not only do these "larger ... debates" shape academic discourse, but also that, in turn, "academic discourse informs public discourse," for example, when political commentators "brand" Bill Clinton "the postmodern president" (Limsky 1F). David H. Hirsch's identification of "the problem of how to continue professing humanist literary criticism in a post–Auschwitz world and in a culture increasingly dominated by technology and antihumanist ideologies" (150) perfectly illustrates Barbara Christian's assertions that "the division between 'the real world' and the world of the academy is not really there" and that "there is not only the text, but ... a context out of which this text is arising" (248). A sensible teaching strategy, then, would be to build fewer primary texts and more of their surrounding contexts into the syllabus. Citing Roland Barthes' *S/Z*, Robert B. Ray points out that the ideology of popular narratives is intertextual. In Barthes's words, "There is no lack of hosts" for such ideology (qtd. in Ray 41). When the lone literary text is situated in an intertextuality of interpretation and theory, it becomes more approachable by being more connected to the "real world" issues of today and yesterday.

This is not to say, however, that undergraduates should be required to read the more abstruse primary sources of literary theory. As Christian laments, such writing is often "problematic":

> I think there are a lot of new and important insights that have come from
> "the new contemporary theory." But the way in which it is written, I think,

indicates something about it that is problematic, and it has a great deal to do with a kind of puritanism, which may be because so much of it is French, but that may be my own bias! But, in other words, it doesn't have a kind of sensuality, and so I think it is very hard to play with it in the classroom [246].

This kind of writing made the news when *Philosophy and Literature* presented its 1998 award for obscurity to Judith Butler, a professor at the University of California, Berkeley, for the following sentence:

The move from a structuralist account in which capital is understood to structure social relations in relatively homologous ways to a view of hegemony in which power relations are subject to repetition, convergence, and rearticulation brought the question of temporality into the thinking of structure, and marked a shift from a form of Althusserian theory that takes structural totalities as theoretical objects to one in which the insights into the contingent possibility of structure inaugurate a renewed conception of hegemony as bound up with the contingent sites and strategies of the rearticulation of power [qtd. in Skube 6C].

Indeed, there is not much that can be said to defend such a sentence, and though this is an extreme example, it certainly is not an isolated one. Focusing on applied rather than on "pure" theory in the undergraduate classroom is one way to reduce the possibility that students will encounter such overblown, even nonsensical, jargon. The St. Martin's Press Case Studies in Contemporary Criticism series, where students are given a summary of the major concepts of the theory under consideration and a critical essay that draws upon these concepts, models just such an approach as does Lois Tyson's *Critical Theory Today: A User-Friendly Guide*, which summarizes theories and then applies them to *The Great Gatsby* in clear and comprehensible essays.

Although it may seem daunting, as Hazard Adams notes, that "never in the history of criticism has there been such a plethora of competing jargons and systems, to say nothing of antisystems" (1), it is precisely this competition, this "contested conceptual space," as John Kucich calls it, that gives the discussion of theory its appeal. Kucich goes on to observe that "contrary to [his] apprehensions, students' engagement with theory depends largely on their being able to see it as an arena of conflict" (47). The livelier participation that results from watching two or more very different adaptations of the same text vie for position in this "contested conceptual space" attests to the truth of his observation.

Given that our students have grown up exposed to a "daily surfeit of words and images" (Hartman, "Fate" 385), it is worthwhile to remind ourselves that "engaging students' imaginations requires an interdisciplinary approach" (Moxley, qtd. in Bizzaro xix), and this interdisciplinary approach could — and probably should — include film.

Several considerations guided the selection of literary texts, critical perspectives, and films that serve as examples in Part I of this study. Because the goal is to improve teaching in a literature class, it seems logical to include not only a novel but also a play and a poem — the so-called broad genres — and to choose ones that are frequently taught in such courses, from introductory to upper levels. Each work could now be described as canonical, although it is only in the last thirty years that *The Awakening* has been reclassified and redeemed from its apocryphal status. *A Streetcar Named Desire* managed to find its own academic niche almost immediately, as it enjoyed success on the popular stage even before it was filmed. And when we turn to Wordsworth's "Ode: Intimations of Immortality," we need only quote Hartman — "I have never been able to get away from Wordsworth for any length of time" (*Unremarkable* xxv).

The adaptations of these works illustrate major theoretical perspectives that inform the kinds of essays that students are likely to find in their library research and whose strategies they might eventually make their own. In each case, the film can be closely related to a critical essay whose argument is grounded, primarily, in the theory under consideration: *The End of August* and *Grand Isle* and psychoanalytic criticism, *A Streetcar Named Desire* and Michel Foucault's cultural criticism, and *Splendor in the Grass* and thematic criticism.

Some adaptation theorists deal with the problem of fidelity by proposing categories based on how closely the film follows its source. In 1975 Geoffrey Wagner, the first to categorize adaptations (but, like Bluestone, limiting his theorizing to novels), establishes three general "modes": the *transposition* (where "a novel is given directly on the screen with a minimum of apparent interference"), the *commentary* (where "an original is taken and either purposely or inadvertently altered in some respect ... when there has been a different intention on the part of the film-maker, rather than infidelity or outright violation"), and the *analogy* (where the film "represent[s] a fairly considerable departure for the sake of making another work of art") (222–27).

In 1993, David Bordwell and Kristin Thompson offer four categories: *referential* (a reference "to things or places already invested with significance"), *explicit* (references "defined by context"), *implicit* (meanings which arise from interpretation), and *symptomatic* ("a manifestation of a wider set of values characteristic of a whole society") (49–52). These concepts are, of course, also applicable to literature. The adaptor reads the text, draws conclusions, and presents, in film form, what he "attributes to the work" (49). In turn, the viewer "reads" the adaptation. Bordwell and Thompson conclude their discussion in reader-response terms: "films 'have' meaning only because we attribute meanings to them. We cannot therefore regard meaning as a simple product to be extracted from the film" (52).

In 2006, John Desmond and Peter Hawkes propose three categories: *close adaptation* ("when most of the narrative elements in the literary text are kept in the film, few elements are dropped, and not many elements are added"), *loose adaptation* (which "uses the literary text as a point of departure"), and *intermediate adaptation* ("when it is in the fluid middle of the sliding scale between *close* and *loose*") (44).

In 2006, Linda Costanzo Cahir also suggests three types of adaptation: *literal translation* ("which reproduces the plot and all its attending details as closely as possible to the letter of the book"), *traditional translation* (which "maintains the overall traits of the book [its plot, settings, and stylistic conventions] but revamps particular details in those particular ways that the filmmakers see as necessary and fitting"), and *radical translation* ("which reshapes the book in extreme and revolutionary ways both as a means of interpreting the literature and of making the film a more fully independent work") (16–17).

Paul Wells even identifies types of animation (including puppetry) and applies them to three versions of *A Midsummer Night's Dream*: "*orthodox* (predominantly industrial 2-D cel animation), *developmental* (2-D and 3-D forms creatively engaging with a range of stylistic and narrational conventions) and *experimental* (principally non-objective, non-linear, avant-garde work)" (Cartmell and Whelehan, *Adaptations* 202). John Canemaker's film *Bottom's Dream* (1983) is the most *experimental*, for it "merely takes two lines from the play as a point of stimulus ["I have had a most rare vision" and "Man is but an ass if he go about to expound this dream"], but nevertheless seeks to encompass the spirit of the whole text" (211). Jiří Trnka's "full-length puppet animation" is *developmental*. Here, "Trnka's fluid and highly mannered puppet movement is located in an impossibly romantic landscape, hauntingly evocative, often using soft-focus photography to mystify and render uncertain the transposition of fairy figures upon rustic spaces" (211). Finally, "Robert Saakiants' version of the play for the S4C / Soyuzmultfilm 'Shakespeare Project' ... works in a much more *orthodox* mode of animation in that it is much more bound up with the overt act of storytelling rather than suggestion" (212), thus being an example of what Desmond and Hawkes call *close adaptation*. And it is Desmond and Hawkes who offer the most interesting and timely example of this type:

> For example, *Harry Potter and the Sorcerer's Stone* (2001), directed by Chris Columbus, is a close adaptation partly because J. K. Rowling, the best-selling author of the Harry Potter series, knew that she had a loyal readership and so in selling the film rights, she stipulated that the film stay close to the Potter text, even insisting on her approval of the director and actors [44].

Commenting on the efforts of Wagner to establish categories and of those who followed him in this task, Brian McFarlane (also limiting the scope of his book to novels) acknowledges the importance of "evaluating the film version of a novel to try to assess the *kind* of adaptation the film aims to be. Such an assessment would at least preclude the critical reflex that takes a film to task for not being something it does not aim to be" and would minimize the risk of implying "the primacy of the printed text" by judging an adaptation solely on the basis of its fidelity to its source (22). Using Wagner's and Desmond and Hawkes's categories with the caveat that there will always be a certain amount of overlap among them, we might classify both *Grand Isle* and *The End of August* as *transpositions* or *close* adaptations of *The Awakening*, the 1951 film version of *A Streetcar Named Desire* as a *commentary* or *intermediate* adaptation, and *Splendor in the Grass* as an *analogy* or *loose* adaptation.

Boyum reminds us that the precedent for a categorization like Wagner's already exists in literary theory — "in particular, in a seventeenth-century treatise by John Dryden, proposing that all translations fall into one of three different categories": *metaphrase*, "or turning an author word by word and line by line, from one language to another"; *paraphrase*, "or translation with latitude"; and *imitation*, "where the translator ... assumes the liberty not only to vary from the words and sense, but to forsake them both as he sees occasion" and take "only some general hints from the original" (69). Thus the work of an adaptor is much like the work of a translator. Both "demonstrate some sort of allegiance to a previously existing work of art" and both "create a new work of art in [their] own particular language[s]." Most important to Boyum, however, is the fact that both are readers. Her background in reader-response theory is obvious, especially since she was both "student and colleague" of Louise M. Rosenblatt (xi). She insists that "an adaptation always includes not only a reference to a literary work on which it is based, but also a reading of it — and a reading which will either strike us as persuasive and apt or seem to us reductive, even false" (70–71).

In a more specialized course that could, for example, be devoted entirely to adaptations, the teacher might also want to incorporate the screenplay into its intertextuality, perhaps not for each film but for one or two that present interesting problems. For example, William Horne argues that whereas Harold Pinter's screenplay of *The Pumpkin Eater* takes the protagonist's mental breakdown seriously, seeing it as a result of a "male conspiracy," Jack Clayton's film reduces "Pinter's acerbic vision" to the level of a soap opera, portraying Jo as just another "silly woman" ("*The Pumpkin Eater*"). Elsewhere Horne insists that "it is crucially important that the screenplay be viewed not only as a shooting script but as an independent *text*" ("See Shooting Script" 53). Similarly, for Hutcheon, the screenplay has a "double semiotic itinerary." It is both a text in itself and an "allusion to another art work yet to be realized" (23). Moreover, Marilyn Hoder-Salmon, concentrating her work on *The Awaken-*

ing, proposes "taking adaptation studies one step further by creating an original screenplay for interpretive purposes" (12). Thomas Leitch notes that Hoder-Salmon's methodology "is readily adapted to the classroom by getting students to write their own adaptations of specific scenes in the novel, turning them from readers looking up to Chopin into writers meeting her on their own ground and on her own level" (18). However, because there is little enough time in the literature class to read the primary source, show the film, review the theory in question, and study at least one representative critical essay, reading and writing screenplays are not included in the discussions here.

One more consideration, this one entirely practical, is the availability of the video cassette or DVD. *Grand Isle*, the 1951 version of *A Streetcar Named Desire*, and *Splendor in the Grass* are "in print" and are affordable. Copies of *The End of August*, though technically "out of print," are occasionally available on eBay.

The survey of adaptation theory presented in Part II is designed for the teacher who is unfamiliar with the state of research in this field. Again, time constraints will most likely preclude a discussion of adaptation theory *per se* in a literature class, but a certain amount of background in the subject will help teachers think more deeply about what they are preparing. For this reason (and because such theory should be explicitly incorporated into courses devoted entirely to film adaptation), Part II of this study deals with adaptations in general by grouping them through image patterns. The past forty years have seen the publication of an array of book-length as well as shorter studies, all of which try to define the peculiar relationship between written text and adaptation. One happy consequence of this attempt in the 1990s is that scholars like Millicent Marcus turn hard-to-read literary theory into a kind of scaffolding for their ideas and in the process make such theory clear. Both parts I and II, then, show how literary theory can enter the classroom: Part I through specific films and critical theories, Part II through what Christopher Orr calls "the discourse of adaptation."

In whatever classroom context an adaptation is used, the teacher should not be put off by the basic, inescapable, and much-written-about difference between the two media — the literary essay belonging to the purely symbolic world of words, the film belonging to the indexical and iconic world of simultaneously perceived images and sounds. This difference is not necessarily a stumbling block but is, rather, an opportunity to introduce both semiotics — through the "parallels and disparities between the two different signifying systems" (McFarlane 6) — and rhetoric — through not only a particular adaptation's attempt, like a critical essay's, to observe, as Aristotle posits, "in any given case the available means of persuasion" but also through one of the "common topics," comparison of similar elements, in this case descriptions of adaptations in general that fall into similar image patterns. Finally, it should be made explicit that not only semiotics and rhetoric but three other theoretical perspectives underlie this entire study. Reader-response theory prizes the idea that students will become conscious of how their own "repertoire[s] for organizing the world and its events" (Fish 529) shape them as readers. Formalism or New Criticism promotes the recursive nature of scrutinizing the specificities of two media, the art of what Hartman calls "slow reading" ("Fate" 386). As Hutcheon puts it, "Adaptation *as adaptation* involves, for its knowing audience, an interpretive doubling ... between the work we know and the work we are experiencing" (139). The third theory is deconstruction, as Derrida's "joyous affirmation of the play of the world" (93) enters the classroom. In this milieu, students can comfortably explore these intertextual webs and intellectually "stand on tiptoe" because it feels good, because it's fun. Teachers, those "perpetual undergraduates on the other side of the lectern," as Norman Holland calls us (336), know that the more serious benefits of stretching taller will naturally follow.

PART I. TEACHING LITERARY THEORY: PAIRING LITERARY CRITICISM WITH FILM ADAPTATIONS

1. Psychoanalytic Criticism

The Awakening by Kate Chopin

The End of August (1982) and *Grand Isle* (1992)

> "Woman, my dear friend, is a very peculiar and delicate organism —
> a sensitive and highly organized woman, such as I know Mrs.
> Pontellier to be, is especially peculiar. It would require an inspired
> psychologist to deal successfully with them. And when ordinary
> fellows like you and me attempt to cope with their idiosyncrasies
> the result is bungling." — Chopin 86; ch. XXII

Doctor Mandelet's words are meant to reassure Léonce that his wife's erratic behavior is innocuous, no more than a "passing whim." However, as Léonce leaves, the narrator reveals that the Doctor "would have liked during the course of conversation to ask, 'Is there any man in the case?'" (87; ch. XXII). A few days later, when he comes to dinner to observe Edna for himself and finds her "palpitant with the forces of life," her speech "warm and energetic," with "no repression in her glance or gesture," and, most tellingly, looking like "some beautiful, sleek animal waking up in the sun" (90; ch. XXIII), he is "sorry he had accepted Pontellier's invitation" for he "did not want the secrets of other lives thrust upon him" (91; ch. XXIII). Now convinced that there is indeed a "man in the case," he "muttered to himself as he walked, 'I hope it isn't Arobin.... I hope to heaven it isn't Alcée Arobin'" (91; ch. XXIII).

Although he may not consider himself an "inspired psychologist," Mandelet's words suggest, both here and during the pivotal childbirth scene when he tells Edna that they might "talk of things" she has never "dreamt of talking about before" (133; ch. XXXVIII), that he is certainly more than one of those "ordinary fellows" who, like Léonce, could be accused of "bungling." His only mistake is to name the wrong man, for it is not Alcée Arobin who preoccupies Edna, though he does indeed become her physical lover, but Robert Lebrun, the courtly lover, who fills her thoughts.

22

Of the two filmed versions of *The Awakening*—*The End of August*, released to theaters in 1981, and *Grand Isle*, produced for television in 1992 — it is *The End of August* that interprets Edna's behavior as Mandelet has done but without his error: Robert is the "man in the case," and Edna's obsession with him leads her to neglect her housekeeping, take up painting more diligently than she had done before, send her children to their grandmother's house in the country, refuse to attend her sister's wedding or accompany her husband on his business trip to New York, move out of the family's mansion, accept Alcée Arobin as her lover, declare her love for Robert, and, most significant of all her actions, commit suicide when he deserts her for the second time.

In his *Texts and Contexts: Writing About Literature with Critical Theory*, Steven Lynn begins his chapter entitled "Minding the Work: Psychological Criticism" with a quote from Freud: "When a member of my family complains that he or she has bitten his tongue, bruised her finger, and so on, instead of the expected sympathy I put the question, 'Why did you do that?'" (151). "Psychology began," Lynn notes, "when the first person, rather than just reacting to another's behavior, wondered instead, Why did you do that?" (151). As Eula Seaton and Leon Heller adapted Chopin's novel for the screen, they surely asked this very question of Edna, the same question that all of Chopin's readers must ask: Why did you commit suicide? Why did you do that? Like Mandelet at this point in the novel, *The End of August* answers with a relatively simple psychological reading: Edna does what she does because of Robert.

Eleven years later, Hesper Anderson faced the same question when she scripted *Grand Isle*. The answer for her, however, was much more complex. While acknowledging that Robert does play a role in Edna's awakening process, *Grand Isle* suggests that forces far deeper, far more personal than the "man in the case" are responsible for the changes that she manifests, changes that ultimately lead her to drown herself. While it is worthwhile to study *The End of August*, especially because its slant mimics not only Mandelet's diagnosis but also the opinions of the novel's earliest critics, it is more challenging and more rewarding to analyze *Grand Isle* and to do so in light of two critical essays: Cynthia Griffin Wolff's "Thanatos and Eros: Kate Chopin's *The Awakening*," published in *American Quarterly* in 1973, and Mylène Dressler's "Edna Under the Sun: Throwing Light on the Subject of *The Awakening*," which appeared in *Arizona Quarterly* in 1992. Both are excellent examples of psychoanalytic criticism. Wolff borrows Sigmund Freud's notion of the "oceanic feeling" from *Civilization and Its Discontents* and R. D. Laing's description of the schizoid personality from *The Divided Self* to explain what she later calls Edna's "un-utterable longing." Dressler blames Edna's despair on her epiphanic realization of Jacques Lacan's concept of the "screen" — "that culturally generated image or repertoire of images through which subjects are not only constituted, but differentiated" (63). As we now judge articles like Wolff's and Dressler's to be "better" than those written by Chopin's contemporary reviewers because they come much closer to doing justice to the novel's complexities, we might judge *Grand Isle* to be the better film precisely because it offers its audience a more complex reading of Chopin's text than does *The End of August*, a reading that is conveyed through the later film's more complex visual and aural elements.

Emblematic of the kind of review that greeted Chopin's book when it was published in 1899 is Willa Cather's article written for the *Pittsburgh Leader* of July 8, 1899. As Margo Culley informs us in a footnote, Cather "is the first of a number of critics to compare the novel to *Madame Bovary*" (170), and it is this comparison that sets the tone of the essay. Although Cather concedes that Chopin's prose style is "light, flexible, subtle, and capable of producing telling effects directly and simply," she denigrates the novel's protagonist. Both Edna Pontellier and Emma Bovary, says Cather, "belong to a class, not large, but forever clamoring in our ears, that demands more romance out of life than God put into it," a class that "really expect[s] the passion of love to fill and gratify every need of life" (171). Though Cather is surprisingly ahead of her time in her view that Robert "was a coward and ran away" (170), she weakens her attack against him when she attributes his flight to the fact that "he was afraid to begin a chapter with so serious and limited a woman" (170–71), a condemnation of Edna not completely erased by feminist criticism but heard far less frequently now than at the end of the nineteenth century. Cather concludes by hoping that "next time ... Miss Chopin will devote that flexible iridescent style of hers to a better cause" (172).

In 1909, Percival Pollard also blames Robert for Edna's awakening — "After she met Robert Lebrun the awakening stirred in her, to use a rough simile, after the manner of ferment in new wine" (179) — and identifies Alcée Arobin as the man who "happened to hold the torch" (181). Although he shares with Cather an obvious discomfort over Chopin's creation, Pollard's tone is not so much denigrating as it is sarcastic. He sees Robert as merely the instigator of Edna's journey, for her desire soon burns out of control, burns past this one identifiable man to Man in general. Edna drowns herself because "it was now merely Man, not Robert or Arobin, that she desires," because "the awakening was too great; that she was too aflame," and thus she "took an infinite dip in the passionate Gulf" (181).

Conveniently for these critics, Edna herself confirms a reading of the novel that points to Robert as both the beginning and end of her awakening. As she leaves him to attend to Adèle, who has gone into labor, she declares,

"I love you, ... only you; no one but you. It was you who awoke me last summer out of a life-long stupid dream. Oh! you have made me so unhappy with your indifference. Oh! I have suffered, suffered! Now you are here we shall love each other, my Robert. We shall be everything to each other. Nothing else in the world is of any consequence" [130; ch. XXXVI].

After 1953, however, when Cyrille Arnavon translated *The Awakening* into French and wrote an introduction that anticipates Wolff's work twenty years later, critics for the most part stop listening to Edna and start attending to other textual elements, such as the comments of the omniscient narrator, who points to Adèle as the source of the awakening. The era of the "male-centered approach to the work, which does not allow that Edna, as a woman, could be stirred by other than a man," in Kathleen Lant's words (115), was by and large over, except, that is, for *The End of August*, produced in 1981, only three years before Lant's essay appeared.

A survey of Robert's role during key episodes of the film's narrative, those episodes that Roland Barthes terms "hinge-points" or "cardinal functions" (McFarlane 13), reveals how *The End of August* privileges Robert (played by David Marshall Grant) as the force that "stirs" the sleeping Edna (Sally Sharp). First, in its early moments, we see Edna and Robert in the surf, splashing each other and squealing like children as Edna proclaims that she doesn't want to get wet. Back from the beach, Edna admits to being "exhausted" and the two greet Léonce (Paul Roebling), who looks closely at Edna and says, "Really, Lebrun, you're letting my wife get burnt beyond recognition." The passage in *The Awakening* reads somewhat differently: "'You are burnt beyond recognition, [Léonce] added, looking at his wife as one looks at a valuable piece of personal property which has suffered some damage" (21; ch. I). The shift in emphasis is such that in *The End of August* Léonce thinks of Robert as a sort of surrogate husband and holds him responsible for his wife's physical condition. In so doing he brings Robert into the substance of the scene in a more complex way than Chopin herself suggests. What is important here, as Christopher Orr notes, is "not whether the adapted film is faithful to its source, but rather how the choice of a specific source and how the approach to that source serve the film's ideology" (72), here an ideology in which Robert will figure prominently.

Robert also has an expanded role in the film's night swim scene on August 28th, perhaps the most important of all the novel's hinge-points. After Mademoiselle Reisz (Lilia Skala) plays the Chopin Prelude (unspecified in the novel; Opus 28, #21 in B-flat Major in the film), Robert (as he does in the novel) proposes a late-night swim, and Edna joins the other party-goers as they walk "in little groups toward the beach" (46; ch. X). What the novel's narrator tells us about her experience with water is relevant here and will become increasingly so later when we turn to *Grand Isle*:

> Edna had attempted all summer to learn to swim. She had received instructions from both the men and women; in some instances from the children. Robert had pursued a system of lessons almost daily; and he was nearly at the point of discouragement in realizing the futility of his efforts. A certain ungovernable dread hung about her when in the water, unless there was a hand near by that might reach out and reassure her.
>
> But that night she was like a little tottering, stumbling, clutching child, who of a sudden realizes its powers, and walks for the first time alone, boldly and with over-confidence. She could have shouted for joy. She did shout for joy, as with a sweeping stroke or two she lifted her body to the surface of the water [46; ch. X].

It is worth reviewing that the film has already established an image of Edna in the water, splashing about with Robert, and though she protests that she doesn't want to get wet, we do see her getting wet. More importantly, we see and hear her having a good time, with no sense of "ungovernable dread" hovering about. Swimming is mentioned somewhat further on in the film when Robert reminds Edna that it is time for her lesson. She refuses to go, claiming to be "very tired" (as she earlier admits to being "exhausted"). Though from time to time we do see Edna on the beach, most importantly when she talks to Adèle (Kathleen Widdoes) about her childhood memory of the meadow, in *The End of August* she doesn't enter the water after the initial splashing scene until the night of August 28th, not at all the situation that the novel itself or *Grand Isle* presents.

In *The End of August*, as Edna swims into the darkness with Chopin's Prelude functioning now as background (non-diegetic) accompaniment, suddenly we hear Robert's sharp "Edna!" She calls back to him, "I'm all right. It's so easy," and swims to shore, where Léonce remarks, "You weren't so far, my dear." She, predictably now, responds, "I'm really tired."

Again, a close reading of Chopin's text clarifies how the film accentuates Robert's role. After the narrator describes Edna "lift[ing] her body to the surface of the water," the omniscient voice continues:

> A feeling of exultation overtook her, as if some power of significant import had been given her soul. She grew daring and reckless, overestimating her strength. She wanted to swim far out, where no woman had swum before.
>
> Her unlooked-for achievement was the subject of wonder, applause, and admiration. Each one congratulated himself that his special teachings had accomplished this desired end. "How easy it is!" she thought. "It is nothing," she said aloud; "why did I not discover before that it was nothing. Think of the time I have lost splashing about like a baby!" She would not join the groups in their sports and bouts, but intoxicated with her newly conquered power, she swam out alone [46; ch. X].

Two comments should be made before we proceed. First, though Edna's remark here that she has lost time "splashing about like a baby" may very well be the source of the film's earlier scene where she and Robert splash each other in the surf, the difference is pertinent. "Splashing about" as one learns to swim is quite a different and more anxiety-producing matter than "splashing about" in a game designed to see who can more thoroughly soak the other. Second, her thought, "How easy it is," becomes in the film, "I'm all right. It's so easy," her shouted reply to Robert's "Edna!" My point remains the same: Robert is privileged, while the emphasis that the text gives to swimming and to the sea itself is suppressed.

Following the narration still further, we read:

> She turned her face seaward to gather in an impression of space and solitude, which the vast expanse of water, meeting and melting with the moonlit sky, conveyed to her excited fancy. As she swam she seemed to be reaching out for the unlimited in which to lose herself.
>
> Once she turned and looked toward the shore, toward the people she had left there. She had not gone any great distance — that is, what would have been a great distance for an experienced swimmer. But to her unaccustomed vision the stretch of water behind her assumed the aspect of a barrier which her unaided strength would never be able to overcome.
>
> A quick vision of death smote her soul, and for a second of time appalled and enfeebled her senses. But by an effort she rallied her staggering faculties and managed to regain the land.
>
> She made no mention of her encounter with death and her flash of terror, except to say to her husband, "I thought I should have perished out there alone."
>
> "You were not so very far, my dear; I was watching you," he told her [46–47; ch. X].

In discussing the difference between "stories told and stories presented," between story-as-novel and story-as-film, McFarlane proposes that one "aspect of the distinction between telling and presenting is located in the way in which the novel's metalanguage (the vehicle of its telling) is replaced, at least in part, by the film's *mise-en-scène*" (29), "the term ... used to describe the arrangement of all the elements within the frame, a term that originated in theater to describe all the stage components" (Cahir, *Literature into Film* 62). In these terms, what has happened at this point in *The End of August* is that there is nothing in the *mise-en-scène* or in the dialogue to suggest the "vision of death," the "flash of terror" that Edna experiences. In the water Sally Sharp plays an unruffled Edna; on the beach she says nothing to Léonce about her fear of "perish[ing] out there alone." Without her introductory line, Léonce's "You were not so very far, my dear" is virtually meaningless.

Borrowing the term "enunciation" from Christian Metz to describe "that which, being dependent on different signifying systems, cannot be transferred from one medium to the other" (vii), McFarlane points out that the "loss of the narrational voice may ... be felt as the chief casualty of the novel's enunciation" (29). Although these elements cannot, like the cardinal functions, be "transferred," they can be "adapted." Some of what the omniscient narrator tells us could have been conveyed in the face of a good actress; and, even more obviously, retaining the original dialogue could have conveyed something of Edna's complex emotions. McFarlane says it very well when he notes that there are "novelistic elements," such as the omniscient narrator's voice, that "offer challenges to the film-maker, especially if he does not wish the experience of his film to shatter a pre-existing reality (i.e. of the novel) but, rather, to displace it" (30). The challenge here, however, was not an especially great one.

Finally, Robert's role becomes once again foregrounded in *The End of August*, ironically, after he has gone to Mexico and Edna has returned to New Orleans. In the novel, dissatisfied with her life as "one of Mr. Pontellier's possessions" (129; ch. XXXVI), Edna begins to walk about the city, visiting both Mademoiselle Reisz and Adèle Ratignolle. On one such excursion she takes her drawings to Adèle, for although she knows that "Madame Ratignolle's opinion in such a matter would be next to valueless," she "sought the words and praise and encouragement that would help her to put heart into her venture" (75; ch. XVIII). Adèle, always the nurturing figure, tells Edna that her talent is "immense" as she "survey[s] the sketches one by one, at close range, then hold[s] them at arm's length, narrowing her eyes, and dropping her head on one side. 'Surely, this Bavarian peasant is worthy of framing; and this basket of apples! never have I seen anything more lifelike. One might almost be tempted to reach out a hand and take one'" (75: ch. XVIII). In *The End of August*, we see that the sketches are all of Robert. As in the novel, Adèle looks at them carefully but must respond differently: "Your talent is immense, my dear. Why, this picture of Robert is just magnificent. Oh my! You really know your subject very well."

To borrow Christopher Orr's and Lant's words, the ideology that *The End of August* serves is decidedly "male-centered." On a certain level, however, its approach is not only understandable but also unavoidable. As William Dean Howells wryly observes in "Novel-Writing and Novel-Reading," a lecture that he gave in 1899, the same year as the publication of *The Awakening*,

> I had many long and serious talks with my friend, Mr. Henry James, as to how we might eliminate the everlasting young man and young woman, as we called them. We imagined a great many intrigues in which they should *not* be the principal personages; I remember he had one very notable scheme for a

novel whose interest should center about a mother and son. Still, however, he is writing stories, as I still am, about the everlasting man and young woman; though I do think we have managed somewhat to moderate them a little as to their importance in fiction. I suppose we must always have them there, as we must always have them in life, if the race is to go on; but I think the modern novel is more clearly ascertaining their place [277].

Interestingly, Doctor Mandelet echoes Howells's sentiment that "we must always have them in life, if the race is to go on" when he tells Edna, at the end of the novel, that "youth is given up to illusions. It seems to be a provision of Nature; a decoy to secure mothers for the race. And Nature takes no account of moral consequences, of arbitrary conditions which we create, and which we feel obliged to maintain at any cost" (132; ch. XXXVIII). As Howells and Mandelet assert (both of them, in my opinion, rather more "inspired" than "bungling" psychologists), Edna's "throbbings of desire" (49; ch. X), the "spell of her infatuation," her "obsession, ever pressing itself upon her," her "incomprehensible longing" (73–74; ch. XVIII) — all aimed at Robert — should not be minimized. He and Edna are, in fact, the "principal personages" of Chopin's story. A "more clear ascertainment" of his place, however, is called for and does finally occur in written criticism, though not for over fifty years. In film, there is no critical exploration of the many more insights that the novel offers into why Edna does what she does until 1992, with the release of *Grand Isle.*

In *Semiotics of Cinema*, Yurij Lotman distinguishes between "unmarked" and "marked" elements. For example, a "natural sequence of events, [when] shots occur in the order in which they were taken," is an unmarked element. On the other hand, when "events occur in a sequence planned by the director" and are thus "re-arranged," the element is marked. Similarly, a shot whose "horizon" is "parallel to [the] natural horizon" is unmarked, while an "upside down shot" or shots of "various types of inclination" are marked. Basing his work on Ferdinand de Saussure's *Course in General Linguistics*, Lotman looks at the "elements and levels of cinematic language" from a structural point of view — that is, in terms of the "mechanism of similarities and differences" (31). In other words, meaning is made through the play between the establishment of "a system of expectations" and the violation (but not the destruction) of such a system. "Consequently," says Lotman, "at the basis of film meaning we find a displacement, a deformation of customary order, facts or appearances of objects" (32), a defamiliarization. It is not at all the case that the marked elements are in any way superior to the unmarked ones. It is the relationship between the two classes of elements that matters:

> When the viewer has acquired a certain amount of experience in receiving cinematic information, he compares what he sees on the screen not only (and

sometimes, not so much) with life, but also with clichés in films which he already knows. In such a case a displacement, deformation, plot trick, montage contrast, in general any saturation of the picture through the occurrence of super-meanings, all become customary and expected, and they lose their informativeness. Under these conditions a return to a "simple" depiction, "cleansed" of associations — an assertion that an object does not mean anything but itself — a refusal to employ deformed shots and harsh montage devices, such an approach becomes unexpected and thus meaningful [32].

Lotman's observation provides an insight into the difference in "look" between *The End of August* and *Grand Isle*. *The End of August* includes only one marked element — the freeze of its last shot. The film's "male-centered" ideology is thus carried by what the characters say and do, not by the "occurrence of super-meanings." Further, the unbroken presence of this "customary" milieu makes the film's approach to the novel seem stable, natural, indisputable. In contrast, the many marked elements in *Grand Isle* not only give the film a quite different look but also bear, along with the characters' actions and words, the weight of meaning. The somewhat disturbing nature of these elements lends an indeterminate or unstable quality to whatever meanings they convey, thus rendering *Grand Isle* the more fertile of the two films. It must be said here, however, that while it may seem that there is very little of a positive nature to say about *The End of August*, this is not so. In *The Anxiety of Influence*, Harold Bloom speaks of the "swerve" as a "corrective movement" made by the "ephebe" (a later poet) who revises the work of his "precursor poet," a movement "precisely in the direction that the new poem moves" (14). How *The End of August* occasionally swerves from its dominant ideological stance will become apparent during the discussion of *Grand Isle*. In Bloomian terms, then, *The End of August* swerves from itself — thus being both "precursor" and "ephebe."

Robert Stam uses the term "reflexivity" to describe how "texts, both literary and filmic, foreground their own production, their authorship, their intertextual influences, their reception, or their enunciation" (xiii). He credits Metz for his "admirably theorized analyses of a broad arsenal of reflexive devices" (xiv), another name for Lotman's marked elements. These include "direct visual address to the camera, verbal direct address, reflexive intertitles, the frame-within-the-frame, the film-within-the-film, [and] subjective imagery" (Stam xiv). With Lotman's, Metz's, and Stam's work in mind, then, the "marked" or "reflexive" elements in *Grand Isle* become obvious. There are two, and only two, extreme close-ups (what Lotman calls "very big close-ups" [33]), six examples of "direct visual address to the camera," fifteen instances where an image is overexposed to a glaring white, and a repeating pattern of "subjective imagery," Edna as a child walking through a meadow. All of these reflexive devices support Dressler's thesis that *Grand Isle* interprets the novel in terms of the Lacanian "screen." The last two become the basis of a Laingian/Freudian reading. In each case, the soundtrack increases the power of the marked element.

In her "Thanatos and Eros: Kate Chopin's *The Awakening*," Wolff uses both Laing and Freud to make her case. In brief, the idea that Edna has "a schizoid affinity for phantasy" is grounded in Laing (241). That her "libidinal appetite has been fixated at the oral level" is an idea drawn from Freud (247). Wolff's essay is also worth studying for its masterful structure. She presents her thesis early on, words it clearly and strongly, and includes what at least some students will recognize as their own response to the novel:

> The contemporary readings of the novel which stress Edna's position as a victim of society's standards do not capture its power; for although it is not a great novel — perhaps it is even a greatly flawed novel because of the elusiveness of its focus — reading it can be a devastating and unforgettable experience.... The importance of Chopin's work ... derives from its ruthless fidelity to the disintegration of Edna's character.... [S]he interests us because she is human — because she fails in ways which beckon seductively to all of us. Conrad might say that, woman or man, she is "one of us" [234].

Further, Wolff's choice of textual citations to support the steps through which her argument unfolds could not be more appropriate. One example, drawn from Laing and especially useful here because it epitomizes her view of Robert's role, will suffice:

> The attachment to Robert, which takes on significance only after he has left Grand Isle, monopolizes Edna's emotions because it does temporarily offer an illusion of fusion, of complete union.... [T]he sense of fusion exists because Edna's lover is really a part of herself— a figment of her imagination, an image of Robert which she has incorporated into her consciousness. Not only is her meeting with Robert after his return a disappointment; ... it moves the static, imaginary "love affair" into a new and crucial stage; it tests, once and for all, Edna's capacity to transform her world of dreams into viable reality. Not surprisingly, "some way he had seemed nearer to her off there in Mexico" [254].

Indeed, one would be hard pressed to devise a better explanation of this intriguing line.

Finally, Wolff models for students how an expert writer can manage the difficult composition problem of bifurcation and what the relationship between different sections of an essay should be: the second cannot seem an afterthought but rather an inevitable evolution of the first. In one brief but finely crafted transitional paragraph, Wolff creates a bridge between the first part of her paper based on Laing and the second part based on Freud:

This [Laingian] description of Edna's defensive patterns is an invaluable aid in understanding the novel; however, taken alone it does not lead to a complete explanation.... [W]e cannot yet comprehend the manner of her dissolution, nor the significance to Edna (which must have been central) of Madame Ratignolle's accouchement or of Edna's own children, who seem to haunt her even though their physical presence scarcely enters the novel. More important, the tone of the novel — perhaps its most artistically compelling element — cannot yet be described or explained in any but the most general terms as a reflection of Edna's schizoid affinity for fantasy. Even the title of the work, *The Awakening*, suggests a positive quality with which Edna's systematic annihilation of self (albeit from the most self-preserving motives) seems oddly at variance. Thus though we might accept the psychic anatomy defined by Laing as schizoid, we must go beyond simple categorizing to understand the novel as a whole [241–42].

It must also be said, however, that even though Wolff provides ample signposts along the way, her work will be problematic for some students. The psychoanalytic concepts will be foreign to some, the academic prose difficult for others. Very few students can express Wolff's thesis in their own words after reading her text by themselves, an exercise that certainly bears out Hartman's remark that "literary commentary may cross the line and become as demanding as literature" (351). In the end, though, students find her essay worth the work. Adding *Grand Isle* to the mix both draws them more fully into the intertextual web and clarifies Wolff, for in its own way, the film too captures the "elusiveness of [the novel's] focus" that Wolff describes (234) and becomes an example of psychoanalytic criticism in its own right.

To review, the reflexive or marked elements in *Grand Isle* that support such an interpretation are the pattern of subjective imagery (the visual refrain of Edna as a child walking through the meadow) and the instances where an image is bleached out to white. The subjective imagery's basis in the novel itself provides us with a starting point.

In *The Awakening*, Edna tells Adèle about her thoughts as the two sit on the porch of their bathhouse on the beach at Grand Isle:

"The hot wind beating in my face made me think — without any connection that I can trace — of a summer day in Kentucky, of a meadow that seemed as big as the ocean to the very little girl walking through the grass, which was higher than her waist. She threw out her arms as if swimming when she walked, beating the tall grass as one strikes out in the water. Oh, I see the connection now!" [34–35; ch. VII].

Adèle asks her where she was going "that day in Kentucky," and Edna replies,

"I don't remember now. I was just walking diagonally across a big field. My sun-bonnet obstructed the view. I could see only the stretch of green before me, and I felt as if I must walk on forever, without coming to the end of it. I don't remember whether I was frightened or pleased. I must have been entertained."

"Likely as not it was Sunday," she laughed; "and I was running away from prayers, from the Presbyterian service, read in a spirit of gloom by my father that chills me yet to think of" [35; ch. VII].

And this is essentially all that they say about the meadow, except that Edna adds, "Sometimes I feel this summer as if I were walking through the green meadow again; idly, aimlessly, unthinking and unguided" (35; ch. VII).

It is only at the very end of the novel, as Edna swims to her death, that Chopin returns to the image of the little girl: "She went on and on. She remembered the night she swam far out, and recalled the terror that seized her at the fear of being unable to regain the shore. She did not look back now, but went on and on, thinking of the blue-grass meadow that she had traversed when a little child, believing that it had no beginning and no end" (137; ch. XXXIX). In the novel's beautiful last sentence, Edna's final sensations of the meadow are aural and olfactory, "sensory, not verbal" (Tyson 34): "There was the hum of bees, and the musky odor of pinks filled the air" (137; ch. XXXIX).

In *Grand Isle*, we see the young Edna in the Kentucky field six times during five different scenes. She appears to be about ten years old, has red hair (as does the film's adult Edna, though in the novel Edna's hair is "yellowish brown" [21; ch. II]), and is wearing a rather simple blue cotton dress with a pink sash. She wears no bonnet. She looks into the camera, sometimes smiles, and turns and runs away before the shot ends. Each occurrence of this visual refrain lasts only a few seconds.

It is during Edna's dream that we first glimpse the girl in the meadow. After Léonce (Jon DeVries) accuses his wife (Kelly McGillis) of being "burnt beyond recognition," as he does in the novel, he leaves her and Robert (Adrian Pasdar) for a night of gambling at Klein's Hotel. When he returns, late, he tries to awaken Edna with "anecdotes and bits of news and gossip that he had gathered during the day" (23; ch. III). In the film we hear his "monotonous, insistent" small talk (24; ch. III) and see that Edna is having difficulty pulling herself out of her dream, whose visuals are accompanied by a dreamy, wind-like score. She manages to tell Léonce that she was dreaming, and he asks, in a rather amorous tone, "Was I in your dream?" When Edna tells him no, that she was "a little girl at home," it becomes obvious, as the novel too relates, that Léonce's mood changes. He becomes angry "that his wife, who was the sole object of his existence, evinced so little interest in things which concerned him and valued so little his conversation" (23; ch. III). What Wolff points out in her 1996 essay, "Un-utterable Longing: The Discourse of Feminine Sexuality in *The Awakening*," holds true for both novel and film: "There is nothing peculiar about the 'action' of this scenario, nor is it difficult to read the subtext: Léonce would like to conclude his pleasant evening with a sexual encounter; his wife is not interested" (6). In revenge, he tells Edna that their child Raoul has a fever and forces her to attend to him, a "profound displacement" that illustrates how, during the nineteenth century, "the language of feminine sexuality became inextricably intertwined with discourse that had to do with child-bearing and motherhood" (Wolff, "Un-utterable" 3–4).

In the novel, Léonce "reproached his wife with her inattention, her habitual neglect of the children" (24; ch. III). After she has assured herself that "Raoul had no fever," Edna "refused to answer her husband when he questioned her." He quickly falls asleep, and then she goes to the porch and begins to cry. With the sea breaking "like a mournful lullaby upon the night," she cries so hard that "the damp sleeve of her *peignoir* no longer served to dry" her tears (24; ch. III). This mood, this "indescribable oppression ... like a shadow, like a mist passing across her soul's summer day" is broken only by the mosquitoes who "made merry over her" (25; ch. III). In the morning, both husband and wife have regained their equilibrium.

In *The End of August*, as in the novel, Edna goes out to the porch after Léonce has upbraided her for being a neglectful mother and has fallen asleep. It is not the sea, however, that sounds "like a mournful lullaby upon the night" but Edna herself who hums "Hush Little Baby, Don't You Cry" as she gazes out into the darkness. In *Grand Isle*, after Edna checks on Raoul, the scene ends with a quick cut to the morning. We do not see Edna cry.

After Edna finally "loosen[s] a little the mantle of reserve that had always enveloped her" (32; ch. VII)—symbolized in both novel and film by her "remov[ing] her collar and open[ing] her dress at the throat" (34; ch. VII)— she is able to tell her dream to Adèle (Glenne Headly) as they sit in front of the bathhouse and stare at the Gulf. Some of the dialogue of *Grand Isle* has been changed to accommodate the fact that Edna is recounting a dream, not a memory. Adèle asks Edna what she is thinking, and Edna answers, "Let me see. The water stretching so far in the hot breeze made me think of my dream a couple of weeks ago when Léonce got so angry." Adèle wants to know why he was angry, and Edna laughingly tells her, "I think because he wasn't in it." She continues, "I was little again and it was a summer day in Kentucky, walking through a meadow that seemed as big as the ocean. I stretched out my arms as if swimming and — Oh, I see." Adèle asks, "And where were you going, walking through the ocean?" Edna replies, "I don't remember. Sometimes this summer I feel as if I'm walking through that meadow again." Adèle's response is "*Pauvre Cherie.*" In answer to Edna's puzzlement she adds, "Because we are grown women now. No more meadows I'm afraid." "And no more dreams?" asks Edna. "No," reiterates Adèle. "Only real husbands and real children to hold us." "That does make me sad. I had such dreams," Edna sighs. Like her earlier line to Léonce — "I was a little girl at home" — this dialogue gives no clue that the dream was based on a real event in Edna's childhood, and she never discusses it again.

We see the refrain a second time during the *soirée* of August 28th, before the crucial night swim. As in the novel, Robert prevails upon Mademoiselle Reisz (Ellen Burstyn) to play, and she chooses a Chopin Prelude. The narrator tells us that "Edna was what she herself called very fond of music. Musical strains, well rendered, had a way of evoking pictures in her mind" (44; ch. IX). But on this night Edna's reaction is quite different:

> The very first chords which Mademoiselle Reisz struck upon the piano sent a keen tremor down Mrs. Pontellier's spinal column. It was not the first time she had heard an artist at the piano. Perhaps it was the first time she was ready, perhaps the first time her being was tempered to take an impress of the abiding truth.
>
> She waited for the material pictures which she thought would gather and blaze before her imagination. She waited in vain. She saw no pictures of solitude, of hope, of longing, or of despair. But the very passions themselves were aroused within her soul, swaying it, lashing it, as the waves daily beat upon her splendid body. She trembled, she was choking, and the tears blinded her [44–45; ch. IX].

Not only does this key passage link Reisz's music to the sea — another voice of "the abiding truth" — but it also stresses that Edna's primal, emotional response, with its passions and tears, has superseded her propensity to conjure up pictures that illustrate whatever music she is listening to. By association, these strong emotions become connected to the sea.

In *Grand Isle*, however, the scene is presented differently. As Reisz begins to play the Prelude #20 in C Minor, the camera pans the room, lingering for a moment on the faces of the significant players in Edna's drama before coming to rest on Edna. She is staring, unblinking, across the room as the camera begins to zoom in, and as we move closer to her face, the Prelude fades away as the abstract windy music arises and then completely takes over the soundtrack as Edna closes her eyes and the girl appears. Her image persists until we hear the Prelude end and see Edna open her eyes to the sound of clapping. There are no tears, no choking contortions — only Edna's visual imagination at work.

Those who are tempted to criticize the way *Grand Isle* has re-imagined this scene might consider, for a moment, what the filmmakers were up against. In order to show that Edna is now, for the first time, seeing nothing when she hears music, they would have had to establish that Edna previously had been in the habit of seeing something. Although added dialogue could, perhaps, have accomplished this and we certainly could have witnessed the emotional component of her experience — tears, choking, etc. — it may not have been clear even then that Edna sees nothing. If it is true, in James Monaco's words, that cinematic language relies upon the index to "deal directly with ideas," ideas that in this case belong to the novel's enunciatory functions and thus cannot be directly transferred to the screen, then what could the possible "concrete representations or measurements" (133) — the indices — of visual nothingness be? In other words, what something can represent a nothing? In terms of this one specific spot in the film, there seems to be no satisfactory answer. If they were indeed caught in this bind, then the filmmakers chose to play up the refrain at the expense of Edna's response as Chopin imagined it: first, seeing no pictures and second, reacting in an intensely emotional way.

In *The End of August*, as Reisz plays the Prelude Opus 28 #21, we see Edna looking out of the window. Her gaze is directed towards two young lovers, backlit by a bonfire on the beach, who have slipped away from the party in search of privacy. In the novel, these unnamed "young lovers," also vacationing at Grand Isle, are paired with another suggestive figure, the unnamed "lady in black." For example, in the novel when Edna and Adèle are sitting in front of their bathhouse, the "lady in black was reading her morning devotions on the porch of a neighboring bath-house. Two young lovers were exchanging their hearts' yearnings beneath the children's tent, which they had found unoccupied" (34; ch. VII). Because *The End of August*, as we have seen, places Robert at the center of Edna's longing, it is small wonder that her fascination with the young lovers is dramatized. There is no lady in black here. On the other hand, *Grand Isle* excludes the young lovers. The lady in black, however, appears on several occasions.

After the night swim with all of its joys and terrors, the "first-felt throbbings of desire" for Robert that she feels while lying in the hammock (49; ch. X) and her sharp retort to Léonce ("Don't speak to me like that again; I shall not answer you") who has commanded that she come to bed (50; ch. XI), Edna wakes early, sends for Robert, and the two set off for mass at the Chênière Caminada. She doesn't make it through the mass, however, and critics are quick to note that she once again is "running away from prayers." Robert takes her to Madame Antoine's where she can rest. As Wolff points out, "Once she is by herself, left to seek restful sleep, Edna seems somewhat to revive, and the tone shifts from one of exhaustion to one of sensuous, leisurely enjoyment of her own body" (246).

> Edna, left alone in the little side room, loosened her clothes, removing the greater part of them. She bathed her face, her neck and arms in the basin that stood between the windows. She took off her shoes and stockings and

stretched herself in the very center of the high, white bed.... She stretched her strong limbs that ached a little. She ran her fingers through her loosened hair for a while. She looked at her round arms as she held them straight up and rubbed them one after the other, observing closely, as if it were something she saw for the first time, the fine, firm quality and texture of her flesh. She clasped her hands easily above her head, and it was thus she fell asleep [55–56; ch. XIII].

Many critics have commented upon this passage, most seeing it as evidence of Edna's awakening sexuality. Wolff, however, finds no "genital significance here." Instead, the scene reinforces her Freudian view that Edna's "libidinal appetite has been fixated at the oral level." "Reduced to its simplest form, the description is of a being discovering the limits and qualities of its own body — discovering, and taking joy in the process of discovery. And having engaged in this exploratory 'play' for a while, Edna falls asleep" (247) and dreams of her young self in the meadow.

In *The End of August*, Edna not only strips to her slip but also appears to masturbate, and this interpretation parallels a major point in both Wolff's and Dressler's arguments. Wolff believes that Edna can feel passion for Robert only when he is absent, for only then can he "be made magically present as a phantom, an object in her own imagination, a figure which is now truly a part of herself" (240). On the Chênière, however, Robert is very much present, and instead of awakening her with a kiss, he "prepares her a meal!" (247) — as if he is somehow aware that "Edna's libidinal energies have been arrested at a pregenital level" and the way to nurture her is not to make love to her but to feed her (247). Similarly, Dressler maintains that "Robert is clearly proximate to Edna's awakenings, but he is never central to them. He may serve, as the novel leads us to surmise, as the initial figure leading Edna to question her life's arrangements, yet her larger desire is finally more personal, more self-centered" (68). In *The End of August*, this "genuinely narcissistic" love affair (Wolff 254) is dramatized by the masturbatory act. In his introduction to *Kate Chopin*, in the series Modern Critical Views, Bloom proposes a similar notion when he notes that "[Edna's] passion is for herself, and this error perhaps destroys her" (1).

Before describing the fourth repetition, it is necessary to examine another of the narrative's hinge-points — the scene during which Reisz allows Edna to read a letter that Robert has written from Mexico, a letter that is all about Edna. He writes to Reisz, "If Mrs. Pontellier should call upon you, play for her that Impromptu of Chopin's, my favorite. I heard it here a day or two ago, but not as you play it. I should like to know how it affects her" (83; ch. XXI). After Edna begs, Reisz hands her the letter and goes to the piano:

Mademoiselle played a soft interlude. It was an improvisation.... Gradually and imperceptibly the interlude melted into the soft opening minor chords of the Chopin Impromptu.

Edna did not know when the Impromptu began or ended. She sat in the sofa corner reading Robert's letter by the fading light. Mademoiselle had glided from the Chopin into the quivering love-notes of Isolde's song, and back again to the Impromptu with its soulful and poignant longing.

The shadows deepened in the little room. The music grew strange and fantastic — turbulent, insistent, plaintive and soft with entreaty. The shadows grew deeper. The music filled the room. It floated out upon the night, over the house-tops, the crescent of the river, losing itself in the silence of the upper air.

Edna was sobbing, just as she had wept one midnight at Grand Isle when strange, new voices awoke in her. She arose in some agitation to take her departure [84; ch. XXI].

In *Grand Isle*, Reisz plays the Nocturne in E Minor — chosen, perhaps, for what James Friskin calls the "wildly passionate" variation on its main theme (107) — while Edna reads the letter. The camera pans the room as the beautiful piano piece progresses, and finally we see that Edna is not sobbing but reclining, resting her head on the arm of the sofa. Once again *Grand Isle* has opted not to privilege Edna's emotional reaction, and it is somewhat surprising that we do not see the little girl at this time. We do not, in fact, see her again until Robert's return.

During one of Edna's visits to Reisz's apartment when the pianist happens to be out, Robert knocks on the door. In the novel, Edna finds in his eyes "the same glance which had penetrated to the sleeping places of her soul and awakened them" (119; ch. XXXIII) and feels "as if her dreams were coming true after all" when he goes home with her (120; ch. XXXIII). In the novel and in both film versions, they begin to talk of their feelings but then retreat into mundane conversation until they are interrupted by Arobin's arrival. Robert almost immediately takes his leave, asking Edna to "convey [his] regards to Mr. Pontellier" when she next writes him, for Léonce is still away on his business trip to New York (123; ch. XXXIV). Arobin settles in, reads the newspaper, smokes a cigar, and invites Edna for a drive. In an interesting bit of dialogue that epitomizes Arobin's character, she tells him to "go away and amuse [himself]." I'll go away if I must; but I shan't amuse myself.... You know that I only live when I am near you," he declares. "Is that one of the things you always say to women?" she asks. "I have said it before, but I don't think I ever came so near meaning it," he answers (124; ch. XXXIV).

After Arobin leaves her, the narrator tells us,

She stayed alone in a kind of reverie — a sort of stupor. Step by step she lived over every instant of the time she had been with Robert after he had entered

Mademoiselle Reisz's door. She recalled his words, his looks. How few and meager they had been for her hungry heart! A vision — a transcendently seductive vision of a Mexican girl arose before her. She writhed with a jealous pang. She wondered when he would come back. He had not said he would come back. She had been with him, had heard his voice and touched his hand. But some way he had seemed nearer to her off there in Mexico [124; ch. XXXIV].

The End of August presents this scene almost exactly as the novel suggests, except that after Arobin tells Edna, "I don't think I ever came so near meaning it," she volleys back at him, "Perhaps another time with someone else you may come even closer to meaning it," a line that indicates that her emotional attachment is still to Robert. In *Grand Isle*, after Arobin leaves as the novel describes, Edna sits quietly on the couch and envisions the girl in the meadow for the fourth time. Now, however, the music that we hear is Chopin's Nocturne in E Minor, not the impressionistic piece that accompanies the first three repetitions of the image. There is another difference as well. For the first time, the girl is preceded by an image of the sea and followed by one of Edna and Robert in an orange grove, with Robert feeding Edna an orange section.

Finally, the refrain appears two more times at the end of the film as Edna is swimming to her death. As we earlier noted, the Edna of the novel thinks of the meadow: "She went on and on. She remembered the night she swam far out, and recalled the terror that seized her at the fear of being unable to regain the shore. She did not look back now, but went on and on, thinking of the blue-grass meadow that she had traversed when a little child, believing that it had no beginning and no end" (137; ch. XXXIX). She thinks of Léonce and her children and concludes that "they need not have thought that they could possess her, body and soul." She suspects that Mademoiselle Reisz "would have laughed, perhaps sneered, if she knew!" She remembers Robert's note, "Good-by — because I love you," and knows that "he did not understand. He would never understand." She reflects that perhaps Doctor Mandelet "would have understood if she had seen him — but it was too late; the shore was far behind her, and her strength was gone" (137; ch. XXXIX). The novel's last paragraph reads,

She looked into the distance, and the old terror flamed up for an instant, then sank again. Edna heard her father's voice and her sister Margaret's. She heard the barking of an old dog that was chained to the sycamore tree. The spurs of the cavalry officer clanged as he walked across the porch. There was the hum of bees, and the musky odor of pinks filled the air [137; ch. XXXIX].

The End of August makes short work of this final chapter of Edna's story. We see Sharp naked from the back as she enters the water, a few seconds of her swimming out to sea, and then the film ends with a freeze frame — its only marked element. In *Grand Isle*, however, Edna's final swim, with the Nocturne as soundtrack, is captured by both underwater and aerial camera work. Kelly McGillis had no compunction about being photographed totally nude from the front, and this sequence uncannily illustrates Sandra Gilbert's thesis that "metaphorically speaking, Edna has become Aphrodite, or at least an ephebe of that goddess" (276). Gilbert suggests that "Aphrodite is, and has her sexual energy, for herself, her own grandeur, her own pleasure" (280), a restatement in mythic terms of what Wolff and Dressler maintain. For Bloom, from whom Gilbert borrows the word "ephebe," *The Awakening* is the "child" of "Out of the Cradle Endlessly Rocking," and it is Whitman's "old crone rocking the cradle, swathed in sweet garments, bending aside" (Introduction, *Kate Chopin* 1) that Edna seeks and finds. Applying Lacan's theory to *The Awakening*, Tyson maintains that Edna is "drawn to the Imaginary Order ... the fantasy union with her mother / her world she experienced in infancy and still unconsciously desires" and therefore "can't be satisfied, not by her art, not by Mademoiselle Reisz's music, not by her own sexual freedom, and not by romance" (33–34).

As in the fourth repetition, *Grand Isle*'s last visions of the little girl are accompanied by other images suggested by the novel itself: first the girl in the meadow, then Léonce and the children, then Robert, then Mademoiselle Reisz, and then the girl again. The film ends with the girl walking away from the camera and dissolving, and we know that Edna is dead.

One of the first generalizations that can be made about this pattern of subjective imagery involves the significance of the change in music — from the other-worldly, windy sound of the first three repetitions to the Nocturne of the last three. As we should recall, Edna does not hear the Nocturne until she returns to New Orleans when Reisz plays it because it is Robert's favorite piece and he has requested in his letter that she play it for Edna. Following Wolff's reasoning, one must conclude that the Nocturne that Edna hears when Robert is absent is far more meaningful to her than even the Prelude, whose power, we are led to believe, inspires her to swim on the night of August 28th. The Nocturne, then, in Wolff's words, becomes the music of the "phantom" Robert, of the Robert who is Edna's "lover" only because he is "really a part of herself" (254). More importantly, as the fourth repetition illustrates, the Nocturne, the sea, the little girl, and Robert seem to have become fused, a fusion that intimates exactly what Robert's role is in Edna's mind.

When Edna and Adèle talk about Edna's dream, they explicitly define its meaning. After Edna tells Adèle, "Sometimes this summer I feel as if I'm walking through that meadow again" and Adèle calls her "*Pauvre Cherie*,"

Adèle goes on to say, "No more meadows, I'm afraid" and Edna answers, "And no more dreams?" Because the image of the meadow has first appeared in a dream and because of this reinforcing dialogue, the meadow of the film is associated with dreams and may even be symbolic of their source, the unconscious mind itself. When an image of Robert follows the fourth scene of the little girl in the meadow and both images are underscored by Robert's favorite Nocturne, the audience can see that Robert belongs to the world of Edna's dreams. As Wolff hypothesizes, because Edna's psychic life is complex, troubled, and immature, she does not really want Robert in a sexual or even in a romantic way. What she has found in her attachment to him is the "illusion of fusion, of complete union" (254). In pointing out that after leaving for Mexico Robert takes "his place among the presences in [Edna's] imagination" (227), Culley concurs with Wolff that Edna has extended herself by "a kind of incorporation of his personality into her own" (239). Even after he returns, Edna needs to keep him in the dream realm, needs to keep him as he was "off there in Mexico," as the film aptly shows through his inclusion in the fourth dream-reverie. As Wolff puts it, deep down Edna knows that "the flesh and blood Robert may prove an imperfect, unsatisfactory substitute for the 'beloved' of her dreams" (255).

It seems clear, then, that *Grand Isle*'s visual and aural refrain reveals something about Edna's character — that elusive quality that Wolff works so hard to define — while it contributes to the general mood and texture of the film as a whole. But the situation becomes more complex. The fifth and sixth images of the little girl which appear during the suicidal swim are joined not only by Robert but by Léonce, the children, and Mademoiselle Reisz as well. This perhaps implies that they, too, have become part of Edna's dream material.

Reisz is connected to Robert, so we can understand her presence here. On a deeper level, as Peggy Skaggs notes, "Even an unattractive, disagreeable artist needs love," so she "resorts to vicarious satisfaction through Edna's intense emotional reactions" (351). Although *Grand Isle*, as we have seen, has eliminated these reactions, we might very well believe in both book and film that Reisz has led "Robert to write to her of his love for Edna, and then she plays stirring love music while Edna reads the letters in her presence" (Skaggs 351). For Hugh Dawson, the relationship between these women is a bit more sinister: "one cannot miss the reciprocal pleasures that the two discover in the aberrant roles of tormentor and willing victim" (13). And, for Elaine Showalter, Reisz "seems to be a surrogate lover" (75). The point is that Reisz is pictured here not only because of her link to Robert, but also because of her link to Edna, whatever this link may be. Putting the above quotation aside, it would be enough to say that Reisz deserves a place in the final refrain because her music serves as a preface to Edna's midnight swim, a swim into the uncon-scious — for like the meadow, the sea, too, represents the source of dreams (Cirlot 345).

Léonce and the children, whom Edna considers "antagonists" at the end of the novel, have also, in the film, been metamorphosed into "presences in her imagination." After all, Edna did acquire them when she was in her "life-long stupid dream" (130; ch. XXXVI). However, in the novel, Edna does also think of three other characters during her last swim, characters excluded from the film's ending. They are Doctor Mandelet, Arobin, and Adèle.

Whereas *The End of August* ends its childbirth scene with the camera focused on Edna's disturbed face as Adèle admonishes her (as she does in the novel) to "Think of the children. Edna. O think of the children! Remember them!" (132; ch. XXXVII), *Grand Isle* includes the subsequent dialogue between Edna and Mandelet (Michael Audley). Mandelet talks of the "illu-sions" through which Nature "decoys" women into becoming "mothers for the race," and Edna replies with a line taken directly from the novel that con-tinues to tease because of what is unsaid: "The years that are gone seem like dreams — if one might go on sleeping and dreaming — but to wake up and find — oh! well! perhaps it is better to wake up after all, even to suffer, rather than to remain a dupe to illusions all one's life" (133; ch. XXXVIII). To find what? Wolff answers this question by reminding us of how the text describes what Edna has just witnessed:

> Edna began to feel uneasy. She was seized with a vague dread. Her own like experiences seemed far away, unreal, and only half remembered. She recalled faintly an ecstasy of pain, the heavy odor of chloroform, a stupor which had deadened sensation, and an awakening to find a little new life to which she had given being, added to the great unnumbered multitude of souls that come and go [131; ch. XXXVII].

In Wolff's view, then, Edna awakens "to separation, to individual existence, to the hopelessness of ever satisfying the dream of total fusion" (257). Her "quest" for "the ecstasy which beckoned," the ecstasy of fusion, "has become in the end merely an 'ecstasy of pain'" (257). Mandelet, who Edna thinks "would have understood if she had seen him" (137; ch. XXXIX), is omitted from the film's final imagery precisely because he "would have understood" these things. He is situated squarely in the world of reality, has been Adèle's partner in this drama of separation, and is thus antithetical to Edna's deep-est desire.

Arobin (Julian Sands), also excluded, belongs to the world of the body, not to the imagination, not to dreams. Culley, who reads *The Awakening* as "an existential novel about solitude" (247), sees in Arobin "another escape from solitude, the deliverance of the flesh" (250). In her view, when the fantasy of Robert has failed Edna and when she can admit to herself that "[t]o-day it is Arobin; to-morrow it will be some one else" (136; ch. XXXIX), "Edna embraces death whose voice she has heard in her aloneness" (251). What Edna "wake[s] up and find[s]" is this aloneness — an awakening that, for Culley, "is particularly poignant because the soul is a female soul, characteristically defined as someone's daughter, someone's wife, someone's mother, someone's mistress. To discover solitude in the midst of this connectedness is surely among the most painful of awakenings" (251). Culley believes with Wolff that Edna has no real feelings for Arobin. At best he is a hedge against solitude. He belongs to the tangible world of the body, and thus he is omitted from the collage of images at the end of *Grand Isle*.

Lant makes a strong case for the fact that it is not Robert who has awakened Edna but Adèle, a position supported by the omniscient narrator:

> That summer at Grand Isle [Edna] began to loosen a little the mantle of reserve that had always enveloped her. There may have been — there must have been — influences, both subtle and apparent, working in their several ways to induce her to do this; but the most obvious was the influence of Adèle Ratignolle. The excessive physical charm of the Creole had first attracted her, for Edna had a sensuous susceptibility to beauty. Then the candor of the woman's whole existence, which everyone might read, and which formed so striking a contrast to her own habitual reserve — this might have furnished a link. Who can tell what metals the gods use in forging the subtle bond which we call sympathy, which we might as well call love [32; ch. VII].

Furthermore, early in the novel Adèle is linked to dreams: "There are no words to describe her save the old ones that have served so often to picture the bygone heroine of romance and the fair lady of our dreams," the narrator tells us (26; ch. IV). With this as a starting point, Wolff tentatively proposes that "if some portion of Edna's self has been arrested in dreams, perhaps Adèle is the embodiment of those dreams" (244). Yet both Wolff and Lant ultimately find in Adèle a much more far-reaching significance. In Lant's view, Adèle teaches Edna that in spite of Edna's desire to "renounce any self or role unsuitable to her, ... there is one self she cannot refuse, for this self is a product of her physical being" (123). It is the self that is a mother. "She cannot renounce her sons; she can only 'elude them,' and she must give up the body to elude her sons" (123). Lant concludes that Edna has "awakened because the feminine Adèle has stirred her to explore her own feminine inner landscape. But tragically, again because Adèle exposes her to the ultimate reality of femininity, Edna awakens to the horrible knowledge that she can never, because she is female, be her own person" (124).

Wolff's argument culminates with a discussion of Adèle and an explanation of why "Edna is intensely involved with Adèle's pregnancy" (256):

Edna's compulsion to be with Adèle at the moment of delivery is, in the sense which would have most significance for her, a need to view individuation at its origin. For if pregnancy offers a state of total union, then birth is the initial separation: for the child it is the archetypal separation trauma; for the mother, too, it is a significant psychic trauma. It is the ritual reenactment of her own birth and a brutal awakening to the world of isolated ego [256].

For both Lant and Wolff, Adèle awakens Edna into what is perhaps most real about the real world, and it is thus her stabbing invocation to "Think of the children," not Robert's "Good-by — because I love you," that seals Edna's fate. Adèle is "the fair lady of our dreams" in name only, and her omission at the end of *Grand Isle* underlines her link to reality, not to the dream world.

The company that the little girl keeps in the fourth, fifth, and sixth refrains, then, is dream material — people, like the little girl herself, who are the material content ("what we actually dream") that underlies the latent content ("what these images actually mean") (Tyson 19). Appropriately, the dissolve is used nowhere else, only in these repetitions of the refrain. As Herbert Zettl notes, dissolves not only "create a surrealistic or dreamlike feeling" but also suggest "a strong relationship between seemingly unrelated events" (202). Here, "strong relationships" are forged among "seemingly unrelated" people — at first glance Léonce and the children may appear to have almost nothing in common with Robert and Reisz — and between these people and the sea. But what of the little girl herself? There are at least three psychoanalytic interpretations that can help us speculate about the nature of her existence, the latent content of this dream.

First of all, although her image in the last three repetitions is joined with and dissolves into other images, it is worth stressing that the little girl is always alone in her scene, emphasizing, perhaps, that Edna is indeed "A Solitary Soul" (the title Chopin initially intended for her novel). When the child looks at the camera, thereby looking at us, we are not really drawn into the meadow with her. She merely looks at us; nothing about her invites us in. Sometimes she even seems a bit unhappy to see us, though, in general, the impression is that she is happy and free. It is significant that she does not wear the restrictive bonnet as she does in the novel and can thus see far more than "the stretch of green" in front of her. In short, one might read this recurring refrain as a representation of what Edna would like to be but cannot — her own person with her own vision, unencumbered by all the blinders that family and society construct for her.

The little girl can also be seen as a personification of one of Edna's character traits. The novel reiterates that she is "capricious," like a child who leaps before it looks, who seeks "no interval of repose between the thought and its fulfillment" (105; ch. XXIX). The book's narrator identifies this trait, as do several characters in both the novel and film — Madame Lebrun (Robert's mother), Robert, Adèle, and Léonce. *Grand Isle* reinforces the presence of Edna's capriciousness through its six glimpses of her as a child. Further, it borrows a visual stereotype when it changes Edna's hair color in both childhood and adulthood from the brownish blonde of the novel to red. In *Grand Isle*, she is indeed presented as impetuous, "hot-headed" both inside and out.

But the little girl also represents something else, something less specific, more "elusive," and this something is Edna's hidden self, willing at last to peek out from time to time to look at the world. Supporting Wolff's observation that in "some sense there are two Ednas" (235), the narrator confides that "Mrs. Pontellier was not a woman given to confidences, a characteristic hitherto contrary to her nature. Even as a child she had lived her own small life all within herself. At a very early period she had apprehended instinctively the dual life — the outward existence which conforms, the inward life which questions" (14). Wolff then cites Laing's "description of the 'schizoid' personality" in order to better "assess the configuration of Edna's personality when she comes to Grand Isle at the novel's beginning" (237). As Laing puts it, "The self, in order to develop and sustain its identity and autonomy, and in order to be safe from the persistent threat and danger from the world, has cut itself off from direct relatedness with others, and has endeavored to become its own object; to become, in fact, related directly only to itself" (qtd. in Wolff 237). Wolff blames Edna's plight on her original family, which "has two faces.... It 'sins' (during the week) with its [horse] racing and land-grabbing; and it 'atones' (on Sundays) with pious condemnations" (235). Quoting from the text, Wolff notes that "Margaret, the oldest, 'has all the Presbyterian undiluted'" and Janet, "the youngest, is something of a vixen" (235). Edna, the middle child, tries to "accommodate both" faces, and she does so by "produc[ing] an 'identity' which is predicated on the conscious process of concealment" (235). Offering a more extreme explanation, Roger Platizky risks the suggestion that the genesis of Edna's "mood changes, boundary problems and suicide" lies in "a previous encounter with sexual violence either as a victim or witness," that she suffers from "a repressed post-traumatic memory" (1). The one clue in the novel that supports that this may be so is given to us by the narrator: Edna's father "was perhaps unaware that he had coerced his own wife into her grave. Mr. Pontellier had a vague suspicion of it which he thought it needless to mention at that late day" (92; ch. XXIV).

Though readers can never know precisely why this hidden self has developed, we can see how fiercely Edna protects it, first by falling in love only with unavailable men — a cavalry officer friend of her father's, the fiancé of a neighbor, and, finally, with a famous actor — and then by marrying a man with whom she would be unlikely to develop a "genuine emotional involvement," for, as Wolff explains, such an involvement would threaten the hidden self: "An intuitive man, a sensitive husband, might threaten it; a husband who evoked passion from her might lure the hidden self into the open, tempting Edna to attach her emotions to flesh and blood rather than phantoms. Léonce is neither, and their union ensures the secret safety of Edna's 'real' self" (237). In this condition, Edna arrives at Grand Isle and is overwhelmed not only by the beautiful, lush island itself, but also by Adèle, whose "beauty derives its power from a sense of fullness, ripeness, and abundance" (244). Edna's self responds and emerges from its desolation, seeking the "resuscitation and nourishment" (250) that the new environment promises.

Unlike *The End of August*, neither Wolff's work nor *Grand Isle* minimizes the role of the sea, certainly the fundamental feature of this new environment. In *A Dictionary of Symbols*, J. E. Cirlot writes that water is "interpreted by modern psychology as a symbol of the unconscious, that is, of the non-formal, dynamic, motivating, female side of the personality. The projection of the mother-imago into the waters endows them with various numinous properties characteristic of the mother" (345). It is not at all surprising, then, that Wolff reads Edna's drowning as "a literal denial and reversal of the birth trauma she has just witnessed, a stripping away of adulthood, of limitation, of consciousness itself" (257). Chopin's text tells us that as Edna stood "naked under the sky," she "felt like some new-born creature, opening its eyes in a familiar world that it had never known" (136; ch. XXXIX). Wolff concludes her essay with an evaluation of Edna's "final act": she "completes the regression, back beyond childhood, back into time eternal. 'The touch of the sea is sensuous, enfolding the body in its soft, close embrace'" (258). The sea is the mother, and Edna has retreated back into the womb, recreating the state of complete fusion possible only before birth. Using Freud's words, Wolff concludes that Edna's "eternal yearning for identity between the ego and nonego, that deeply buried original desire to reachieve the condition once experienced, to repeat the human dream that was once realized in the mother's womb, is fulfilled" (256).

Grand Isle does justice to the sea's role in Edna's outer and inner landscapes by keeping the waters of the Gulf always before us. The film opens with an extended beach sequence which includes a view of Edna being coaxed into the surf by Robert and several children. As they move into deeper water, she hangs back, refusing to go further. Then in the next sequence we see Edna and Robert approach Léonce, who notices that Edna is "burnt beyond recognition," seat themselves on the porch steps, and talk about how Edna "sank like a rock." Edna predicts, however, that "the rock will rise."

The film's second swimming scene is derived, in part, from the novel. At the end of Chapter V, Robert asks if Edna will go bathing. She tells him no, but with "a tone of indecision…. Her glance wandered from his face away toward the Gulf, whose sonorous murmur reached her like a loving but imperative entreaty" (31; ch. V). He insists that "the water must be delicious; it will not hurt you," and, as the feminist critics point out, he then acts in a rather peremptory way: he "reached up for her big, rough straw hat that hung on a peg outside the door, and put it on her head" (31; ch. V). Chapter VI belongs entirely to the omniscient narrator who reveals that Edna follows Robert "in obedience to one of the two contradictory impulses which impelled her." A "certain light was beginning to dawn dimly within her,—the light which, showing the way, forbids it." This light "bewilder[s]" her and "move[s] her to dreams, to thoughtfulness, to the shadowy anguish which had overcome her the midnight when she had abandoned herself to tears." "In short," says the narrator, she "was beginning to realize her position in the universe as a human being, and to recognize her relations as an individual to the world within and about her." This "ponderous weight of wisdom," however, takes on an ominous quality, for "the beginning of things, of a world especially, is necessarily vague, tangled, chaotic, and exceedingly disturbing. How few of us ever emerge from such beginning! How many souls perish in its tumult!" This chapter closes with words that are echoed at the novel's end:

> The voice of the sea is seductive; never ceasing, whispering, clamoring, murmuring, inviting the soul to wander for a spell in abysses of solitude; to lose itself in mazes of inward contemplation.
>
> The voice of the sea speaks to the soul. The touch of the sea is sensuous, enfolding the body in its soft, close embrace [32; ch. VI].

This chapter is dramatized in *Grand Isle's* second swimming scene, composed of ten shots. I have called the accompanying music, written for the film by Elliott Goldenthal, the sea theme. It is a haunting, slow piece set in a minor key. The scene contains the two "very big close-ups" that Lotman would identify as marked elements. The first is an extreme close-up of Edna's light green right eye as she says, "Listen, Robert" as the sea theme and natural sounds, especially the sound of waves coming ashore, provide a context for her words. The second extreme close-up is of Robert's brown eyes, look-

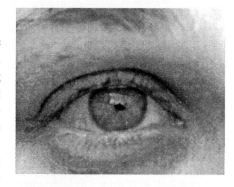

In *Grand Isle*, a 1992 Turner Picture produced by and starring Kelly McGillis as Edna Pontellier, who at this point in the novel is afraid to try to swim, listens to the sound of the sea and fearfully tells her friend Robert LeBrun, "Listen, Robert."

ing to sea and then turning to Edna as he says, "You don't have to be afraid," but Edna doesn't "want to swim today" and the scene ends by its bleaching out to white. An interesting aside is that in the Burton-Zeffirelli adaptation of *The Taming of the Shrew* the first sight we have of Kate is a "very big close-up" of Elizabeth Taylor's violet eye as she peers out of a window to gaze at the goings-on in the street below.

The expression on Kelly McGillis's face as she gazes into the camera, her body language, and the nature of the dialogue manage to capture some of Edna's bewilderment as she confronts the "tangled, chaotic, and exceedingly disturbing" nature of the "beginning of things." The sea's musical signature, the sea theme, represents the "voice of the sea," a seductive voice, but at this point in Edna's journey, a fearsome one.

Lant would approve, perhaps, of the fact that in the film it is Adèle, not Robert, who proposes that everyone go to the beach after their *soirée* on August 28th. Shot through a blue filter, the entire scene has an eerie quality, in character with Edna's two responses to her first real swim. She is both "intoxicated with her newly conquered power" (46; ch. X) and then the victim of a "quick vision of death" (47; ch. X). Her remark to her husband that she "thought [she] should have perished out there alone" (47; ch. X) is a chilling premonition of the end of the novel.

As the details of these swimming scenes show, *Grand Isle* manages to render much of the novel's enunciatory material into cinematic terms and to illustrate Arnavon's observation that "the attraction the water holds for [Edna], symbolizing a return to a pre-natal existence, becomes gradually stronger" (187). Wolff might say that at this point, however, Edna is still holding her hidden, mother-hungry self at bay. In comparing *The Awakening* to Emily Dickinson's J. 520 ("I started Early — Took my Dog —"), Timothy Cramer makes a similar point: "Like Dickinson's speaker who is afraid that the sea 'would eat me up —/ As wholly as a Dew,' Edna is afraid that she would be swallowed up before reaching the safety of society" (54). Later, it is this very swallowing up that she will seek and find.

The fourth swimming scene in *Grand Isle* is also rooted in the novel. After Robert leaves for Mexico, Edna's "whole existence was dulled, like a faded garment which seems to be no longer worth wearing" (65; ch. XVI). She takes comfort in swimming, "a diversion which afforded her the only real pleasurable moments that she knew" (65; ch. XVI). Just before the Creoles return to New Orleans, Reisz trails Edna to the beach. Reisz herself does not swim, "on account of her false hair, or the dread of getting the violets wet, ... [or] the natural aversion for water sometimes believed to accompany the artistic temperament" (67; ch. XVI). Edna urges her to talk about Robert until the conversation turns to Mariequita, the Mexican girl linked to both Robert and his brother, Victor. To escape Reisz's "venom," which made her "depressed, almost unhappy," Edna goes swimming "with an abandon that thrilled and invigorated her. She remained a long time in the water, half hoping that Mademoiselle Reisz would not wait for her" (68; ch. XVI).

In *Grand Isle*, this scene functions as a transition. As in the midnight swim, its music is the sea theme. There are, however, some striking new features that anticipate Edna's final plunge. First, she swims easily, doing a strong and leisurely crawl, not hesitating to put her face into the water. It is not at all the tiring dog-paddle, with her head awkwardly sticking up, that we see during the night swim of August 28th. Also, she has not put on her bathing cap, the turban-like affair that she has worn on each previous occasion in the water, perhaps a foreshadowing of the more radical disrobing to come. Her long red hair is braided. At the film's end it will be entirely loose, a long free-form tangle that also suggests the Aphrodite of Gilbert's essay. Finally, the camera work hints at but does not match the photography of the last sequence. In this fourth scene, the camera is held just at the water's surface so that sometimes we see the green below, sometimes the blue above, and sometimes both. By contrast, the camera of the earlier swimming scenes is never actually in the water, and during the last swim, it is sometimes so deep that we see Edna swimming above us.

During the long New Orleans sequences, *Grand Isle* reminds us of the sea's role when it incorporates a shot of the beautiful, sparkling waves into the fourth repetition of the refrain. We see these waves again, of course, at the film's end. As we have already noted, McGillis, who not only starred in this film but produced it as well, was willing to be photographed nude. Her strong, full body and her obvious ease in the water fairly depict the narrator's comment that Edna "lifted her white body and reached out with a long, sweeping stroke.... She went on and on" (136–37; ch. XXXIX). In the film Edna dives, surfaces to look around, floats on her back, and envisions, as we have seen, the little girl, Léonce and the children, Robert, Reisz, and then the girl again. The soundtrack is one unbroken rendition of the Nocturne. At the very moment that the Nocturne ends, the girl disappears.

Along with the refrain, the other marked element that can be associated with Wolff's work is the repetition of overexposures, those fifteen spots where the final image of one shot bleaches out before the next begins. Fourteen occur between scenes. One scene ends, for example, with Robert's face whited out as he smiles conspiratorially with the other guests over a bit of eccentric behavior on the part of Mademoiselle Reisz. The following shot is the first repetition of the refrain, Edna's dream on the night that Léonce returns from Klein's Hotel. Only one white-out, the sixth, occurs within a scene, the one where Edna rests in Madame Antoine's bed. A close-up of Edna's relaxed face bleaches out, and the next shot reveals that Edna is again dreaming of herself as a child. The other thirteen, though, have nothing to do with the refrain and occur seemingly at random, some introducing major hinge-points (for example, a close-up of Edna reading Robert's "good-by" note, a white-out, then Edna walking towards the sea at Grand Isle), some minor ones (Robert and Edna talking about Creole life, a white-out, then the guests assembling for dinner). Although it does not seem possible, therefore, to discover an overall design or to attach a meaning to any individual incidence, these striking visual events, taken together, evoke a mood out of which an interpretation may evolve.

In the spirit of Lotman's remark that the viewer "compares what he sees on the screen ... with clichés in films which he already knows" (32), we might consider two articles concerning Peter Bogdanovich's adaptation of *Daisy Miller* that provide a clue as to how we might read the overexposures in *Grand Isle*. First, Boyum describes "the film's final scene at Daisy's graveside": "Here, the other mourners having left, Winterbourne is shown standing alone, the camera slowly moving farther and farther away from him. Thus Bogdanovich emphasizes both his physical and emotional isolation, further underscoring the total emptiness of both man and moment by bleaching the image before us to a blank and jarring white" (149). J.J. Liggera writes in similar terms of the scene where Mrs. Walker literally gives Daisy the "cold shoulder" by turning "her daringly exposed shoulders" towards her: "The huge priggish image holds for a moment with the mustachioed Winterbourne revealed in splendid isolation. He is pretentiously and awkwardly suited after the European style, an American become a stuffed shirt. The image then bleaches out in a soft gold, a stinging conviction of Winterbourne, whose lovelessness proved lethal" (141). Not only do both critics point to Winterbourne's isolation, but they also share a negative reading of the bleaching out technique. It suggests an "emptiness," a "stinging conviction" associated with "lethal" "lovelessness." In *Grand Isle*, the bleachings are perhaps even more negative, for the force of their connotation builds as the incidences increase, and there is no "soft gold" here — only the "blank and jarring white" that Boyum sees in *Daisy Miller*.

In supporting her argument that "Edna's central problem, once the hidden 'self' begins to exert its inexorable power, is that her libidinal appetite has been fixated at the oral level" (247), Wolff cites a passage from a scene in the novel that is not included in *Grand Isle*. It is the dinner party scene where Edna entertains her guests one last time in Léonce's house. As Wolff notes, the "dinner party itself is one of the longest sustained episodes in the novel; we are told in loving detail about the appearance of the table, the commodious chairs, the flowers, the candles, the food and wines, Edna's attire — no sensory pleasure is left unattended. Yet even this indulgence fails to satisfy" (248). The passage reads as follows:

> There was something in her attitude, in her whole appearance when she leaned her head against the high-backed chair and spread her arms, which suggested the regal woman, the one who rules, who looks on, who stands alone.
>
> But as she sat there amid her guests, she felt the old ennui overtaking her; the hopelessness which so often assailed her, which came upon her like an obsession, like something extraneous, independent of volition. It was something which announced itself; a chill breath that seemed to issue from some vast cavern wherein discords wailed. There came over her the acute longing which always summoned into her spiritual vision the presence of the beloved one, overpowering her at once with a sense of the unattainable [109–10; ch. XXX].

Wolff observes that it "is not specifically Robert that Edna longs for," that "the beloved one" exists in an "indefinite perpetual image," that her longing is "an immortal one" (249). She concludes that the "indefinite quality of Edna's longing thus described has an ominous tone, a tone made even more ominous by the rising specter of those 'vast caverns' waiting vainly to be filled" (249). These internal "vast caverns" have, perhaps, their external counterpart in the sea with its invitation to "the soul to wander for a spell in abysses of solitude" (32; ch. VI) and its "vast expanse of water," the metaphoric "unlimited" in which Edna might "lose herself" (47; ch. X). The "stretch of water" between her and the land prompts the "vision of death," "the flash of terror" that so "appalled and enfeebled her senses" the night of August 28th. These caverns and abysses, orchestrated by internal wailing "discords" that find their echo in the "never ceasing, whispering, clamoring, murmuring" voice of the sea (32; ch. VI) singing its "mournful lullaby" (24; ch. III), are represented by the white-outs. We might pause here to recall Melville's diction in "The Whiteness of the Whale": "Is it that by its indefiniteness it shadows forth the heartless voids and immensities of the universe, and thus stabs us from behind with the thought of annihilation, when beholding the white depths of the milky way?" (212). An interesting aside is that students who have seen the film starring Patrick Stewart as Ahab (Captain Picard of *Star Trek: The Next Generation* fame) are still not willing—or able—to read more than a few pages of Melville's masterpiece. Here we might review Boyum's contention that the "early views about the mission of adaptation," where "the great unwashed mass [was] the target audience," now involves "just about everyone" (77). Students who have seen the film at least know something about the plot of *Moby Dick*, not the best outcome but not the worst either.

Caverns and abysses, indefinite voids and immensities do speak of annihilation, but the annihilation in Chopin's book, according to Wolff, is connected not to nothing, but to something, to the "ecstasy of death," the ultimate fusion with "time eternal" (258), the moment when, in Freud's words, an "identity" is achieved "between the ego and the nonego" (qtd. in Wolff 256). This is why such a general sense of impending annihilation, unlike the specific nothing that Edna sees when she hears Reisz's music, can be represented at all. The white-outs in *Grand Isle* mirror the "monumental white shroud" (Melville 212) in which the sea — the symbolic nonego, the unconscious, the mother — will wrap her returning child. It is into this something that the last image of the girl in the meadow dissolves.

At almost every turn there is an element in *Grand Isle* that corresponds to a facet of Wolff's argument. Missing from the film, however, is the novel's — and Wolff's — emphasis on food. Wolff writes that "an astonishing proportion of that part of the novel which deals with Edna's sojourn at Grand Isle is paced by the rhythm of her basic needs, especially the most primitive ones of eating and sleeping" (245–46) and that "those who care about her typically feed her; and the sleep-and-eat pattern which is most strikingly established at the beginning of the novel continues even to the very end" (247–48). Wolff uses this sleep-and-eat pattern, of course, as further evidence of Edna's being arrested in the oral stage. In the film, however, the many shots of elaborate meals being laid out by servants seem to function rather superficially as an index of Edna's wealth. In other words, nothing calls any special attention to what and when she eats, and the little girl in the meadow, whom we have identified as Edna's hidden self, is not pictured as the "voracious, omnivorous, and insatiable" self that Wolff describes (242). Thus, the omission of the dinner party scene is not particularly problematic, especially since the crucial information included in this scene — that Edna's interior landscape includes a "vast cavern wherein discords wailed" (109; ch. XXX) — is depicted elsewhere: in a very interesting close shot that occurs as Edna enters her lavish Esplanade Street home and, her head photographed against a bare white wall with the ticking of a clock the only sound, looks about with a blank expression that Chopin herself would have perhaps identified as the "old ennui" (109; ch. XXX); in a shot of her burning her drawings, one by one, as if to suggest that her art has become "not a defense against inner turmoil, merely a reflection of it" (Wolff 252); in her expression of bemused fatalism — as if to say, "I expected as much." — as she reads Robert's "Good-by — because I love you" note; and in the cumulative effect of the white-outs.

Admittedly, Dressler's 1992 article "Edna Under the Sun: Throwing Light on the Subject of *The Awakening*" is less accessible to students than Wolff's — physically less accessible since it has not been included in any of the handy collections of Chopin scholarship and intellectually less so as well since students are far more likely to know something about Freud's thought before-hand than about Lacan's. The Bedford Case Studies edition, however, does devote three full pages to a summary of Lacan's revision of Freud in Ross Murfin's "What Is Psychoanalytic Criticism?" — the chapter that precedes Wolff's essay — but even if students are not using this edition, they are bound to encounter the Lacanian vocabulary that has recently become more and more apparent in both literary and film criticism. In short, if the teacher interested in psychoanalytic readings of *The Awakening* should wish to include an example of a Lacanian interpretation, Dressler's is a good choice, espe-cially since the marked elements in *Grand Isle* — the extreme close-ups, the visual direct address to the camera, the refrain, and the white-outs — paral-lel the main points of Dressler's work.

Like Wolff, Dressler begins her essay with a brief refutation of those scholars whose readings of the text in some way fall short, a rhetorical strat-egy that the teacher might well point out. Then, she presents her thesis:

> Although *The Awakening* has traditionally been explored as a stirring into sexual consciousness, I would like to suggest now that the novel also and specifically addresses its title as a trope for *eye-opening* — for an entry, that is, into structures of seeing and being seen commonly theorized under the rubric of the "gaze" or "look," and which, for my own purposes, have been best enunciated by Kaja Silverman in her formulations on Lacan. What is it that might be gained by such an approach? It is my own belief — my own particu-lar bent of thought — that, with Edna newly viewed as a subject engaged fun-damentally with the problems and realities of the gaze — problems which are given scope and shape in the novel by the presence of light and sun — her ending likewise becomes newly formulated: as one which refers not to tran-scendence, or defeat, or even to a hopeless ambiguity, but rather to limitation and possibility as they exist within a construct of Lacanian illumination [60].

Dressler reminds us that for Lacan, we are all determined by "the gaze that is outside" (61). In the novel, Edna is "from the outset ... placed within the landscape of an other's particularly masculine way of seeing," best exemplified, perhaps, by Mr. Pontellier's "scopophilic" comment: "You are burnt beyond recognition" (61). Though initially the sunshade under which we first see Edna in the novel may appear to shield her from Mr. Pontellier's "look," the situ-ation is, in fact, otherwise: the "shade is of course intended to preserve Edna as an object for visual consumption," a condition to which Edna initially acquiesces (61).

Soon, however, Edna's awakening, her "*eye-opening*," begins and pro-ceeds through a series of eight stages. The first occurs after Léonce comes home from Klein's Hotel, wakes Edna up, and then scolds her, and the narrator com-pares Edna's "indescribable oppression," her "vague anguish," to "a shadow, like a mist passing across her soul's summer day" (25; ch. III). Citing also Chopin's references to Edna's "inward life," to the existence of some "hidden, 'truer' self" (14), Dressler asks two pertinent questions: "But who might this truer self be? And which is the shadow which has intervened?" (63). Although she doesn't answer the first question until her discussion of the sixth stage, she answers the second here. The shadow is the "screen"—in Lacan's words, "that culturally generated image or repertoire of images through which subjects are not only constituted, but differentiated," a construct "something like a mask, a double, an envelope" (qtd. in Dressler 63). In the novel, the screen is "dramatized by the intervention of apparently benign presences — sunshades and hats, gloves and veils, a multitude of tents, shawls, and umbrellas — all articles of protection which nevertheless encase, shield, and define the subject (in Edna's case as woman, mother, wife, and possession) who without such screening would lack identity altogether" (63). The sets and costumes in both films well illustrate such a dramatization. The general items listed above plus mosquito nets surrounding beds, veils on hats (particularly in *Grand Isle*), and the layers of clothing that we see Edna shed in *The End of August* when she prepares to nap at Madame Antoine's bring the screen, as it were, to the screen. Edna, unlike the other characters, has "vaguely intuited the images that enclose her" but also senses that "intuition may not necessarily lead to independence from such images" (Dressler 63). This gain in awareness represents the second stage of Edna's awakening.

The third stage is best exemplified during the soirée when Edna first hears Reisz play. Dressler suggests that Reisz "interestingly takes up positions both as looker and looked-on." Though she is "impervious to the glare of social looking," she is a spectacle of sorts, with her "rusty black lace" and the "comic 'bunch of artificial violets'" that she wears in her hair. At the same time, she has "eyes that glowed" (64). What is most important, however, is that Edna's emotions have been laid bare by "what she has not seen. It is as though for the moment Edna has been able to elude the insistence of the pictorial, the inevitability of seeing which necessarily implies its converse, or what Laura Mulvey has described as 'to-be-looked-at-ness'" (65). This is the beginning of Edna's flight from "traditional scopic forces" into a place where she can "establish a self entirely apart" (64). The place she finds, of course, is the sea. Here, in the "dark and shapeless" Gulf, in the "not-see of darkness," Edna glimpses "that the only place which is apart from the world of the seen, and apart from the world of the represented, is the dark house of nothingness itself; the only space where a self constructed by its images sheds that self, and its images, finally and for all" (65). Here, Edna experiences the "quick vision of death," a terrible vision that is matched only by its opposite — her husband's reminding her that "as long as she is living, she will never really be outside the field of his vision. 'You were not so very far, my dear,' he tells her. 'I was watching you'" (65).

The fourth stage is characterized by Edna's "struggles to seize the structure of looking that has shaped her — to fashion, that is, her own image of self" (67). Dressler's illustration from the text is the undressing scene at Madame Antoine's. She notes the contrast between how Edna looks at her hands after Léonce accuses her of being "burnt beyond recognition" and how she looks at her body here. With Léonce, she "held up her hands, strong, shapely hands, and surveyed them critically, drawing up her lawn sleeves above the wrists" (21; ch. I). Alone in Madame Antoine's bed, to review, she "looked at her round arms as she held them straight up and rubbed them one after the other, observing closely, as if it were something she saw for the first time, the fine, firm quality and texture of her flesh" (55–56; ch. XIII). In Lacan's terms, however, the change is merely an "illusory usurpation of the authority of the gaze," for in "seeing herself seeing herself, Edna has found a space in which she can *seem* to control her body as it is imaged" (Dressler 67).

In her awakening's fifth stage, Edna "moves forward in her attempts to structure her own way of seeing herself" but only when Robert departs for Mexico (68). Now, she takes up her art with renewed interest and in so doing "has taken on the role of looker rather than of looked-upon" (69). The problem, however, is that "the image of the artist is itself another screen, another construct allied not to the dark lash of imageless waves but to the land and to the visible" (69). After all, Dressler notes, Reisz, the artist, exhibits a "natural aversion for water" (69). Thus, as artist, "Edna stands in danger both of duplicating the imagistic force of the look (as she stares at others) *and* of recasting herself as simply another social construct" (69). What she discovers is that "looking also exposes the full extent to which she herself is imaged, the extent to which it is impossible for her 'to see [herself] without the intervention of representation'" (71).

For a moment after Robert returns from Mexico, Edna believes that "she may yet forge herself an Edna-generated image that will include Robert in its self-sufficient circle" (71). However, her belief is soon dashed as she watches Adèle give birth and is "confronted finally and irreversibly with the limitations of her subjectivity" (71), the "limitation" to which her "ending ... refers" (60). What she witnesses, in Lacanian terms, is the "reality of imaged existence as it is duplicated and expressed within the visible world" (72). The essence of the sixth stage, and the point at which Dressler answers her first question — "But who might this truer self be?" — is that "Edna, in looking at Adèle, can only look at herself looking at herself as she is imaged — as another woman, on the bed before her, in the throes of a labor that is the physical, visible, corollary to her specular assignation in the world. There is no hidden, invisible, 'truer' self that she might bring forward to counter this visible image" (72). Edna's realization that the "moment a child, a self is brought into the world, it enters representation" leads her to acknowledge that she has "never really 'possessed' the gaze. And she is left 'dazed' by the revelation of it" (72).

One of the strengths of *The End of August* is that during this childbirth scene, Edna is completely transfixed, riveted by what she is witnessing — a stronger reading of the novel than the busy Edna of *Grand Isle*, helping the doctor and maid, wringing out bloody rags. The problem with *The End of August* in general, however, is that when one particularly evocative shot or scene occurs, not only is it not "marked" but it also is not embedded into some kind of pattern that would help to foreground it. Thus it remains in the background, unobserved, unread.

Although it may seem that Edna's epiphany that there is no "truer" self would signal the end of Dressler's argument, this is not at all the case. To continue, Dressler uses Lacan's distinction between the "look" and the "gaze." The "look" is "fundamentally local and focused at the eye" while the "gaze" is "not coterminous with any individual viewer, or group of viewers" but is, in Lacan's words, "'unapprehensible,' issuing 'from all sides.'" Possessing an "abstract status," the nature of the gaze is "best formulated in [Lacan's] impersonal phrase, 'point of light'" (66). Analogous to de Saussure's distinction between *langue* ("the system of language in general") and *parole* ("any particular usage within it") (Adams and Searle 645), an analogy that reflects Lacan's interest in language, the difference between the gaze ("issuing 'from all sides'"), parallel to *langue*, and the look ("fundamentally local"), parallel to *parole*, allows Dressler to analyze the role of the sun in Chopin's novel. It is this role that affords a positive reading of Edna's end, the "possibility" to which her "ending ... refers" (60).

Throughout the novel, Edna is "closely linked to the sun." She "is burned by it, and consistently described as a being who thrives in it, reminding Doctor Mandelet of 'some beautiful sleek animal waking up in the sun,' and prompting Mademoiselle Reisz to exclaim, as Edna enters her apartment, 'Ah! here comes the sunlight!'" (66). For Dressler, the sun is the "figure" of the gaze. It "dominate[s] this novel" and stands for "something very like Lacan's 'point of light'" (66).

The important idea is this: "for Lacan the object-in-sight — the 'spectacle' which is illuminated by the 'light' of the gaze —... is also always as well the source-origin of yet another 'point of light.'" This formulation again reflects Lacan's concern with language, here with the endless chain of role-shifting signifiers and signifieds that make it a slippery affair to arrive at a final, meaningful signified. Further, the gaze "generate[s] a look" (as *langue* generates *parole*) and as Silverman writes, it is a look that "in effect looks back at the viewer" (qtd. in Dressler 73). At the same time, Edna is at this moment both a spectacle under the sun/gaze and the sun/gaze herself, as her association with the sun suggests. The seventh stage is the answer to Dressler's final question: if "Edna in this moment, 'absolutely alone,' lit by the sun on her naked body, represents the conflation of gaze and spectacle, to whom is she looking back at as viewer?" Possibly, suggests Dressler, the "gaze-force of the sun itself," but also, and most importantly, at "the *reader* itself" (73). As Edna's "limitations and possibilities as a human subject" are revealed, the reader is confronted "with the nature of its own subjectivity" (73), with the "inevitability of the function which *is* the look that gives the self" (74).

Finally, although Lacan writes that "all binarizations of spectator and spectacle mystify the scopic relations in which we are held," he does "allow for some *freedom* within that mystification" in the form of "'playing' with the gaze through a manipulation of the screen" (74). Such play is "hinted at ... in the figures of the mockingbird and parrot, who from the beginning of the book speak in a borrowed language" (74). Dressler's conclusion is that although Edna "chooses rather to die than to live by manipulating the images that cloud her life," Chopin herself engages in such play by "slipping the mask of her heroine onto her readers, asking them at the last to see, not Edna, but themselves" (74). The eighth stage involves "the challenge which has perhaps always been embedded in Edna's ending ... a challenge, finally, not to defeat or success, but to seeing as seen. And it leaves the reader with Edna, exposed — in the harsh white light of a page" (74).

Although, as we have noted, both *Grand Isle* and *The End of August* beautifully picture the accoutrements that Dressler identifies as the novel's "dramatization" of the screen, it is again mostly to *Grand Isle* with its marked elements that the teacher should turn in order to help students come to grips with Dressler's essay, an essay that ends with the kind of wordplay that can frustrate even the most able student. The film's fifteen white-outs can be read as reminders of the "omnipresence of the 'gaze'" (66), technological sunbursts that mimic the sun itself, the ultimate "point of light" in Chopin's text. Just as they could not be individually analyzed in relation to Wolff's essay, they have no individual meaning in relation to Dressler's. In other words, they do not seem to represent the "look" of any particular character. Rather, their insistent presence throughout the film becomes an image of the insistence of the "gaze" itself.

Individual looks, however, are also highlighted in *Grand Isle*. This is accomplished, first, through the use of extreme close-ups which occur (and occur only) during the swimming lesson scene detailed earlier. To review, in this scene we see Edna's green right eye filling the screen as she says, "Listen,

Robert." The film's music, its "sea theme," coupled with natural sounds (birds calling, waves splashing), represents the "voice of the sea" of the novel, a voice that is "seductive; never ceasing, whispering, clamoring, murmuring, inviting the soul to wander for a spell in abysses of solitude; to lose itself in mazes of inward contemplation.... The voice of the sea speaks to the soul. The touch of the sea is sensuous, enfolding the body in its soft, close embrace" (32; ch. VI). Here, as the cinematography makes clear, Edna's "look" is directed not towards Robert, though she invokes him to "listen," but towards the sea, towards what Gerri Brightwell calls the "great wordless voice" (6), towards Dressler's "not-see of darkness" where Edna will eventually escape both the gaze and the confines of patriarchal language which "refuses to allow its women a language of their own" (Wolff, "Un-utterable" 7). At this point, however, Edna is engaged in what Dressler defines as the third stage of her awakening, and the film's emphasis on her eye signals that "she will seek to establish a self entirely apart from traditional scopic forces" (64).

The situation with Robert, however, is quite different. Again to review, the next shot is an extreme close-up of his brown eyes, first looking with Edna at the sea but then turning towards her as he replies, "You don't have to be afraid." The sea holds no special attraction for Robert, who, like most of the other Creoles, enters the water "as though into a native element" (46; ch. X). But Edna interests him intensely, as the shift in his look indicates. As John Rowe points out, "In public, her husband and her lovers possess her body, treating it as 'a valuable piece of personal property,' the intentional object of masculine desire" (117), of the "masculine gaze" (130). Just as Léonce insists upon Edna's maintaining her white skin, a sign of her leisure and his wealth, Robert too, as Dressler notes, "is careful to take Edna's 'big, rough straw hat' and 'put it on her head' before one of their walks" (62), a walk whose destination is the sea — and the very scene in the film which we are discussing here. If Edna's look at the sea marks the third stage, then Robert's look at her prefigures the fifth — her discovery that "looking also exposes the full extent to which she herself is imaged" (Dressler 71).

Finally, *Grand Isle* dramatizes the "look" in yet another way — the inclusion of visual direct address to the camera. *Grand Isle* was produced for television, but its stars made their names in movies shown in theaters. Thus, on one hand, we "do not expect film actors to turn to us from time to time and include us.... We still suffer from a slight psychological shock when being discovered watching the happening on the screen" (Zettl 223), a shock that Groucho Marx (or more recently, Matthew Broderick in the splendid *Ferris Bueller's Day Off*) exploits for comic ends and that Samuel Beckett exploits for existential ends when he made *Film* and broke "the fourth wall," allowing us to see an elderly Buster Keaton involved in the "search of non-being in flight from extraneous perception breaking down in inescapability of self-perception" (11). Therefore, Zettl's comment that we "accept" television "actors addressing us directly during a story and thus drawing us into their plot" (223) whereas we are "shocked" when this happens in film is not entirely true. In the case of *Grand Isle*, the device invites the viewer to think about this marked element rather than to simply accept it as an oddity.

Edna as her adult self looks once and only once into the camera. During the first shot of the swimming lesson scene, with a kind of unhappy resignation, she stares at the back wall of the bathhouse (the location of the camera and, by extension, of our eyes) and finishes buttoning her bathing suit as the sea's theme begins. Although the extreme close-up of Robert's eyes will tell us that Edna is indeed the object of the male look, Edna's look at us, even though a worried one, reinforces Dressler's notion that at this point in her journey Edna is no longer entirely passive. She is now an emergent looker, readying herself to "seek to establish a self entirely apart from traditional scopic forces" (64). Moreover, since we are positioned at the bathhouse wall and since Edna is buttoning her suit while looking at us, we are, in effect, functioning as a mirror. On a literal level, we might well expect a mirror in this location so that the bathers, especially the women, could check their appearances before coming before the eyes of the public. In other words, the mirror is an instrument through which the "scopic forces" project their abstract power into the concrete terms of everyday life.

On the figurative level, however, the shot implies much more. Since 1975, when Mulvey published her "Visual Pleasure and Narrative Cinema" in *Screen*, it has become a commonplace in film studies that the spectator is in "direct scopophilic contact with the female form displayed for his enjoyment" and, through the male protagonist, gains "control and possession of the woman within the diegesis," the story (13). Dressler makes a similar point in terms of the novel when she notes the difference between the way that Chopin describes Léonce and the way she describes Edna:

> Contrary, for example, to the terse illustrations of her husband's physical appearance, Edna Pontellier will have descriptive passages lavished upon her, details of her hair, coloring, and dress brought forward, of her "captivating" features, of her "firm, round arms" and her "bare insteps." She is described as having a body of "clean ... symmetrical" lines (later the painterly "living tints" of her flesh are invoked), and one which requires "feeling and discernment" in order to appreciate. What is notable here is Chopin's deftness in (re)activating the reader's gaze even as she cloaks it in a vocabulary of artistic apprehension (read, connoisseurship). Yet what we are left with is nothing more than Edna still as object-in-sight, recognized primarily for the "charm" of her physique and for "the noble beauty of its modeling" [62].

If Edna, then, looks into the mirror that is the viewer, what she sees reflected is herself as "object-in-sight." She sees, because we see, exactly what Léonce and Robert see, not some other "Edna-generated image" whose possibility teases her imagination. Although hopeful that "in the future ... women may find themselves in mirrors" — and by "themselves" she means "selves" not constituted by the masculine gaze — Helen Emmitt laments that now, as in 1899, "for the woman who cannot find a mirror to reflect her, the embrace of the water provides self-fulfillment" (316–17, 318).

It is Mademoiselle Reisz whom Dressler singles out as the other woman in the text who "takes up positions both as looker and looked-on" (64) and, interestingly enough, it is Reisz who also looks into the camera — again, once and only once — at the very end of *Grand Isle* in the image that Edna sees as she is swimming away. To review, the sequence of these final images is as follows: the little girl, Léonce and the children, Robert, Reisz, and the little girl again. Edna sees Reisz in a medium shot at the piano, her room with its oriental rug lovely in the sunlight. Then the camera moves in for a close-up of Reisz's face as she blinks, nods her head, then smiles knowingly. What she appears to know may be what the Edna of the novel suspects:

> She thought of Léonce and the children. They were a part of her life. But they need not have thought that they could possess her, body and soul. How Mademoiselle Reisz would have laughed, perhaps sneered, if she knew! "And you call yourself an artist! What pretensions, Madame! The artist must possess the courageous soul that dares and defies" [137; ch. XXXIX].

Yet, she is not sneering, and it may be that *Grand Isle's* Reisz knows something other than that suggested above, for the visual situation is somewhat complex. Here, Reisz is an image, a product of Edna's mind (as is Robert, "off there in Mexico"), and we must assume that Edna envisions Reisz looking at her. But in looking into the camera, she is also looking at us. We, then, momentarily, become Edna, for we see as she sees. And what we see, in Dressler's terms, is that Edna has chosen once and for all to reject "another screen, another construct allied not to the dark lash of imageless waves but to the land and to the visible" (69). In Edna's projection, Reisz knows that she herself has settled for the screened existence, that she herself has chosen her screen, and that she understands Edna's rejection of this and all screens. And she approves. Further, as in the bathhouse shot when Edna in looking at herself in the mirror looks also at us, so too does Edna's image of Reisz look at us when it looks at her. The difference here, however, is that Edna is able to look at the image looking at us. The corresponding point in Dressler's work occurs when she notes that at the novel's end Edna gazes at "the *reader* itself" (73). This moment in the novel, which according to Silverman, "unsettles because it threatens to expose the duplicity inherent in every subject, and every object" (qtd. in Dressler 73), finds its filmic parallel in the "duplicity," indeed the multiplicity, of the shot in question — Reisz, in Edna's image, looks at Edna and at us as well, but as Edna's image it is really Edna "seeing herself seeing herself" (67) and Edna seeing herself seeing us, "confronting [us] with the nature of [our] own subjectivity" (73).

Finally, Edna gazes at herself and at us most directly and most often when she sees herself as the child in the meadow. As we have seen, this repeating image represents, in Wolff's terms, the hidden self; in Dressler's, perhaps, an expression of the third stage of Edna's awakening, the stage where she "seeks to establish a self entirely apart from traditional scopic forces" (64). Robert Collins's work with the novel's garment imagery — specifically with the bonnet as what Dressler would call a "symbol-symptom" of these "scopic forces" — clarifies this point. Claiming that Edna is mistaken in her belief that "her unsuccessful attempts to learn how to swim that summer at Grand Isle have triggered the memory" of herself as a girl in the meadow, Collins proposes that "what in fact has triggered the memory is Edna's subconscious realization that the role she has been fated to as a woman has obstructed her view of life just as the sunbonnet obstructed her view that day in Kentucky, making it impossible for her to see anything more than what is immediately before her..." (183). The absence of the bonnet in *Grand Isle*'s refrain, then, depicts the early stages of Edna's quest for an "Edna-generated image" (Dressler 71), of her first inclinations to be one who looks at the world without blinders, not merely one who is looked upon, and to be one who is unconcerned with how she looks, for the purpose of the bonnet, after all, is to keep the sun off her face. The bare-headed child corresponds to the part of her adult self that does not care if she becomes sunburned, for she seems to notice her skin "critically" only when her husband comments on it.

The girl in the meadow looks into the camera during four of the six sightings. As does her image of Mademoiselle Reisz, Edna's image of her young self represents her "seeing herself seeing herself," but there is a difference. Reisz's gazing image persists until the shot ends, whereas the little girl behaves as the adult Edna does in the bathhouse: she looks but then turns her back to the camera. When our looking at her exposes her looking, she is removed from the "space in which she can *seem* to control her body as it is imaged" (67) and is once again "restore[d]," in Dressler's words, "to her position as an object-in-sight" (70). From this she flees.

Lacan's notion of "the drive" also helps us to read meaning into the little girl's turning her back on us. In Joan Copjec's words, "What's involved in the drive, Lacan tells us, is a *making oneself heard or making oneself seen*; that is to say, the intimate core of our being, no longer sheltered by sense, ceases to be supposed and suddenly becomes exposed" (qtd. in Mellard 401). This "intimate core" corresponds to what Wolff calls the "hidden self" and to what *Grand Isle* pictures as the little girl in the meadow. Further, as James Mellard explains in a helpful endnote,

> Drive seems to be allied with enjoyment of *jouissance*. Both drive and *jouissance* represent pleasure that has become pain, express a compulsion to transgress oedipal law, and represent Thanatos, or the death drive. Desire operates within the pleasure principle, *jouissance* beyond it. Thus, whereas desire is lawful and seems allied with consciousness, enjoyment or *jouissance* is unlawful and is allied with the unconscious [406].

Clearly Edna is a "victim" of *jouissance,* not of desire.

This brief outline of Lacan's "late theory" (406) is helpful here in two ways. First, in reminding us of Lacan's connection to Freud, Mellard provides a way for us to link Dressler and Wolff, for Lacanian thought holds that "the unconscious is centered on lack or absence of the desired object" (Adams and Searle 733), exactly Wolff's position in "Thanatos and Eros." Further,

> Lacan refers to this lost object of desire as *objet petit a,* or "object small a," with the letter *a* standing for *autre,* the French word for *other....* Why a small *a* (*autre: other*) instead of the capitalized *Other* Lacan uses ... to refer to a particular quality of the Symbolic Order [the world of language that follows the child's immersion in the Imaginary Order]? Perhaps it's because our relationship to our *objet petit a,* to our lost object of desire, is so personal, so individual, so utterly private, whereas our experiences in the Symbolic Order are not. *Objet petit a* is the "little other" that belongs only to me, that influences only me.... *Other* with a capital *O,* in contrast, influences everyone [Tyson 28].

The "look," as we have seen, not only is loosely synonymous with *parole,* but also with *objet petit a.* The "gaze," on the other hand, is connected not only to *langue* but also to the *Other.*

Second, Mellard provides yet another bit of evidence for those critics who steadfastly maintain that *The Awakening* was far ahead of its time, for his essay identifies the postmodern novel *Damage* and its film adaptation as artifacts that attest to the "postpatriarchal, postoedipal universe" in which we now live and which was foreseen only in Freud's late works (396). Our major point here, however, is simply that the last shot of *Grand Isle*, the little girl's retreating back as she runs deeper into the meadow, dramatizes not only Dressler's idea that "Edna Pontellier chooses rather to die than to live by manipulating the images that cloud her life" (74) but also Mellard's reading of Lacan's "late theory" (406), where *jouissance* "is allied with the unconscious." The little girl, the exposed intimate core, who, we should recall, appears first in a dream and is thus constructed of material from the unconscious, dissolves, before our eyes, back into the unconscious, here symbolized by the meadow, that "ocean of waving grass" (Chopin 36; ch. VII) that parallels the sea itself, into whose depths Edna simultaneously swims.

If Zettl is at least partly right that the direct looks of the characters cause us to "suffer from a slight psychological shock when being discovered watching the happening on the screen" (223), then *Grand Isle* offers its viewers exactly what Dressler claims the novel offers its readers — "a challenge ... to seeing as seen" (74). We are, and have been, "with Edna, exposed," not only "in the harsh white light of a page" but also in the fifteen overexposures, those white-outs, that represent the gaze itself. Edna flees the gaze, dissolving into the primordial nonego, the empty meadow held for a moment or two before our eyes until it fades to black. Our lot is considerably easier. We can close the book — or stop the DVD.

2. Cultural Criticism
A Streetcar Named Desire by Tennessee Williams
A Streetcar Named Desire (1951)

> We all have in our conscious and unconscious minds a great vocabulary of images, and I think all human communication is based on these images as are our dreams; and a symbol in a play has only one legitimate purpose, which is to say a thing more directly and simply and beautifully than it could be said in words.
>
> Symbols, when used respectfully, are the purest language of plays. Sometimes it would take page after tedious page of exposition to put across an idea that can be said with an object or a gesture on the lighted stage.— Tennessee Williams [qtd. in Jackson 26]

The introduction to this book cites Geoffrey Wagner's work in categorizing adaptations. The two versions of *The Awakening* are what he would call *transpositions*, where, to review, "a novel is given directly on the screen with a minimum of apparent interference." As we have seen, while both films closely follow Chopin's text, there is much to say about the differences between *Grand Isle* and *The End of August*. Wagner would likely call the 1951 adaptation of *A Streetcar Named Desire* a *commentary*, where "an original is taken and either purposely and inadvertently altered in some respect ... when there has been a different intention on the part of the film-maker." This "different intention" arose in part because of the Censor Board, but the major changes illustrate what we are interested in here: exploring the relationship between the film and Foucault by connecting the film primarily to the work of Nicholas Pagan and William Kleb. Briefly stated, in the 1951 adaptation of *Streetcar*, violence is characteristic of what Foucault calls the Same, while timidity or weakness is associated with the Other. Otherness implies diversity and permissiveness, qualities which do not need to be supported by violence. Sameness implies conformity and suppression, which must be imposed by violence. Stanley represents the Same, as do Stella and Mitch, and it is the increased violence in the film that bonds them even more closely to Stanley than they are in the play. Blanche, of course, belongs to the realm of the Other. The role of the audience is also included in this discussion, for, as Anca Vlasopolos suggests, the "force of this 'problem' play is to disquiet us" (338).

Before introducing students to the kind of cultural criticism practiced by Michel Foucault, it is important to note what they can already say about *Streetcar*. What might please Williams himself is that what they seem to respond to most fully when they study this play is its symbolism. They can easily identify the paper lantern that Blanche buys to cover the naked light bulb in Stella and Stanley's bedroom as a symbol of illusion, her way of hiding the truth that the light bulb can reveal. They see symbolic gestures in Mitch's putting the lantern in place, in his being the first to tear it down, angry enough to want to "take a look at [Blanche] good and plain!" (117; scene 9) and, at the play's end, in Stanley's "tearing it off the light bulb," his final assault against Blanche, causing her to cry out "as if the lantern was herself" (140; scene 11). Students find meaning, sometimes ironic, in the symbolic names of the streetcars (Desire and Cemeteries) that bring Blanche to Elysian Fields, itself a richly allusive place name, as is Belle Reve. They enjoy exploring the suggestive nature of the names of the major characters. "Blanche DuBois" and "Stella" are names which Blanche herself defines (her name, "the two together mean white woods. Like an orchard in spring!" [55; scene 3] [and] "Stella for Star" [18; scene 1]). Blanche's simile — "like an orchard in spring" — is quite in character with her desire to be young again. "White woods," however, could also be "like winter trees in snow," but this would be a threatening simile for Blanche, conjuring up images of age and winter, not youth and spring. "Stanley" means "stone clearing" ("Behind the Name"), suggestive of his streak of heart-hardedness, and "Eunice" means "Good Victory," specifically "her happy sexual victory" with her husband, Steve (Kolin, "Eunice Hubbell" 106 and 109). "Harold" is the given name of "Mitch" (from his last name, "Mitchell") and is a form of "Herald," an "officer having the duty of making royal or state proclamations, and of bearing ceremonial messages between princes or sovereign powers" (*Oxford English Dictionary*). In this sense he is the officer under Stanley — the putative "sovereign power" — who announces the unpleasant truths about Blanche. Students can also see that the Young Man "collecting for *The Evening Star*" (82; scene 5) is Desire personified and that the blind Mexican Woman selling "Flores para los muertos" is Death, whose "opposite is desire," as Blanche tells Mitch (120; scene 9). They may discuss how Blanche symbolizes what Thomas Adler calls "the beauty, culture, and grace of the old," while Stanley is symbolic of the "increasingly utilitarian new" (39).

When they watch the 1951 film version, students notice that not only are these symbols from the play itself still present in the movie but also that Elia Kazan has added others. When the broken bottle with which Blanche attempts to defend herself during the rape shatters the large, ornate oval mirror that they have seen throughout the film, students recognize, as does Maurice Yacowar, that the "mirror is an image of Blanche's shattered composure and self-respect" (20). The shot of the fire hose washing away the street trash that immediately follows the rape is, to students, a clichéd symbol of Stanley's "phallic forcefulness" (Yacowar 20), but when they are reminded of Eunice's line to Stanley — "I hope they do haul you in and turn the fire hose on you, same as last time!" (60; scene 3) — they can also observe, again as does Yacowar, that "Stanley, formerly a victim of the hose and treated as trash by the regularizing forces in society, is now enjoying a kind of revenge by bringing Blanche down to his level" (20).

These observations, however, are relatively superficial, but with the help of several critical texts the students can take their ideas to a different level by becoming familiar with the postmodern theories that challenge what Williams presumes in the introductory quote: that if one chooses one's signifiers with care, the signified — the "idea" or the "thing" — can be "said." If students were to encounter, for example, Edward Said's notion that "*presence*, or the transcendental signified," is a "tyranny and [a] fiction" (166) or, in a more likely scenario, if they were to discover in Pagan's fascinating *Rethinking Literary Biography: A Postmodern Approach to Tennessee Williams* that in *Of Grammatology* "Derrida is extremely wary" of the "security," "confidence," and "tranquil assurance" of any commentary — including the author's — that "leaps over the text toward its presumed content, in the direction of the pure signified" (86), they would be at a loss. But a book like Pagan's, which opens, in his words, "a new way for literary biography to consider the relation between author and text" (10), is the very sort of book that might prompt students to question not only Williams's presumption about symbols but also Thomas Adler's method of setting up dichotomies through which the play's themes emerge. Adler's book, one of Twayne's Masterwork Studies that has gone out of print but is available in libraries, was well liked by students because the reading level and what we might call the idea level are both comfortable. Pagan challenges the "tranquil assurance" with which Adler (whom Pagan erroneously calls Alfred, not Thomas) uses "the supposed opposition between Blanche and Stanley" (100) to identify the play's themes (his last chapter is titled "The Themes"), the inevitable signifieds toward which, for him, the signifiers necessarily point. Indeed, from Pagan's postmodern point of view, what Adler says about Blanche's past — that her "remembering and partial reinventing of a past that perhaps never was at Belle Reve, and assuredly never was in Shep Huntleigh" (84) — could be said about Adler's own "remembering and partial reinventing" of the play's themes, its "pure signifieds." In the following chapter, "'Ode: Intimations of Immortality from Recollections of Early Childhood' and Thematic Criticism," we will revisit thematics in a kindlier, gentler, and more complex light.

While Pagan, writing in 1993, does concur with Adler, writing only three years previously, that Stanley is "predator, victimizer/executioner" and Blanche is "moth/victim," and that "Desire (Eros)" belongs in Stanley's world while "Death (Thanatos)" belongs in Blanche's, Pagan finds it "easy to question" his own neat categories (92). Rather than thinking of Blanche as "moth/victim," he suggests that she "may be thought of as predator — she preys on young men," and, furthermore, positioning himself as a feminist would, he asks, "Why are we to assume that the desire named in the title or the desire that names the streetcar is Stanley's desire, men's desire? What about Blanche's desire? What about women's desire?" (92). These are fair and important, though simplistic, questions to pose to students. Though Pagan names the reward of working through a not-quite-so-comfortable book like his own — "an active, on-going, and playful relation" (11) among reader, text, and "paper-author" (the term Roland Barthes uses to indicate that the "flesh and blood author is inaccessible; or, at least, is knowable only as a function of discourse, not as a pre-linguistic entity" [10]) — his point is stated much more simply by Bert Cardullo who suggests that Williams's characters are complex "human beings *first*," not "social symbols or gender representatives" that can be neatly categorized as "victor-victim, oppressor-oppressed, or working man-decadent woman" (169).

Though Pagan's book is a valuable addition to the Williams scholarship, it is perhaps too difficult and too long (128 pages) to include in an already crowded undergraduate course. As we saw in the chapter devoted to *The Awakening*, the inclusion of one or two short critical essays is a more manageable strategy. Kleb's "Marginalia: *Streetcar*, Williams, and Foucault," written expressly for Phillip Kolin's *Confronting Tennessee Williams's* A Streetcar Named Desire: *Essays in Critical Pluralism*, covers some of the same semiotic ground as Pagan's book, but because it introduces students to the kind of cultural criticism practiced by Foucault, it goes beyond Cardullo's easy-to-read formalism. In other words, it occupies a workable middle ground. First, we will examine how Blanche represents the Other, second, how Stanley represents the Same, and, finally, how Stella and Mitch also represent the Same, more so in the film than in the play.

Just before Stanley rapes Blanche, he upbraids her: "And look at yourself! Take a look at yourself in that worn-out Mardi Gras outfit, rented for fifty cents from some ragpicker! And with the crazy crown on! What queen do you think you are?" (127; scene 10). While Stanley's words embody the source of his rage against Blanche — the threat that her queenship will supplant his kingship — and thus provide a prologue of sorts for the rape-as-punishment about to follow, they also paraphrase, in dramatic terms, Kleb's thesis:

> ... Williams's plays construct and animate the same shifting ontological landscape mapped out by Foucault; situated at the margin where death, madness, and sexuality intersect and interact, they focus, as does Foucault in his most important texts, on the struggle to control (through the power of knowledge and the manipulation of "truth") a definition of the Same and the Other [27].

When Stanley demands that Blanche look at herself in her outlandish, cheap costume, he wants her to recognize her otherness and his sameness and to thereby acknowledge the extent to which she has disrupted his household. She, of course, does not comply (at this point she cannot) and retreats instead into a rescue fantasy that centers around the quasi-mythical Shep Huntleigh.

Kleb bases his work on Foucault's *Discipline and Punish, History of Sexuality, The Order of Things,* and *Histoire de la folie.* Although he finds the English translations of the first three "complete and adequate," he notes that the English translation of the fourth is "radically abridged," and thus he chooses to translate passages himself and preserve the French title (41). In keeping with Foucault's suggestion that "his writing be viewed as a 'tool box' containing a variety of ideas and strategies that might be used when appropriate and without regard for a totalizing system" (41), Kleb freely draws upon Foucault's four texts and others as well to structure his argument.

He begins by characterizing the play as a continuation of a "discourse on sexuality" that began during the late eighteenth century "when the human sciences and the concept of social welfare began to emerge" (28). Sex becomes "*the secret* that must be revealed — or 'confessed,' as Foucault puts it," and this "repressive hypothesis, then, sex as secret, contributes to the proliferation of discourses on sexuality that has characterized modernity" (28). Finding it meaningful that *Streetcar* opened on Broadway on December 3, 1947, and Alfred Kinsey's *Sexual Behavior in the Human Male* was published in January of 1948, Kleb locates their essential similarity in a "central strategy" of "talk," of "self-revelation," which in *Streetcar* becomes "a series of confessions, some forced, others voluntary, in which the marginal figure (Blanche) is reclassified as an object of purely sexual knowledge" (29). It is not only Stanley who engineers such a reclassification, for "Blanche was immediately and widely perceived as a sign for sexual maladjustment" by audiences and critics alike. To read Blanche solely in these terms, however, is to make the kind of mistake Pagan accuses Adler of making — in other words, of obscuring

> an understanding of the power relations at work in Williams's play by restricting awareness of the true scope of Blanche's power. Surely sexuality is a key

term in Williams's configuration of the otherness of Blanche DuBois, but it is by no means the only term, and it becomes, in fact, the term that finally limits her power, allows her to be contained, silenced, excluded, and confined [Kleb 30].

As Foucault's work demonstrates, the modern clinic, prison, and asylum "operate by dividing individuals into categories: sick/healthy, criminal/law-abiding, mad/sane," the same kinds of bipolar categories that Pagan questions in Adler and in himself. These institutions, according to Foucault, had their beginnings in the "houses of internment" of the seventeenth century. Here, "anyone regarded as a threat to society at any point or level might be confined" (Kleb 31). "The poor, the unemployed, the sick, venereals, homosexuals, prostitutes, the sexually promiscuous, blasphemers, witches, profligates, free thinkers, libertines, the insane" could find themselves in serious jeopardy, and those "noisy women, prodigal sons, and daughters whose passions were overexcited by reading too much romance literature" could be confined on the strength of "a *lettre de cachet en famille*" (31). All of the above, "housed together" and alienated from Reason, became the embodiment of Unreason — a "huge, polymorphous, all-encompassing term of otherness — anything and everything that threatened the Same" (31).

Since Blanche, whom Stanley explicitly describes as a "noisy woman" (110; scene 8), belongs to the world of the Other, her strategy for survival is "to defend herself by taking control of the Same; to reconstitute her otherness (her difference) as sameness" (Kleb 31). As Kleb sees it, her defense is a triple attack against "Stella, Mitch, [and] the flat itself" (31). First, because "Blanche stands for Stella's psychological inheritance, a threat not only to her marriage but to the baby in her womb," Stella must "reaffirm her new life with Stanley," a reaffirmation dramatized by Scene 3 where Stella reunites with Stanley after he has beaten her and where Blanche is left "separated from the site of healthy sexual union" (Kleb 32), though the word "healthy" could certainly be questioned. Second, Blanche attempts to "take control of the Same" through Mitch, who lives with his sick mother and is associated with "unmanly sensitivity, disease, arrested adolescence, even sexual confusion," all traits that connect him "to the symbolic value of Allan Grey," Blanche's young homosexual husband who commits suicide after Blanche confronts him with her disgust. "Blanche's presence threatens to make these seeds grow" in Mitch (Kleb 33). Like Stella, however, Mitch too is "rescued" by Stanley and thus "escape[s] the sexual fate [Blanche] represents, with its connections, finally, to madness and death" (34). Blanche also attacks the apartment itself when, first, "she tries to establish its difference (from Belle Reve), then she tries to transform it, and finally her mind, her imagination, threatens to consume it" (34). In Scene 10, when "the walls of the flat disappear and a tawdry vision of life at the sexual margins materializes," her madness becomes "a kind of fury that threatens not only to consume the mind but to destroy the world" (Kleb 36).

It is against these attacks, then, that Stanley defends "his control of the Same by reaffirming Blanche's difference" (Kleb 34). Using the language of semiotics, Kleb suggests that Stanley does this by "redefining the 'truth' about Blanche solely in terms of her sexual misdeeds.... In short, he transforms her from an exploding symbol of Unreason to a contained sign (the rape is the signifying act) linking sexual promiscuity and madness" (34). Similarly, Pagan thinks of Blanche as the wild card, for "it can dispense with the role that it usually plays and play a great variety of other roles" (116). Her wild card status, however, makes it difficult for us to "envisage a 'real' Blanche DuBois, a Blanche DuBois outside of her role-playing" (Pagan 120). For Kathleen Hulley, "Blanche is literally and symbolically dangerous because she is too multivalent to be contained; she opens too many possibilities" (116), while Stanley "restricts the powers of the symbolic function to their most socially expedient level" (118). In other words, in terms of Pagan's metaphor, Stanley "transforms" or names the wild card once and for all when he rapes her, pinning down both her body and her identity. In Stanley's eyes, she has become "the woman in the traveling-salesman joke, the stereotype of the nymphomaniacal upper-class girl, ... the whore of his history who provokes and enjoys yet another encounter" (Vlasopolos 333).

Furthermore, for Kleb, Blanche — as the "exploding symbol of Unreason," or what he later calls the "expanding symbolist shadow" (36) — can ultimately be identified as the "primordial feminine Other in its most threatening and entrancing (to the male) aspects: enchantress, witch, and faery queen" (36). This, then, is Kleb's answer to Stanley's question "What queen do you think you are?": she is the "ancient Soul — desperate, lost, and out of time — that ultimately challenges Stanley's power" (36). Drawing on Julia Kristeva's *Black Sun*, Calvin Bedient sees a similar but not identical significance: Blanche represents "the primitivism of feminine abjection, the pull of the archaic mother," the figure, reified as the sea, to which we have already been introduced in Wolff's psychological interpretation of *The Awakening*. In fact, Blanche tells Stella and Eunice that she "can smell the sea air. The rest of my time I'm going to spend on the sea. And when I die, I'm going to die on the sea" (136; scene 11). She even wants to wear a "silver and turquoise pin in the shape of a seahorse" on her jacket (132; scene 11). But Blanche's fantasy about the sea never comes true as Stanley becomes the defender of "patriarchal order" who "stands as a bulwark" against "the abject identity-threatening corporeality that the mother, in her archaic guise, represents," who stands against, in Kristeva's terms, "the archaic 'Thing'" itself (Bedient 47).

Pagan has a different and even more playful answer to Stanley's question "What queen do you think you are?" Noting that Stanley Hyman "has suggested that Williams employs 'the Albertine Strategy,' that is to say, disguises homosexual males as females as Proust had done in changing the name Albert to Albertine in *A la recherche du temps perdu*," Pagan asks us to "notice that Stanley Kowalski offers us the possibility of reading Blanche as gay male when he says, 'What *queen* do you think you are?'" (65). Pagan also cites Mitch's observation, "I was fool enough to believe you was *straight*," as further support for his contention that "in her numerous sexual experiences with boys, Blanche may be regarded as both heterosexual woman often described by critics as 'nymphomaniac' and as gay male" (66). The quotation marks in Blanche's reply, "Who told you I wasn't 'straight,'" draw attention to the word (117; scene 9). Pagan even recalls that in "Kazan's movie version of the play, the word *straight* receives even more emphasis because Blanche replies to Mitch's question by herself asking a question: 'What's straight? A line can be straight or a street. But the heart of a human being?'" (103). Further, noting that "in his monumental *History of Sexuality*, Foucault points out that the Greeks apparently referred to the act of having sex with a boy as 'doing the thing'" (71), Pagan comments that "Blanche moves from talking about the 'thing' that Allan himself could not speak about (his homosexuality) to 'the terrible thing at the edge of the lake,' ... Allan's dead body" (71). Blanche's use of "thing," the fact that her name can be read as "Blanche DuBoys — Blanche of or from the boys — " (Pagan 68), and the gender confusion inherent in her name — "the adjective *blanche* would have to be *blanc* to agree with the noun *bois*, which is masculine" (Pagan 64) — seem to clinch his case, unless we put credence in one particular statement by Williams himself: "The most stupid thing said about my writing is that my heroines are disguised transvestites. Absolutely and totally none of them are anything but women. It's true about my work, as it's true about Albee's in *Virginia Woolf*. I understand women, and I can write about them" (Hanks 122, note 16). One wonders what Pagan might have made of Stella's accusation of Stanley in Scene 3 — "*Drunk — drunk — animal thing, you!*" (57) — or of Kristeva's identification of the primitive feminine principle as the "archaic 'Thing'" (Bedient 47).

While many labels may be assigned to Blanche — witch, fairy, archaic mother, or even gay man (if we accept Pagan's argument) — far fewer are assignable to Stanley, who "represents the Same." Though Kleb agrees with the general consensus that Stanley is an "icon of male heterosexual power," he also finds in him "something more" dangerous: "If the 'classical' figure of Unreason can help to illuminate the true range and reach of Blanche's power, then another key figure (according to Foucault) from this same period can throw additional light on Stanley — the absolute monarch, the source of all *political* power" (Kleb 37). As Kleb notes, *Streetcar* itself reinforces this identification. Stanley speaks with "lordly composure"; he has "an impressive judicial air"; he "represents the Law, and he summons the Napoleonic Code to support his case for a stake in Stella's property"; he is "the king around here" (37). "He is the Phallus through which going ahead is possible" (Bedient 46). But most of all, he is the punisher. As Foucault observed, "In brief, at the same time that the houses of internment were confining a broad range of social misfits under the category of Unreason, criminal acts (infractions of the Law) were more often dealt with not by internment but by immediate punishment, in serious cases by the public infliction of bodily pain" (qtd. in Kleb 37). When Blanche calls Stanley "my executioner," she recognizes on some level that "he lives in a different (premodern) world, where the 'will to knowledge' is exercised through interrogation, and punishment is registered physically" (Kleb 37). In other words, she recognizes that he is more dangerous than the relatively benign, though primitive and messy, ape to which she earlier compares him.

Kleb reads the play's final scene, then, as a *supplice*, a "publicly staged corporal punishment" (37) where Stanley's "people are brought together (thus the problematic poker game at such an odd moment) and made to witness a final demonstration and reassertion of the king's power and control" (38). These people, who for Hulley constitute the play's "chorus and community," champion the "principle of prohibition" that Stanley guards as they support his limiting "the possible interpretations of Blanche's role to their most fundamental level" (119). For students who may still find all this difficult to grasp, Mark Winchell gives voice to what many of the male students in the literature class are privately thinking:

> As males, we have secretly cheered the bad boy on as he proves something we have always wanted to believe, that the sententious schoolmarm is really a secret nympho. There is even a sense in which the male who has allowed himself to identify with Stanley can see *Streetcar* as having a fairy tale ending. The witch has been dispatched (if not to the hereafter, at least to the loony bin); the home is safe; and the prince and princess of Elysian Fields live happily ever after — seeing colored lights unsubdued by magic lanterns [140].

Winchell then asks, "But what of the woman spectator?" His answer focuses not on Blanche but on Stella, who in "purely Darwinian terms ... is clearly the heroine of the play. She has survived because she has successfully adapted herself to changing circumstances" and "has no illusions about the desirability of a world in which women are worshipped but not supported" (141). In short, Winchell believes that for men, the play "is a fantasy of complete domination; for women, one of complete submission" (142) — sexual submission to be sure — but also social submission to her "changing circumstances."

Cardullo even believes that "Stanley may even have resorted to force to get Stella, who thought [Stanley] was 'common' upon meeting him for the first time but who 'loved it,' in his words, when she got pulled down from the grandiose columns of her Southern aristocratic past" (175–76). In this regard, W. Kenneth Holditch finds a striking similarity in Blanche, Edna Pontellier, and Harry Wilbourne of William Faulkner's *The Wild Palms*: for all three "romance is frustrated by the harsh reality of economics, social convention, religion, and the biological reality of birth and death, all those hereditary and environmental forces with which the Naturalistic writers from Zola to Dreiser were concerned, even obsessed" (164–65). Stella, however, is different. "But of course there were things to adjust myself to later on," she tells Blanche (24; scene 1), indicating that she has managed to substitute an adjustment to the "harsh reality" of Stanley's world for what could have been her own Blanche-like frustration with it.

In Foucauldian terms, Stella submits to the Same. Kleb believes that in the play's final scene, it is not Stanley but Stella who becomes the operative "guardian of the Same" (39). Foucault points out that

> by the late eighteenth century ... modes of punishment founded on spectacle and physical pain were gradually being replaced by the reformist penal institutions characteristic of modern society — institutions based on continuous surveillance (discipline in the original sense of the word), sites for the observation, analysis, and instruction of confined individuals. The object of punishment, therefore, shifted from the body of the condemned to the personhood, the soul [Kleb 38].

Although it may seem, says Kleb, that Stella has helped Blanche by rescuing her "from Stanley's *ancien regime*, ... such a reading ... seems questionable" because, as "Foucault sees it, internment, whatever the rationale, is always a kind of exorcism, a rite of purification, an emblem of anxiety" (39). What awaits Blanche in the state mental hospital is a "new regime of power," one which forces inmates to assume "the personae of acceptable social types" (39). When the Doctor orders the Matron to release her hold on Blanche and then calls her "Miss DuBois," the audience can see that the persona she will adopt fits the "genteel social role ('the kindness of strangers')" that she has been intermittently practicing all along. In Foucault's terms, however, this rescue attempt is "simply a different style of subjugation" (39).

As Stella and Eunice are trying to keep Blanche occupied until the Doctor arrives, Stella tells Eunice, "I couldn't believe her story and go on living with Stanley" (133; scene 11). Kleb suggests that "Stella may not 'believe' Blanche's accusation, but she knows it as a possibility" (40). Pagan cites Elia Kazan's opinion that "Stella will see Stanley differently following Blanche's calling her attention to her sell out" (94). And despite Pagan's attempts to set himself apart from Adler, Adler has earlier concluded that Stella's line is a rationalization that gives way to "her doubt about her husband: things can never be the same between them again" (63). These critics, however, differ in how they read Stella's withdrawal. For Pagan, Stella's decision to believe Stanley is "a reflection of patriarchal power," and Stella "will surely remain firmly entrenched within that traditional economy, within the family which [Luce] Irigaray calls 'the privileged locus of women's exploitation'" (94). For Adler, their baby is the one who now "intrudes between Stanley and Stella." Stella becomes the "nurturing mother [who] takes preeminence over the wife and lover" so that, in the end, "Stella may be there *for* Stanley's use as a sex object in the future, [but] she indicates she will never again be totally *with* him as energetic lover" (63–64). It is Kleb's Foucauldian spin, however, that is most interesting:

> As each of Williams's "normal" characters responds to Blanche's presence, she individualizes him or her in terms of what she represents, aspects of her condition and character. Her perceptions uncover and reveal the "secret" elements within: who each truly is (or might become). At the heart of Stella's love (her loyalty and devotion), Blanche locates sexual addiction and infantilism. In Mitch's natural gentility, she reveals a mother fixation, moral cowardice, and the potential for sexual assault. Finally, she reconstitutes Stanley's paternalism as a kind of domestic tyranny where rape and adultery are male prerogatives [40].

Thus, "as Stanley (defender of the Same) pins down Blanche (proliferating Other) as a controllable sign for sexual lunacy, she pins him down as a sexual outlaw. She implants her otherness *in him*" (40). It is this otherness that comes between Stella and Stanley even as "his fingers find the opening of her blouse" (142; scene 11). In short, Kleb proposes that "Williams's project" is the same as Kinsey's and Foucault's — "to relocate the Other within man's own nature, within the Same" (41).

Pagan's work with phonics supports Kleb's conclusion that Stella has recognized the Other — "domestic tyranny where rape and adultery are male prerogatives" — in the Same — "Stanley's paternalism" (40). Again attacking the kind of thematics that he sees typified by Adler, Pagan begins by quoting Derrida: "Thematicism necessarily leaves out of account the formal, phonic, or graphic affinities that do not have the shape of a word, the calm unity of the verbal sign." It "necessarily ignores the play that takes the word apart, cutting it up and putting the pieces to work" (102). In this deconstructive spirit, Pagan traces the "phonic signifier *st* and *bl*" (103), pointing to words like "straight," "streetcar," "Stella," "star," "Steve," "stud," "stone," and, of course, "Stanley" and to words like "blue," "blood," "bleed," "blows," and, of course, "Blanche." Although he can conclude that these intertwining chains of signifiers constitute Williams's "inimitable idiom" (112), his "stylistic signature" (110), he stresses that they are "independent of any signifying intention" (110):

> Although our starting point for the *st/bl* opposition was the opposition between Stanley and Blanche, we cannot privilege them as fundamental signifieds in their respective chains. As a signifier, Stanley may be no more important than Stella, Steve, straight, stud, stone, and story in that series; and as a signifier Blanche may be no more important than blue, blues, blood, bleed, blows, and blank in that series. It may not be the case that the two chains are rigorously divided. Stanley, for example, may wear *bl*ue jeans, or the *bl*ues may be associated with *St*ella rather than *Bl*anche; but nevertheless, it is difficult to deny that a clear pattern is established; and the *bl* and the *st* offer themselves up as more important signifying structures than any of the individual links in their respective chains [105].

Though at first Pagan speculates that "the *bl* may be seen as assigning a place for marginalia" — and, in a list much like and published the same year as Kleb's (1993), he details these "marginalia" as "not only women and homosexuals, but also rootless wanderers, poets, blues musicians, the chronically shy, ... the fragile, ... and those with a chronic need for alcohol" (104) — he later saves himself from the kind of dichotomizing that he finds in Adler's work by acknowledging that "the *bl* cannot always represent the margin, the world of women and homosexuals, any more than the *st* can always represent the male world or the 'straight' world" (111). It is Stella who makes Pagan aware of the insidious attraction of his own dichotomy because, since "the *st* world" includes Stella, it is "not reducible to the so-called masculine order" (103). At first blush it might also appear that the *st* world corresponds to the gender-transcending world of the Same, the world that Stella represents when she commits Blanche to the state hospital. Continuing to question and to deconstruct his own argument, however, Pagan suggests that "the themes established by the *bl* may not be rigorously divided from those established by the *st*" (111), and his recognition of the *bl/st* conflation might be seen as a restatement, in different terms, of Kinsey's, Williams's, and Foucault's "project" as Kleb defines it: "to relocate the Other within man's own nature, within the Same" (41).

Kleb ends his article by analyzing the role of the audience, indeed by implicating it not only in Blanche's fate but in Williams's as well. When Stanley and Stella "subjectify Blanche as a manageable sign linking sexual abnormalcy and mental disorder, the audience, relieved, can now focus simply and safely on the psychosexual pathology of Blanche DuBois — and her creator. The theatre itself becomes the asylum to which Blanche, and Williams, are condemned" (41). As Hulley puts it, Blanche's "flood of signs" makes not only the folk of Elysian Fields — the "chorus and community" — uneasy, but the play's audience as well. It too likes manageable signs. It too requires "a fixed point from which to view the shifting possibilities" (118).

As Stella's presence in the *st* chain alerts Pagan to the dangers of dichotomizing, so too does her role as audience of Blanche's play help Hulley understand more about the role of *Streetcar*'s audience: "Like the audience she has been watching a play performed for another — Blanche's 'play for' Mitch. Like the audience, she knows more about Blanche's play than does Blanche's intended audience. In this position Stella can form the point of view which will allow Blanche's 'play' to continue, or which will terminate it" (120). When Stella does choose and tells Eunice in Scene 11, "I couldn't believe her story and go on living with Stanley," she is "not deluded by Stanley; rather, her decision is the deliberate preservation of social order" (120). Like Stella, the audience too has experienced a crucial moment of choice, only that moment has occurred earlier, during Scene 10, the rape scene, "when the walls dissolve and hellish flames shadow the room while the *Varsouviana* of Blanche's memories dominates any exterior sound" (119). Although Williams's stage directions do not mention the *Varsouviana* here — rather, "the night is filled with inhuman voices like cries in a jungle" (128; scene 10) — Hulley is right about the overall effect of the staging and what it represents: "The disintegration at the level of setting is thematically mirrored in Stanley's transgression. When he rapes his wife's sister, he too exceeds the limits of his world. At this climactic moment, every category is threatened; desire transcends bounds. Music, light, space collude in a cacophony of disorder" (119). "This," says Hulley, "is the crucial moment for the audience, the moment in which either it allows the disintegration to continue or it restores order" (119). "This is the moment," she continues, "when each member of the audience decides either that Blanche has gotten what she asked for, or that Stanley's insensitive dominance exceeds any sympathy" (119). It is Hulley's next observation, however, that relates explicitly to Kleb's work: "No matter what attitude we adopt, ... to choose is to carve space up once again into socially accepted territories. Any judgment grants power to Stanley; even to hate him is to impose limits on the unbearable violation" (119). For Hulley, as for Kleb, Stanley is the imposer of limits and therein lies the source of his power.

Vlasopolos and June Schlueter shed additional light on the part that *Streetcar*'s audience plays in Blanche's exile and punishment. In her emphasis on what she optimistically believes is the audience's perception of, in Kleb's words, "the power relations" that operate in Elysian Fields, Vlasopolos also enters Foucauldian territory:

> ... It is the conflict between two versions of history struggling for authority that should be salient for us in the light of twentieth-century historical experience.

> The lucidity of Williams's representation appears in the impartial view of the
> combat which he gives us between two antagonists and in a resolution that
> does not sentimentalize the victimization of the loser as an ascension to a
> more glorious world. Swayed by alternating sympathetic identifications, audi-
> ences arrive at a sense of the arbitrariness involved in history-making and its
> attendant victimization. They perceive that historical discourse depends on
> power, not logic, for its formation [325].

Moreover, she acknowledges that "the most disquieting revelation of the play
is the audience's willing submission to a character's mastery of a situation,
and in the end to that character's version of events" (326). When Stanley "taps
into the dominant discourse of patriarchy and is thus able to reduce Blanche's
story to an all-too-common denominator," in other words when he reduces
her to a manageable sign, he — and we the audience — can "vanquish her"
(332).

Drawing on Hans Robert Jauss's division of the "reading process into
two hermeneutic acts: understanding and interpretation," Schlueter makes the
same point. "Because the first reading does not provide the reader with
fulfillment of form until the final line," it is only through the "'second' reading, which follows and is activated by the end of the first," that a reader can
"understand the ways in which each segment of the text and each reading
moment contributes to the whole" ("'We've had this date'" 73). Whatever the
reader might think about the rape in moral terms, "as terminal event in both
Stanley's and Blanche's narratives of each other" it "offers satisfaction, for it
provides the reader with a sense of the aesthetic whole" at the end of the first
reading (76). Schlueter's point is that in

> the second reading, Stanley's story of Blanche has priority, for the reader now
> knows that it has prevailed. Her desperate effort to construct herself as a
> woman of breeding and refinement, of poetry and beauty, has yielded its
> credibility to Stanley's construction, which, the reader knows, has been legit-
> imized through completion.... Having experienced the force of Stanley's script
> and its terminal action, the reader reevaluates Blanche's past in the prevailing
> author's (i.e., Stanley's) terms ["'We've had this date'" 76–77].

Yet, although Vlasopolos, Schlueter, Hulley, Bedient, Kleb, and Pagan
all avow Stanley's power to deconstruct Blanche, they all — each in his or her
own way — disavow his injustice. As Mark Lilla puts it, "It turns out that there
is a concept — though only one — resilient enough to withstand the acids of
deconstruction. That concept is justice" (39). In Derrida's words, it is the
"'infinite idea of justice,' though it cannot and does not penetrate our world"
(Lilla 39), that incites these critics to uncover Williams's subversive practices.

Vlasopolos, for example, finds a problem in "the audience's pragmatic
shrug at the end of the play" (337). Although she admits that "the authority

of history is on Stanley's side," she concludes that the "force of this 'problem' play is to disquiet us so that perhaps we might hear, if not speak for, those whom history has silenced" (338). Further, Williams "intends to subvert the story-tellers, the history-makers," the Stanleys of this world through his disquieting "stage business," especially through the "backdrop which becomes transparent at crucial moments and the contest between types of music and jungle noises" (326). In effect, the "visual and aural effects contradict the triumph of the narrative version accepted by all the characters" except Blanche, "who is stripped of authority, dispossessed of authorship" (326).

For Schlueter, the reader, "attracted by the integrity and the pleasure of the aesthetic whole," has accepted "Stanley's final fiction"—we might even be tempted to call it his "final solution"—and has thus been "seduced into a hegemonically masculine and conventionally generic reading of the play" ("'We've had this date'" 78). But Schlueter also identifies *Streetcar*'s subversive function:

> Blanche's reliance on the kindness of strangers, even as family and acquaintances assemble to witness, not to prevent, her expulsion, may alert the reader to how little kindness his or her own reading has shown her. For the reader uneasy about allowing the play to end so neatly, at Blanche's expense, yet another retrospective reading will deliver him or her back to scene 10, this time to question his or her own agreement to the closure it urged ["'We've had this date'" 79].

Similarly, Hulley contends that although "any judgment grants power to Stanley" (119) because any judgment involves setting limits, the play as a whole questions "social law":

> The problem Williams presents is that to limit the productive power of the symbol is repressive, while to allow the symbol unlimited power is chaos. By representing the either/or categories of contextual control through the death of desire, Williams surpasses the issues of "sane" or "insane," "truth" or "illusion" to expose the ambivalent social law which makes those terms significant [122].

And like Vlasopolos, Hulley credits the role of the set in this project: the set is transformed "into an artificial, unreal space which functions like a mask to disarm the audience" (121).

For Bedient, "the play sacrifices Blanche, or 'feminine' abjection, however reluctantly, in favor of the transparent social system. When the cards are down, the playwright"—and I would add, his audience—"prefers identity-sustaining law to the engulfing archaic mother" (56). But although Williams has sculpted his plot to rid "the symbolic order of contaminants," he has also raised two important questions: "Is Stanley's 'deliberate cruelty' the same thing as a necessary social violence?" and "How *much* violence can be justified in keeping at bay the castrating Phallic Mother?" (56–57).

Although Kleb initially suggests that the audience, with Stanley and Stella, has "relieved" its anxiety by committing Blanche to the asylum and Williams to the theatre, this is not the end of the story for him either. "Reading *A Streetcar Named Desire* by way of Foucault can help to free the play, and its author, from this ironic confinement, this 'disciplinary' site. And it can return them both to the dangerous, disruptive, and marginal world where they both belong" (41).

Finally, for Pagan as for Kleb, Blanche and Williams escape their sad ends. Although Pagan does not explicitly address the issues surrounding Stanley's alleged triumph at the end of the play, he does, as we have seen, rescue Blanche from being "caught in a signifying structure that places her in opposition to Stanley Kowalski" (91). He also rescues Williams. In a paragraph where he explores whether Williams would have perhaps laughed at the manner of his own death ("A bottle cap lodged in his throat and he suffocated"), Pagan cautions that although Williams's laughter is "almost legendary, ... one should be careful ... not to be taken in" by it. As Truman Capote wrote, "Tennessee was an unhappy man, even when he was smiling the most, laughing the loudest" (qtd. in Pagan 84). Through his writing, however, "Williams enters the game, a game that is not merely 'play for the sake of play,' but a game which all who read or see his plays may also enter, and in so doing, enable the playwright to live on, to survive" (124). Further, Pagan claims, "Through play, ... something (a piece? a trace? a biographeme?) of the author may enter our own lives" (125).

Obviously, Williams, who once proclaimed "I am Blanche," inhabited the margins. Kazan writes of the "struggle it must have been for Tennessee to face his homosexuality in a society where it was thought shameful. There had to have been an early anguish in his way of life and a separation from the 'normal' society around him" (348). More specifically, Kazan suggests that Blanche's attraction to "the man who is going to destroy her" is a "reference to the kind of life Tennessee was leading at the time.... [He] was aware of the dangers he was inviting when he cruised; he knew that sooner or later he'd be beaten up. And he was" (351). Pagan's point is well taken: when we truly engage with Williams's texts, we necessarily enter into the "dangerous, disruptive, and marginal world" of the Other.

It might be said that although the critics cited above draw upon different theoretical bases — semiotics, narratology, biography, deconstruction, reader-response, feminism, and cultural criticism — they have all found "'resistances' within [*Streetcar*] which destabilize the prevailing ideology that the text would appear to support" (Newton 124). My premise here is that these "resistances" can best be presented to students through Kleb's essay. His Foucault-based cultural criticism subsumes the theories named above and clearly drives home the message that this "prevailing ideology" is one which privileges sameness and marginalizes otherness. The point that Stephen Greenblatt makes about Renaissance texts, however, serves as a warning relevant not just to literary analysis. K. M. Newton paraphrases: "The resistances or subversive elements, which on the surface undermine the ideological discourse of such texts, function rather to immunize that discourse against being seriously threatened since subversion is both generated and contained by the dominant ideology" (124–25). Subversion is sanctioned by the Same and might be seen as merely a sort of irresistible pacifier that the Same offers the Other in a self-protecting strategy. Newton, however, spins Greenblatt's frightening vision of the Same's co-opting project in a positive direction, conceding that although it seems to prohibit the possibility of social change, there is an "indirect" way out: "Greenblatt could still argue that [such criticism] promotes change indirectly by revealing how this process operates. The reader of such criticism is then in a better position to understand his or her contemporary cultural situation and can act to alter it" (125). In Christopher Norris's rephrasing of Jürgen Habermas, "[T]here must be certain positive norms — structures of rational understanding — which allow thought to criticize the current self-images of the age" (qtd. in Newton 124). However, as Mylène Dressler so pointedly writes of *The Awakening*, "[W]e are left with ... nothing more than Edna still as object-in-sight" (62), and thus we worry that Habermas' optimism is perhaps misplaced and "current self-images" will not be open to criticism.

The speculations about Stella's emotional response to Stanley after the play ends illustrate the struggle between these two positions. The stage directions tell us that she "is crouched a few steps up on the stairs" as Blanche is taken away by the Doctor and the Matron. She calls her sister's name three times as Eunice "descends to Stella and places the child in her arms." Then Eunice enters the kitchen as Stanley "stands at the foot of the steps looking at Stella." He "uncertainly" addresses her as she "sobs with inhuman abandon. There is something luxurious in her complete surrender to crying now that her sister is gone." As Stanley "kneels beside her and his fingers find the opening of her blouse," he "voluptuously, soothingly" says to his wife, "Now, honey. Now, love. Now, now, love. Now, now, love. Now, love." The play's last stage direction and last bit of dialogue sound a decidedly sexual note: "The luxurious sobbing, the sensual murmur fade away under the swelling music of the 'blue piano' and the muted trumpet" as Steve announces, "This game is seven-card stud" (142; scene 11).

Does Stella resist the control of the Same? And if so, is her resistance meaningless ("subversion is both generated and contained by the dominant ideology") or meaningful (one can "understand his or her contemporary cultural situation and can act to alter it")? Although, as we have seen, the critics appear to largely agree with what Kazan wrote in his "notebook for *A Streetcar Named Desire*" — that "Stella will see Stanley differently following Blanche's calling her attention to her sell out" (qtd. in Pagan 94) — this statement should be read in light of his later (1988) autobiography where he seems to be adamant that Williams' intention was that Stella would not feel "an enduring alienation from her husband":

> Stanley was the father of her child. Stanley had turned on the "colored lights" for her. Above all, Stanley was there. As he'd declared, they'd been perfectly happy until Blanche moved in. The implication at the end of the play is that Stella will very soon return to Stanley's arms — and to his bed. That night, in fact. Indifference? Callousness? No. Fidelity to life. Williams's goal. We go on with life, he was saying, the best way we can. People get hurt, but you can't get through life without hurting people. The animal survives — at all costs [Kazan 351].

Taken together, Kazan's two statements probably do fairly suggest what Williams had in mind when he ended the play as he did, though in *Where I Live: Selected Essays*, Williams denies that he did, in fact, always have something in mind. He "has shown his awareness of the limitations of intentionality when he suggests that as far as a play is concerned, 'many of its instants of revelation are wayward flashes, not part of the plan of an author but struck accidentally off'" (Pagan 91–92). Yet, for two good reasons one suspects that the ending of *Streetcar* was not "struck accidentally off." The first is Williams's desire to ground his plays in a "fidelity to life," the second, his always meticulous arrangement of material. Given that the whole of the Williams canon is a study in the aesthetics of repetition and balance (the repeated use of the lantern, for example, or the balanced presentations of the Young Man and the Mexican Woman) and given that the ending of the 1951 film serves just such an aesthetic (Stella again flees, as she did in Scene 3, up the stairs to Eunice's apartment, and Stanley again bellows her name), it seems obvious that Williams could have ended, but chose not to end, the play in this way. In other words, writing for the Broadway stage, he sacrificed the pleasures of repetition on the altar of "fidelity to life," the tough life of working-class New Orleans.

With Blanche's "story" echoing in her ears and Stanley's "fingers find[ing] the opening of her blouse," Stella can "see Stanley differently" and at the same time not feel an "enduring alienation." Although "things can never be the same between them again" (Adler 63), Stella may still feel enough desire for Stanley to allow her to stay, raise their child, and carry on. She may be unable to sustain a sense of alienation towards the father of her child. She may still be able to take pride in the "drive" that makes Stanley "the only one of his crowd that's likely to get anywhere" (50; scene 3). Williams presents a number of interpretive options, and what he writes about Brick in *Cat on a Hot Tin Roof* seems to apply equally well to Stella:

> The bird that I hope to catch in the net of this play is not the solution of one man's psychological problem. I'm trying to catch the true quality of experience in a group of people, that cloudy, flickering, evanescent —fiercely charged!— interplay of live human beings in the thundercloud of a common crisis. Some mystery should be left in the revelation of character in a play, just as a great deal of mystery is always left in the revelation of character in life, even in one's own character to himself [85; act 2].

Partly because of its revised ending, it is the 1951 film — not the play itself or its 1983 and 1995 made-for-television adaptations — that most fully dramatizes the struggle between the pessimistic, naturalistic view that requires us to see a Stella totally immersed in the Same and the more optimistic view that offers a shred of hope that she will be able to "act to alter it" or, at least, "criticize the current self-images" that it perpetuates. Paradoxically, the 1951 film is the most postmodern of the adaptations; ironically, the Censor Board's stipulations made it so. Of course, the position that Stella is allied with Stanley and defends his "control of the Same" (Kleb 38) surfaces in the play and all three adaptations when Stella commits Blanche to the asylum. As Eric Bentley points out, "Can a sister just send someone to an asylum without any medical advice? If so, which of us is safe? And even if Blanche is mad at this moment, will she remain so?" (qtd. in Kleb 39). But the 1951 film, unlike the other texts, also pictures Stella's sameness through her violence, oddly enough directed toward Stanley, the master of the Same. Kazan felt that "the censorship took away some of the ambivalence from the character of Stella (Kim Hunter): the fact that she could be both angry at Stanley (Marlon Brando) and attracted to him at the same time" (qtd. in Phillips, "*ASND*" 232). For example, one of the "dozen trims" that the Legion of Decency demanded — or it would issue a "C" (condemned) rating — involved the "series of close and medium shots ... [that] conveyed Stella's anger melting gradually into forgiveness" (Phillips, "*ASND*" 233) as she descends the stairs to a remorseful Stanley:

> There was a brilliant close-up — I'm speaking of Kim Hunter's performance, not my direction — of her coming down the stairs to her husband when he's called desperately for her to come back. This close-up had been cut short and with it the piece of music Alex North had written. The shot and the music were both considered "too carnal" [Kazan 435].

With the release on video in 1994 of the "Director's Cut," audiences were finally able to see this remarkable close-up for themselves. I would argue, however, that Stella's ambivalence was never really lost, for the 1951 film gives ample evidence of both Stella's desire for Stanley and her violent anger at him. In the 1951 release, desire is a characteristic of both the Same and the Other. Violence is a characteristic only of the Same.

The fact that Stanley is more violent in the film than in the play is well documented, especially by Ellen Dowling, who contrasts how play and film begin:

> The play begins with a rather favorable portrayal of Stanley as he returns home, stopping only long enough to rouse his contentedly reclining mate and toss a package of meat at her before heading off to the bowling alley with Stella following happily after. In the film, on the other hand, our first view of Stanley is an entirely negative one. We first see him in the midst of a violent altercation with the members of an opposing bowling team; he is wearing a sweaty T-shirt and "bellowing" at the other team's captain. On the screen, we share Blanche's revulsion at this sight of a violent male who so obviously dominates the members of his own sex; on the stage we share Stella's excitement at the entrance of her common yet physically attractive husband [237].

While some might quibble that neither Blanche's reaction nor ours to seeing Stanley fighting is one of "revulsion"—indeed, it may be better characterized as the thrill of seeing Stanley's physicality in action, a physicality bound up with the "vibrant, close-to-the-nerve sexuality" that Brando brought to the role (Schlueter, "Remake" 141) and that lies at the heart of the male "fantasy of complete domination" as well as the female fantasy of "complete submission" (Winchell 142)—and while it might also be said that Kazan's and Williams's decision (surprisingly, not the Censor's) to omit the rather sexually crude meat-tossing episode may have been a function of their decision to shoot the film in black and white, where the "red-stained package from a butcher's" would lose its visual impact, it is true that Stanley, Mitch (Karl Malden)—as we will soon see—, and Stella are all more violent in the film than in the play.

Several examples of Stella's greater violence should suffice here. The first occurs during Scene 2 when she informs Stanley that Belle Reve has been lost. In the play, Stanley, alluding to the Napoleonic Code, rifles through Blanche's trunk, looking for evidence of her thievery. Though the stage directions describe his behavior in the active verbs that persist throughout the play—he "jerks out an armful of dresses," "blows on" Blanche's fur-pieces, "hurls the furs to the daybed," "jerks open a small drawer in the trunk and pulls up a fist-full of costume jewelry," and finally "kicks the trunk partly closed and sits on the kitchen table"—Williams is silent about what Stella has been doing. She does verbally challenge Stanley, even to the point of calling him an "idiot," but Williams has not explicitly directed that she respond physically until, the tirade over, she "snatches up her white hat and gloves and crosses to the outside door" (35–37; scene 2).

In the film, Stella does not passively listen. She pulls on Stanley's arm as he toys with Blanche's belongings, stares at him, and again tries to pull him away. She smoothes out, rearranges, and attempts to put back Blanche's things as he continues to scrutinize what he suspects has been paid for by the loss of Belle Reve.

Secondly, during Scene 3, after Blanche (played by Jessica Tandy on stage and Vivien Leigh on screen) and Stella return from Galatoire's, the poker game is still very much in session. Stanley is irascible because Mitch has declared himself out of the game, and when Blanche turns on the radio in the bedroom, Stanley displaces his feelings and "jumps up" to turn the radio off. It soon becomes clear that Mitch has quit the game for good with "seven five-dollar bills in his pants pocket folded up tight as spitballs" (52; scene 3) in order to investigate the charming new woman in the bedroom behind the curtains. Almost immediately Mitch and Blanche establish a bond based on their sorrowful pasts. After Blanche asks him to hang the paper lantern over the light bulb — "I can't stand a naked light bulb, any more than I can a rude remark or a vulgar action" — she turns on the radio again. As she "waltzes to the music with romantic gestures" and Mitch "moves in awkward imitation like a dancing bear," Stanley "stalks" into the room, "snatches" the radio, "shouts" an oath, and "tosses" the radio out the window (57; scene 3). Stella blames his behavior on alcohol: "Drunk — drunk — animal thing, you!" she cries as she "rushes through to the poker table," telling the men to "please go home!" Then Stanley "charges after Stella, ... there is the sound of a blow, ... and Stella cries out" (57; scene 3).

Again, in the film, Stella does far more than rush into the next room. She slams the men's coats onto the table, sends the hanging lamp spinning wildly, overturns furniture, and, in general wrecks her own kitchen before Stanley corners her and strikes. Stella's physical display seems to be an outgrowth of the anger she verbally expresses earlier in the scene, first when Stanley "whack[s] ... his hand on her thigh" and she scolds him, "That's not fun, Stanley," confiding to Blanche, "It makes me so mad when he does that in front of people" (48; scene 3). The ambiguity here is interesting. Does it always make Stella angry when he "whacks" her? Does she become angry only when he does it "in front of people"? A bit later when Stanley tells her and Blanche to "hush up!" she replies, "This is my house and I'll talk as much as I want to!" to which Blanche cautions, "Stella, don't start a row" (51; scene 3). The point is simply that the film's audience witnesses Stella's anger in action just moments before it watches her desire come alive as she descends the stairs, falls into Stanley's arms, and rakes his back with her fingernails. It would be hard to imagine a juxtaposition that suggests her ambivalence more fully. A third example occurs after Blanche tells Stella that she does indeed "*want* Mitch ... *very badly!*" (81; scene 5). In the play, Stella reassures her that "it will happen," and then as "Blanche sinks faintly back in her chair with her drink" and Eunice and Steve exhibit their own brand of sexuality, "Stanley and Stella twine arms as they follow, laughing" (82; scene 5).

Again, the film paints a different picture. After Blanche confirms her desire for a future with Mitch, the camera takes us outside, where we see Steve chasing Eunice. As Steve passes by Stanley, Stanley reaches for him and tears his shirt. Then Stella enters the shot, but instead of twining arms with her husband, she avoids his embrace, telling him to "let go" as she pulls away and follows after Eunice and Steve.

Although it may seem as if Stella's sometimes violent behavior in the film would make her a woman stronger than the "little woman" of the play, not merely content to "trot along behind the men and watch them bowl, to countenance, up to a point, their card playing and loud drinking because of what will happen later in the bedroom" (Adler 61), and a more able opponent of what she recognizes as Stanley's idiocy, from Kleb's perspective it is the Stella of the film who is Stanley's "little woman," a woman who belongs to and with him, for her physical violence towards him identifies her with the Same. This identity supports Greenblatt's pessimistic contention, again paraphrased by Newton, that "subversion is both generated and contained by the dominant ideology" (124–25).

Mitch, too, behaves more violently in the film than in the play, especially in Scene 9. The visual effect of his violence depends, in part, upon Kazan's stunningly right choice to film *Streetcar* in black and white, a choice which, as we have seen, may have been responsible for the omission of Stanley's "heav[ing] the package" of red meat at Stella at the play's beginning (14; scene 1). The photography underscores one of the central motifs of the play: that Blanche hides from bright light, symbolic of Stanley's literal world of facts, refusing to go out until after dark and manipulating the environment of the apartment to maximize shadow, especially by having Mitch place the "adorable little colored paper lantern" that she bought at a "Chinese shop on Bourbon" over the naked light bulb in Stanley and Stella's bedroom. As soon as Mitch performs this significant action, creating what Blanche calls "magic," he becomes a party to her efforts to hide fact with illusion and her sad personal history with "what *ought* to be truth" (117; scene 9). In Scene 9, which takes place on the disastrous evening of Blanche's birthday party, "a while" after Stanley takes Stella to the hospital (113), Mitch finally shows up. In the play, Blanche "rushes about frantically," trying to pull herself together, and finally "rushes to the door in the kitchen and lets him in" (113; scene 9).

In the film, however, it appears that Mitch is too impatient, too angry about what he has learned about Blanche's past to wait for her to properly admit him. He pounds on the door and then kicks it open. His interrogation, which leads Blanche to confess her sexual history, mimics Stanley's in Scene 2, the scene that, for Kleb,

> mirrors the overall dramatic shape of Williams's play (Blanche's exposure and defeat); employs its central interactive strategy (interrogation and confession); and states the major dramatic question: Who is this strange woman — moth-like, "*incongruous*" — who has arrived unannounced and uninvited, at night, claiming kinship and a place at the hearth? [30].

Then, in a particularly cruel move that anticipates the rape in Scene 10 even more than his "fumbling" attempt to get what he has "been missing all summer" (120; scene 9), Mitch "tears the paper lantern off the light bulb" and holds Blanche's face under its harsh light to "take a look at [her] good and plain!" (117; scene 9). The change in lighting from a fuzzy softness to a sharp chiaroscuro is instantaneous, and bizarre shadows objectify Blanche's deterioration. With the lantern gone, Vivien Leigh's heart-shaped face, with its high forehead and cheekbones, big eyes, and slightly sunken cheeks, is especially vulnerable to lighting. Commenting on the effectiveness of the film's close-ups, Kazan describes her as looking "pathologically drawn and aged" (385). With the lantern in place, however, she looks as young as she looked in *Gone with the Wind*, an inevitable comparison since Leigh's Oscar-winning, enormously popular portrayal of Scarlett O'Hara firmly situates the 1939 film and *Streetcar* in the same intertextual web. With the lantern's removal, however, she ages twenty years and hardens before our eyes. Mitch's putting up the lantern, his tearing it down, and then Stanley's tearing it down for good at the end of the play make it what Herbert Zettl calls a "dramatic agent" (35), one whose effect depends upon the wide range of light/dark contrasts that black and white film affords. Mitch's violence, heightened by the dramatic changes in Blanche's face, firmly links him, with Stella, to Stanley, the primary guardian of the Same.

The film further reflects Kleb's work through its own unique vocabulary — the visual and aural composition of the shot, the basic unit of filmmaking. Harry Stradling's marvelous, studied photography establishes *Streetcar*'s overall look through, for example, the barred shadows created by the apartment's shutters, the stroboscopic effects of ceiling fans, flashing lights coming from the street, cigarette smoke swirling about, and, of course, the contrast between the soft light of the lantern and the harsh glare of the light bulb. But three shots do stand out and become "marked elements," Lotman's term that served us so well in the previous chapter. All three support Kleb's notion that at the play's end Blanche is "being handed over to a different, newer 'technique of power,' the mental institution" (38).

The first is the shot that opens Scene 9. With Stanley and Stella gone to the hospital, Blanche, exhausted by the emotional losses on the evening of her birthday dinner, appears to be sleeping upright, leaning against the arm of her chair, a bottle on the floor at her side. What marks the shot is that the camera is situated above and slightly to the left of the ceiling fan, shooting directly down on Blanche. With the sound of the door buzzer (it's Mitch, coming for the sex that he thinks the "unclean" Blanche now owes him), the shot ends.

The second, its partner, occurs at the end of this scene, after Mitch tells Blanche that she's "not clean enough to bring in the house with [his] mother." Blanche, in the play, begins to scream "Fire! Fire! Fire!" (121; scene 9). In the film, she tells him, "Get out of here quick before I start screaming, screaming" and then chases him outside and does begin to scream with all her might. A quick cut to a down-shot from high above the street, a bit above roof level, shows us Blanche, still screaming and then collapsing, silent, head down, leaning on the ornate railing that leads up to Eunice's apartment, a small figure in the middle of a banked circle of galleries with spectators gazing at her from all sides. The shot is held for several seconds until a voice inquiring "You all right lady? What's wrong lady?" returns the camera to ground level.

Gene Phillips disparages this "addition to the original play" because it "serves only to slow down the tempo of the action temporarily and adds nothing to the audience's understanding of Blanche or her situation, since her increasing withdrawal from the threatening, inquisitive outside world has been thoroughly documented by this point in the film" (*The Films* 77). Phillips, however, is paying attention to verbal content rather than to cinematic vocabulary. This shot and its earlier counterpart not only frame Scene 9, but they also allude, I believe, to a startlingly surreal shot from the 1948 film *The Snake Pit*, where the camera travels up and away from Virginia Cunningham (Olivia de Havilland) until we see that she, with the other female inmates, is in a huge pit. Thus the two down-shots of Blanche illustrate Foucault's point regarding "surveillance" and foreshadow the end of the play. In both instances, as we look down on Blanche through the eye of the camera, we are positioned as if we were, like the doctors in *The Snake Pit*, charged with this patient's surveillance. Eight years later, in 1959, Joseph L. Mankiewicz will similarly position Catharine Holly in his film adaptation of *Suddenly Last Summer*.

The third marked shot, occurring during the sequence at the end of the play where the Doctor (Richard Garrick) and the Matron (Ann Dere) come for Blanche, both confirms this analysis and extends it. Williams's description in the play of the Matron's "Hello, Blanche" is applicable here. Her words are "echoed and re-echoed by other mysterious voices behind the walls, as if reverberated through a canyon of rock" (139; scene 11). The film reproduces this effect, taking us into Blanche's mind as it does when we hear the Varsouviana, the music that was playing on the night that Allan took his life. The echoes pile up as Stanley and the Matron ask Blanche what she has forgotten and continue as Blanche holds her ears and frantically stumbles along the windows behind the gauzy curtains like a trapped "moth beating its wings against a wall" (Kazan 384). The echoes end only when Stanley asks, "You want the lantern?" In a very effective move by Alex North, who won an Oscar for the film's music, Stanley's line is immediately reinforced musically by a strong, full chord that underscores the drama of the question and reminds us of what the lantern has meant to Blanche and to us. Then, Stanley rips the lantern down, holds it towards Blanche, and she lunges at it, grabbing it away from him and clutching it to her heart. All that we hear now are her gasping cries as she wrestles with the Matron.

In both play and film, the Matron, who has now pinned Blanche down on the floor, hands behind her back, comments, "These fingernails have to be trimmed," and then asks, "Jacket, Doctor?" He answers, "Not unless necessary" and then firmly says Blanche's name — "Miss DuBois." Again, the non-diegetic music is a powerful element. What we hear is a haunting, minor-key melody that rises as the Doctor looks down at Blanche and opens her eyes with his fingers. Luigi Zaninelli describes it as "a kind of music which is clearly American yet still undeniably European. The thematic material takes its inspiration from American popular music of the 1940s but the treatment, harmonically and polyphonically, is inspired by elements not unlike those found in the music of Ravel, Debussy, Prokofiev" (McCraw 7). What we see is Blanche's face and twisted torso, her body lying along the vertical (Y) axis, so that it looks as if she is hanging upside down on the right side of the frame, what Lotman would call an "upside down shot" (31). The camera shoots over the shoulder of the crouching Doctor, who occupies the left side. Blanche says, "Please —"; he interrupts, answering the Matron's "Jacket, Doctor?" with "It won't be necessary"; and Blanche finishes, "Ask her to let go of me." He quietly says, "Yes, let go." For a full thirty-four seconds, there are no words — only the music — as the Doctor helps Blanche to her feet, circles from the left of the frame to the right, removes his hat, offers his arm, and begins to lead her out of the room, as she delivers her most famous line, "Whoever you are — I have always depended on the kindness of strangers." From the Matron's "Hello, Blanche" to Blanche's last line, three minutes and two seconds have elapsed. Over a third of this time — one minute, twenty-two seconds — is

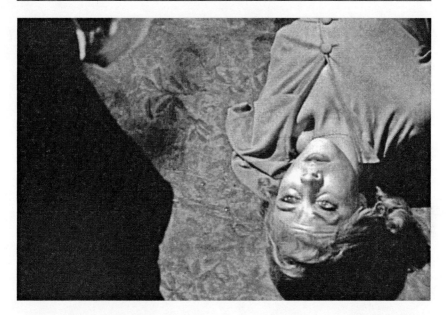

At the end of the 1951 Warner Brothers version of *Streetcar* is a fascinating shot of Blanche DuBois, played by Vivien Leigh, literally hanging upside down in the frame. She will be rescued — visually righted — by the Doctor, whose shadow we see here and who will be Blanche's last "kind stranger."

devoted to this one powerful shot whose extraordinary length, moving music, and precise choreography create an incredibly riveting experience for the audience.

If ever one needed to show how the elements of film — *mise-en-scène,* montage, sound — can be coordinated to influence the audience's emotions, this sequence would surely be an example to cite. At first, as Kleb notes of the play, "Like Eunice, the audience perceives Blanche as an outsider" (40). In both play and film, her "incongruous ... fluffy" clothes (15; scene 1) and her poetic speech reinforce this perception. In the film, the contrast between Leigh's classical acting style and "Brando's method acting ... heighten[s] the distinction between Stanley Kowalski, a reality pared to its dynamic essentials, and Blanche DuBois, the skilled purveyor of illusion" (Cahir, "Artful" 73). Almost immediately, however, notes Kleb, Blanche "gathers our gaze and we begin to see the world through her eyes" (40). In the film, our vision of her world culminates with this shot and her last bit of dialogue. The intense three minutes and two seconds that we have just endured are enough by themselves to make us "see the world through her eyes" and acknowledge that what Kleb says of the play is even more true of the film — "no matter how her difference is defined and displayed, something of this point of view remains" (40).

While this scene does make us sympathize with Blanche and realize that she has been treated unjustly, it also graphically displays the point in Kleb's argument that we have previously noted, that Blanche is "urged" to assume a "genteel social role." When we see the on-screen Blanche literally upside down and then watch as the Doctor helps her to again be upright, we have no doubt that Blanche will indeed be "reconstituted" and will probably never again step outside of her prescribed role, the role that she prophetically announces to Mitch when she first meets him in Scene 3: "Married? No, no. I'm an old maid schoolteacher!" (55; scene 3).

When we look at the changed ending that the Breen office and the Catholic Legion of Decency demanded, we see that, ironically, where they sought to restrict, as Hulley would put it, "the powers of the symbolic function" (118), they instead expanded the possibilities. Yacowar tells the story as follows:

> ... The censor insisted on the removal of the hint that Blanche's first husband was homosexual. Kazan was amenable on this point because he preferred the victim to be considered weak, rather than deviant. But when the censor required the removal of the rape scene, both Williams and Kazan opposed him adamantly.
>
> Williams and Kazan labored to find an acceptable compromise, but they refused to remove the rape scene, which they argued was the crux of the action. Finally it was agreed that the rape would remain but that the rapist would not go unpunished. The film ends with Stella rejecting Stanley ("Don't you touch me. Don't you ever touch me again.") and assuring her baby that "we're not going back in there. Not this time. We're never going back. Never, never back, never back again" [22].

Yacowar doesn't point out the obvious, but the obvious is precisely the point — Stella speaks these lines to the baby and, of course, to herself but not to Stanley, as she runs up the steps to Eunice's, just as she does at the end of Scene 3. In that scene, Stanley's desperate "heaven-splitting" cry of "STELL-LAH-HHHH!" (60; scene 3), immortalized by Brando and now firmly entrenched in American popular culture, is answered by an amorous, forgiving Stella. At the film's end, the "mature moviegoer" has no doubt that Stanley's identical pleas will again be identically answered. As Phillips puts it,

> This was a shrewdly ambiguous way to end the movie, since the unsophisticated viewer could believe that Stella would make good her resolution. The more mature moviegoer, however, would realize that Stella had left Stanley earlier in the film, in the wake of a domestic quarrel, and then returned to him when he begged her forgiveness; and hence there is ample reason to believe that she will do so again ["ASND" 232].

Murray Schumach makes much the same observation: "Thus the twelve-year-olds could believe that Stella was leaving her husband. But the rest of the audience would realize it was just an emotional outburst of the moment" (qtd. in Cahir 76). Linda Cahir puts Joe Breen in the company of these youngsters, for the change seemed to satisfy him as well (76).

While Williams, Kazan, and the "mature moviegoer" could appropriately "read" the film's ending, the "twelve-year-olds," Joe Breen, and the Legion of Decency could not, and thus the scales seem to tip towards the more pessimistic point of view — that Stella returns to her man. The film's "shrewdly ambiguous" ending, however, does not so much tip the scales as set them rocking. It accommodates both Greenblatt's insight that "subversion is both generated and contained by the dominant ideology" (Stanley as the primary embodiment of the Same, sets up and controls — indeed, makes a game of — Stella's recurrent impulse to leave him) and Newton's rereading that holds out the possibility that one can "understand his or her contemporary cultural situation and act to alter it" (Stella, ironically the "author" of the *lettre de cachet en famille* that decides Blanche's fate, is finally able to subvert the Same by fleeing upstairs). In other words, we can indeed choose to believe that Stella will break the pattern that we've already witnessed or that she will once again, in Jonathan Dollimore's words, be "folded back into a dominant ideology" (qtd. in Newton 123).

The play and the 1983 and 1995 adaptations (all exempt from Censor Board control) end in a more limited way. The belief that Stella will to some extent or another draw away from Stanley depends solely upon speculation about what will happen post-diegetically — how, for example, the baby will affect Stella's feelings for Stanley after Blanche's departure. In the 1951 film, however, there is at least the possibility that Stella's second flight to Eunice's apartment (what Philip Kolin calls "sanctuary," a "safe house," "an almost god-like, god-benevolent location" [115]) is more than a move in a sexual game. It may indicate that Stella finally understands what Blanche has known from the beginning — that "Stanley's paternalism [is] a kind of domestic tyranny where rape and adultery are male prerogatives" and, concomitantly, that her "loyalty and devotion" are really "sexual addiction and infantilism" (Kleb 40). Because the 1951 film lets us visualize (not merely speculate about) this possibility, it, not the play itself or its later television adaptations, best embodies Kleb's insight that "Williams's project," like Foucault's, is "to relocate the Other within man's [or in this case, woman's] own nature, within the Same" (41).

Like Stella, Mitch may also come to understand that Stanley harbors the Other. In the play, as Mitch listens to Blanche scream as "the Matron steps boldly toward her," the stage directions describe him "start[ing] toward the bedroom. Stanley crosses to block him. Stanley pushes him aside. Mitch lunges and strikes at Stanley. Stanley pushes Mitch back. Mitch collapses at the table, sobbing" (141; scene 11). In the film, dialogue is added to these actions. When he hears Blanche struggling with the Matron, he cries, first to Stanley, "You done this to her," and then to Steve (Rudy Bond) and Pablo (Nick Dennis), "He did this to her." Stanley replies, "You must be nuts. What're you looking at? I never once touched her."

From the point of view of the Censor Board, Mitch's affirmation that Stanley "done this to her" is part of Stanley's punishment. Being accused by a crazy woman is one thing, but being accused by one's "best friend," as Stanley calls Mitch in Scene 7 (103), is quite another. What this added dialogue and Mitch's physical attack signify, however, is not fixed. Though it could be true that Mitch's accusation does originate in his having located, like Stella, the otherness within Stanley, it could just as easily be true that it arises from his having located, in himself, as pointed out earlier, the "seeds" of "unmanly sensitivity, disease, arrested adolescence, even sexual confusion" that Blanche "threatens to make ... grow" (Kleb 33). In blaming Stanley, Mitch may have projected the accusation that really should have been directed against himself onto his "best friend." Or Mitch, as well as Stella, may have been visited by both terrible epiphanies.

One more change in Williams's story as it moved from stage to film is important to discuss. In the play's Scene 9, after hearing Blanche's confession, Mitch accuses her of having told him "lies, lies, inside and out, all lies," to which she pitifully responds, "Never inside, I didn't lie in my heart." At this moment, a "Vendor comes around the corner. She is a blind Mexican Woman [Edna Thomas] in a dark shawl, carrying bunches of those gaudy tin flowers that lower class Mexicans display at funerals and other festive occasions. She is calling barely audibly. Her figure is only faintly visible outside the building" (119; scene 9). "*Flores. Flores. Flores para los muertos. Flores. Flores,*" she calls. With the woman now at the door, Blanche opens it, "frightened," and the woman repeats, "*Flores? Flores para los muertos?*" to which Blanche responds, "No, no! Not now!" as she "darts back into the apartment, slamming the door." The woman continues to chant "*Flores para los muertos*" and "*Corones para los muertos, Corones ...*" as Blanche continues to tell Mitch about "regrets — recriminations ... Legacies!" (119; scene 9), what Wolcott Gibbs calls "the gathering horrors of Belle Reve" (57). "*Corones*" also links Blanche to the funeral wreaths sold by the Mexican Woman when Stanley wants Blanche to "look at [herself] ... with the crazy crown on!" (Thomas Brown). Indeed, she is literally wearing her own funeral crown, her cheap tiara, as Scene 10 moves quickly towards its culmination, Stanley's rape of Blanche.

In the play's Scene 10, "a few hours later that night," Stanley returns from the hospital. Drinking beer and feeling certain that in the morning he will hear the words "You've got a son!" he makes Blanche an offer: "Shall we bury the hatchet and make it a loving-cup? Huh?" (125; scene 10). When Blanche refuses, calling him "swine" and proclaiming that she has given Mitch "his walking papers," Stanley's fires are restoked. He follows Blanche into the bedroom, and her "Don't come in here!" signals the beginning of a bit of surreal stagecraft. Suddenly, "lurid reflections appear on the walls around Blanche. The shadows are of a grotesque and menacing form" (128; scene 10). As she attempts to call Shep Huntleigh, the night becomes

> filled with inhuman voices like cries in a jungle. The shadows and lurid
> reflections move sinuously as flames along the wall spaces. Through the back
> wall of the rooms, which have become transparent, can be seen the sidewalk.
> A prostitute has rolled a drunkard. He pursues her along the walk, overtakes
> her and there is a struggle. A policeman's whistle breaks it up. The figures dis-
> appear. Some moment later the Negro Woman appears around the corner
> with a sequined bag which the prostitute had dropped on the walk. She is
> rooting excitedly through it [128; scene 11].

This is, perhaps, an echo of Stanley's rooting through Blanche's trunk at the play's beginning. Stanley interrupts her telephone call when he comes out of the bathroom "in the brilliant silk pyjamas" (129; scene 10) that he "break[s] out on special occasions ... [and] wore on [his] wedding night" (125; scene 10). When he begins to "interfere" with Blanche in earnest, she "smashes a bottle on the table and faces him, clutching the broken top." "Tiger — tiger!" he demands. "Drop the bottle-top! Drop it! We've had this date with each other from the beginning!" As the scene ends, "he picks up her inert figure and carries her to the bed," and when "the hot trumpet and drums from the Four Deuces sound loudly" (130; scene 11), we know that the wild card has been named, the wild cat tamed.

Two changes were made when Scene 9 moved to the screen. First, perhaps reflecting the notion that the cinema serves the entertainment needs of the common man while the Broadway stage belongs to a more exclusive clientele, the Mexican Woman's first line is translated. She says to Blanche at the door, "*Flores. Flores para los muertos*," then, in a southern accent, "Flowers. Flowers for the dead." More importantly, though, in the film we can see in a close shot that she is not blind. She looks into Blanche's eyes, and Blanche scrutinizes her face.

The changes in Scene 10 are far more radical. Though Kazan does take liberties when he allows us to hear the Varsouviana or the torturing echoes of the last scene, that is about as far as he can go without destroying the film's basic realism. The transparent walls of the Broadway play he directed have no place in his film. Neither do the "inhuman voices like cries in a jungle," for these do not arise from Blanche's memory (like the Varsouviana) or from the dialogue (Stanley's and the Matron's words). The surrealism that a theatre audience could easily accept would look and sound ridiculous here. Kazan, however, had begun to develop a kind of philosophy of place that would hold him in good stead as he planned the filming of *Streetcar*:

> I asked Jack Ford once, I said, "Where do you get your ideas of how a scene should be directed?" And he said, "From the set." He said, "I go out on the set in the morning, the set I've chosen, way before anybody else, an hour before the crew, and I walk around and look at the set — where they come in and where they go out, what there is, what there isn't, and so on." And when I thought about it, it's a very important thing. That is, the physical life of the scene is determined by whether the set squeezes people together or whether the set has an escape place in it [Schickel].

Because a set that "squeezes people together" is exactly what *Streetcar* required, Kazan had the set constructed in an unconventional way: "We had the walls of Stanley and Stella's home built in small sections that could be removed, so making the set grow smaller as time passed, more constricting and more threatening to Blanche. This is an eerie effect, and it worked" (Kazan 384). It is indeed a subtly eerie effect, a wonderful reinforcement of Blanche's feeling that she's "caught in a trap" (128; scene 10) of Stanley's frustration in having an outsider in his apartment made for only two. As Alan Ehrlich argues, "The household was too crowded for a sister-in-law, as she is an outsider to the established order, the marriage; but for a son there is plenty of room" (qtd. in Cardullo 179, note 4). Moreover, violent action in a small space makes the space seem even smaller and magnifies the violence. Though John Erman calls his own television version of *Streetcar* "naturalistic" and Kazan's "surrealistic," Pamela Hanks's term for Kazan's film — "heightened realism" — is probably a better description (117). The shrinking set and the disturbing music and echoes in Blanche's mind, all of which become emblematic of her madness, manage to fall within the codes of cinematic realism.

We can also accept the reappearance of the Mexican Woman in the film's rape scene. As in the play, feeling increasingly threatened by Stanley's drunken taunts, Blanche snatches up a few meager belongings and heads for the door. As she open it, the silhouette of the Mexican Woman materializes through the New Orleans fog and slowly approaches. While the Woman is still a good distance away, though, Blanche speaks to her, again whispering, "Oh no. Not now," and, again terrified, she backs into the apartment, where Stanley's cat-and-mouse game continues to intensify until the scene ends with Stanley's "hands firmly clasped around Blanche's wrists as the frightened woman flails her head violently. Defeated, she throws back her head to expose her long neck in the shattered mirror" (Schlueter, "Remake" 144–45). While it would have been possible to have glimpsed, through a window, the background scene with the prostitute, the drunk, and the Negro Woman, all of whom represent the Other, its absence supports my contention that in this film, violence is a characteristic only of the Same.

In terms of the kinds of symbols that are discussed at the beginning of this chapter, the Mexican Woman clearly represents Death. "She seems to stalk Blanche, even as death blindly stalked the DuBois family at Belle Reve" (Cardullo 171). She is the on-stage embodiment of the personification that Blanche offers to Mitch, hoping that it will help him understand why she behaved as she did. Telling him about her mother, Blanche pictures Death: "I used to sit here and she used to sit over there and death was as close as you are.... The opposite is desire. So do you wonder?" (120; scene 9). The audience has already seen the personification of Desire in the figure of the Young Man (Vito Christi) who appears in Scene 5 to collect money for the Kowalskis' newspaper, *The Evening Star,* and whom Blanche wants to "kiss ... just once, softly and sweetly on [the] mouth!" (84; scene 5). With the appearance of the Mexican Woman, the picture of the most mighty of literary opposites — Thanatos and Eros — is complete.

Cardullo reads the Mexican Woman's blindness in three ways. First, evidently suggesting that Death, like Justice, is not prejudiced, she "becomes, in her blindness, a symbol of all the deaths at Belle Reve that helped to deplete Blanche's finances and break her will" (171). Next, "since she is blind, obviously she moves slowly. The effect of the Mexican Woman's movement, combined with her calls, is haunting. It is to make us feel that Blanche is haunted by her past ... that her past can never leave her" (173). Finally, and most intriguing of all, Cardullo works with Williams's stage directions that follow Blanche's last line, "Whoever you are — I have always depended on the kindness of strangers," to link Blanche and the Mexican Woman and argue that Blanche is experiencing a spiritual death. Williams writes,

> The poker players stand back as Blanche and the Doctor cross the kitchen to the front door. She allows him to lead her as if she were blind. As they go out on the porch, Stella cries out her sister's name from where she is crouched a few steps up on the stairs. "Blanche! Blanche! Blanche!" Blanche walks on without turning, followed by the Doctor and the Matron. They go around the corner of the building [142; scene 11].

Cardullo's connecting Blanche with Death depends not only on the Woman's being blind but also on her being Mexican:

> The Mexican Woman represents all that Blanche once thought she was above, and all that she has now become: a foreigner of sorts in New Orleans without a penny, whose language is not understood by Stanley and goes unheeded by Stella; a woman whose heavy makeup and costume jewelry can no longer hide her ravaged looks; a silent woman by the end of the play who does not heed Stella's desperate cries and who "allows [the Doctor] to lead her [out of the Kowalski apartment] as if she were blind" [173].

Cardullo's point, however, can be taken even further by contemplating Blanche's reaction to the Mexican Woman. Even though Blanche acknowledges to Mitch in Scene 6 that she believes that Stanley will "destroy" her, will become her "executioner" (93), she runs from him only in Scene 10 when his physical threat becomes all too real. One might be tempted to wonder why Blanche, in both play and film, having lived through the heartbreak of her husband's suicide and the hard life that she subsequently carved out for herself, would react so strongly to the Mexican Woman, who, unlike Stanley, poses no physical threat to her whatsoever. The answer may lie in the somewhat odd literary situation of a character's recognition of the symbols within her own story. The lantern is a case in point. When Stanley says to Blanche in Scene 11, "You left nothing here but spilt talcum and old empty perfume bottles — unless it's the paper lantern you want to take with you. You want the lantern?" and then "seizes the paper lantern, tearing it off the light bulb," and she "cries out as if the lantern was herself" (140), we know that the lantern is, to her, not just a way to soften the light and hide the age in her face. Blanche's strong response to the Mexican Woman similarly indicates that she does indeed "read" the woman in the same way that the film's audience does. In truth, Blanche has already "died" many times — with Allan Grey's suicide (his last name is not accidental), with the DuBois family's "long parade to the graveyard" (26; scene 1), with the loss of her job, and with her expulsion from Laurel. Emily Dickinson could have been writing about a specific someone like Blanche, as well as about the general human condition, when she contrasts the lives of trees — "Green People" — to the lives of humans: "We — who have the Souls — /Die oftener — Not so vitally —" (J. 314). Perhaps no one in American literature has died "oftener" than Blanche DuBois, and perhaps no one has more soul.

The Mexican Woman of the film presents us with different interpretive options. Not only does the film twice confirm Cardullo's point that the Mexican Woman is a symbol of Blanche's spiritual death, but her two appearances, once in Scene 9 and once in Scene 10, also connect Stanley's actual rape of Blanche to Mitch's attempted rape: "Using evidence supplied by Stanley," notes Kleb, "[Mitch] forces Blanche to confess the whole truth about her secret sexual life, and this confession elicits not compassion, forgiveness, the promise of salvation, but severe physical punishment — rape. It is carried out by Stanley after Mitch is unable to do it himself." Mitch and Stanley have "redefin[ed] the 'truth' about [her] solely in terms of her sexual misdeeds," and such redefinition demands such punishment (34). In a more subtle way, however, the Mexican Woman can perhaps teach us something about what lies behind the whole notion of Same and Other, why this powerful dichotomy arose in the first place, and how it can be transcended.

The Mexican Woman appears to be the true Other — Death — the Other that the Same, in its preoccupation with power, its obsession with the "struggle to control ... a definition of the Same and the Other" (Kleb 27), cannot bear to acknowledge simply because this ultimate Other defies definition and always triumphs. In order to distract itself from the mystery and power of the true Other, the Same goes to devastating lengths to construct a manageable Other out of those persons previously listed — "the poor, the unemployed, the sick, venereals, homosexuals, prostitutes, the sexually promiscuous, blasphemers, witches, profligates, free thinkers, libertines, the insane ... noisy women, prodigal sons, and daughters whose passions were overexcited by reading too much romance literature" (Kleb 31) — who inhabit the "dangerous, disruptive, and marginal world" (Kleb 41) that is as much a part of life as the orderly and central, albeit sometimes violent, site that the Same stakes out for itself. This is why it is significant that Stanley never sees the Mexican Woman. He has adopted a philosophy of positive thinking that he credits, for example, for his survival of the battle of Salerno: "I believed I was lucky. I figured that 4 out of 5 would not come through but I would ... and I did. I put that down as a rule. To hold front position in this rat-race you've got to believe you are lucky," he tells his poker buddies (131; scene 11). Unable to tolerate the thought of his own death and perfectly able to fulfill his role as "guardian of the Same," he has envisioned the flesh-and-blood Blanche, not Death Herself, as what Kleb calls the "primordial female Other" (36). Stanley cannot face the traumatic message that there is only one real separation in this world — the living and the dead. It is this separation that D. H. Lawrence (whose work Williams especially admired) so clearly captures in "Odour of Chrysanthemums" when Elizabeth Bates is washing the body of her husband, Walter, who has suffocated in a mining accident: "She looked at his face, and she turned her own face to the wall. For his look was other than hers, his way was not her way" (301).

And yet, even the life/death dichotomy can be transcended. Cardullo argues that the Mexican Woman's flowers, with their "gaudy tinniness," are symbolic of "all the cheap, good times that Blanche enjoyed with strangers" (172). His interpretation is flawed, however, for these "cheap, good times" are something more — the key to Blanche's emotional survival. Without them, death would have overwhelmed her. The life-saving role of desire, "the opposite" (120; scene 9) of death, should not be considered "cheap." As the narrator of *The Awakening* points out, Edna Pontellier's sexual encounter with Alcée Arobin, though based on lust, not love, lifts a "mist ... from her eyes, enabling her to look upon and comprehend the significance of life, that monster made up of beauty and brutality" (104; ch. XXVIII). Associated, then, with both Death and Desire, the Mexican Woman is not the Grim Reaper to whom Blanche alludes in Scene 1: "Why, the Grim Reaper had put up his tent on our doorstep!" Blanche tells Stella as she recounts the story of the deaths of the last members of the DuBois family. Because she is female, the Mexican Woman belongs to a set of images of Death that include, for example, Whitman's "*Dark mother always gliding near with soft feet*" ("When Lilacs Last in the Dooryard Bloom'd") or, again, as we cited in the chapter on *The Awakening*, the "old crone rocking the cradle, swathed in sweet garments, bending aside" ("Out of the Cradle Endlessly Rocking"), images that find their genesis in the Triple Goddess of antiquity, maiden and mother and crone, the goddess of the ever-turning cycle of life itself. The Mexican Woman represents the face of the crone, the hag associated with the waning moon, the destroyer, the face that demands recognition and acceptance. Lost in a denial pattern of her own, Blanche, like Stanley, cannot locate this Other within her own nature. At sixteen, when she married the young homosexual Allan Grey, she lost not only the bliss of the romantic love she had felt for him but also the chance to be a mother. With his death, she assumed the burden of guilt that requires her to periodically relive, aurally, that terrible evening, from the Varsouviana to the gunshot that signals the end of the flashback. Now thirty and "played out" (118; scene 9), Blanche would like to start over, but all the paper lanterns in the world covering all its naked light bulbs won't bring back her youth, and Stanley's ruining her chances with Mitch has robbed her a second time of the possibility of motherhood.

Looked at from this feminist, archetypal position, we can see why, effectively cheated out of enjoying all the stages of her life, Blanche flees from the Mexican Woman, telling her twice in the film, "Not now." She is not ready to see the crone in herself, to be the "old maid schoolteacher" that — desperate for a compliment from Mitch — she represents herself as being in Scene 3.

Henry Schvey argues,

> Stella's baby, born at approximately the same time as Blanche's violation by Stanley in the previous scene, is associated with Blanche in the final moment of the play.... Williams clearly suggests an identification between the tragic fall of one and the birth of the other.... Blanche's symbolic death has ultimately resulted in new life.... Thus Blanche's fall is actually part of a process which goes beyond death and hints at something like heroic transcendence ... [at] spiritual purification through suffering [109].

Schvey locates visual confirmation of transcendence in Blanche's donning a Della Robbia blue jacket as she prepares for what she thinks will be a sea voyage with Shep Huntleigh. Her wearing blue associates her with both the Virgin in Renaissance art and with the Kowalskis' baby boy, bundled in a "pale blue blanket." Further, Leonard Quirino, in his work with Blanche's compulsive bathing, observes that "Williams ... denies the memory-haunted Blanche the full powers of the river Lethe," the "watery purgatory where the dead are cleansed of all taint of memory and desire before they can be considered fit for reincarnation," until the "very end when he allows her the refuge of madness" (81). (As we have already noted, Blanche wishes to die at sea and wears a seahorse-shaped pin on her jacket.) Symbolically, then, Blanche's time of suffering is over. She has found a "refuge" and is cleansed and prepared for "heroic transcendence," even mustering enough old-fashioned grace to say to the poker players as she walks through the kitchen, "Please don't get up. I'm only passing through," interestingly a line that Bob Dylan has incorporated into the excellent lyrics of "Things Have Changed," only adding the word "gentlemen" after "Please don't get up," a word that Williams would certainly not object to. He probably also would not object to — and maybe even laugh at — "The Simpsons" episode where Marge Simpson as Blanche rolls her anger at her husband, Homer, onto Ned Flanders who is playing Stanley. Marge, then, like Marlon Brando, could have found herself in Lee Strasberg's Actors Studio where The Method was taught and practiced. We see another pop culture reference to *Streetcar* when Woody Allen wakes up in *Sleeper*, thinking himself to be Blanche DuBois, and recovers only when Diane Keaton assumes the role of Stanley: "I say — Ha! — Ha! Do you hear me? Ha — ha — ha! (128; scene 10).

Like violence, the possibility of "heroic transcendence" can be seen in both play and film, but, like violence, it is more powerfully depicted in the film. When the Doctor and the Matron first arrive, Blanche tells the Doctor, "You are not the gentleman I was expecting," and then whispers to Stella, "That man isn't Shep Huntleigh." After the struggle with the Matron and her rescue by the Doctor, who, as we have seen, literally turns her around and helps her to her feet, Blanche's demeanor changes. In the film, we must also recall, the Mexican Woman is not blind, and at the film's end, the Doctor does not lead Blanche out "as if she were blind." She takes his arm, and in a peaceful, dignified way, she walks out of the apartment looking into his face. This nameless old Doctor, this "Whoever you are," has encouraged Blanche to see the southern gentleman in him. This look, this walk, and the symbols of transcendence give the film's audience hope that when the Mexican Woman again arrives, as of course she will, Blanche will be able to again look into her face but do so this time without terror. Though she was never a mother in the biological sense of the word, perhaps she could find in herself the archetypes of maiden and mother and crone, thus experiencing a transcendence (a deconstruction of the binary oppositions, as it were) where Same and Other are One.

3. Thematic Criticism

"Ode: Intimations of Immortality from Recollections of Early Childhood" by William Wordsworth

Splendor in the Grass (1961)

What though the radiance which was once so bright
Be now forever taken from my sight,
  Though nothing can bring back the hour
Of splendour in the grass, of glory in the flower;
  We will grieve not, rather find
  Strength in what remains behind; — Wordsworth [ll.
177–82]

Wordsworth's poem and William Inge and Elia Kazan's 1961 film are obviously not related in the same way that *Streetcar* and *The Awakening* are to their adaptations. On the surface, it may seem that the Ode amounts to just one small moment in the film's story, chosen to highlight the emotions of a teenage girl who is devastated by the loss of her boyfriend. The Inge scholarship reinforces this erroneous impression, for while there is ample discussion of *Splendor in the Grass*, only a few critics even mention Wordsworth's lines, and they but briefly. Although in Wagner's categorization the film would be considered an *analogy* and in Desmond and Hawkes's a *loose adaptation*, a closer look reveals that poem and film are intricately connected through shared themes whose exploration may bring students closer to Wordsworth's great poem.

As Ralph Voss points out, we know that Inge "developed a vital interest in reading" during high school and that his "interest in literature went well beyond whatever study was necessary for good grades in his English classes" (25). Before the success in 1950 of the Broadway production of *Come Back, Little Sheba*, he had been a high school English teacher and then, after completing his M.A. in English, taught composition and drama at Stephens College in Columbia, Missouri, and at Washington University in St. Louis. Inge particularly liked Wordsworth, "whose poetry would later lend both themes and titles" to his own work (Voss 25). In terms of titles, the one-act play *The Glory of the Flower* was incorporated into *Splendor in the Grass*; in terms of themes, Voss comments that not only Deanie and Bud of *Splendor* but "many other Inge characters, like Evelyn in Inge's novel *Good Luck, Miss Wyckoff*," "find/Strength in what remains behind" (260).

The first reviews of *Splendor in the Grass* are mostly negative (Voss 196). Of those critics who did like the film, Arthur Knight, writing for the *Saturday Review*, calls it a "constantly fascinating" study of "the drives, motives, and psychological quirks" of "youth in revolt against parental authority," and the *Newsweek* critic finds that it "brings into the open Inge's unique talent for sympathetic satire in a dramatic story" (qtd. in Leeson 18). Tim Dirks notes that in the "quasi–*Romeo and Juliet* script, Warren Beatty marked his screen debut ... and co-star Natalie Wood received a Best Actress nomination ... for one of her finest (if not *the* best) screen roles" (2). On the other (and more representative) hand, Robert Hatch, writing for the *Nation*, slammed the film's turning "tragedy into sentimental slapstick" through "superficial" characterization and "ludicrous" effects, and R.M. Hodgens of *Film Quarterly* sarcastically pronounces it a "long film that treats familiar material as thoroughly as possible" (qtd. in Leeson 19). Nonetheless, it won Inge an Academy Award for Best Original Script, and although Voss suggests that "perhaps the Warner Brothers hype netted Inge his Academy Award nomination" (197), one would certainly like to believe that Wordsworth's influence on Inge's interior life and what C.M. Bowra calls the Ode's "stately" presence (78) in the script contributed to his triumph.

Warren Beatty's remark that the "unpretentiously worded" script "has such a feeling for young people" (qtd. in Thompson 7), those "burgeoning numbers of teenage filmgoers" toward whom Kazan "directed his efforts" (Pauly 233), still proves true almost fifty years later. Quite differently from most of those professional reviewers, my students unabashedly love *Splendor in the Grass* and complain when we have to stop the movie at the end of class. "The conflict between natural desire and responsibility which the young lovers face" (McClure 58) is quite real to them, as are the other kinds of conflict typical of the parent/child, brother/sister, friend/friend relationships that are also portrayed. But it is Deanie's response to Wordsworth's poetry that makes students want to thoughtfully read and reread the Ode and to explore its role in Inge and Kazan's film.

Elia Kazan's film of *A Streetcar Named Desire* is now a canonical text in its own right, and *The End of August* and *Grand Isle* are such close transpositions of Chopin's *The Awakening* that they require no plot summary. But *Splendor in the Grass* is different. It is not a retelling, in a different medium, of the "story" of the Ode. Kazan and Inge turned one of Inge's unpublished novels into the screenplay, published by Bantam later in 1961. This screenplay, now out-of-print, is the basis of H. Baird Shuman's chapter on *Splendor in the Grass* in his 1965 *William Inge*, volume 95 of Twayne's United States Authors Series, a chapter that is a bit misleading because the finished film does not always follow its script. In the 1989 revision of this book, the same problem exists. F. Andrew Leslie's stage adaptation of the screenplay, a very different rendition altogether, is not particularly helpful where the film is concerned. Thus, a detailed synopsis of what we actually see on screen seems in order.

Wilma Dean "Deanie" Loomis (Natalie Wood), the only child of a comfortably well-off grocer and his wife, and Arthur "Bud" Stamper (Warren Beatty), the only son of a newly rich oil man and his wife, are high school seniors in love and tormented by the desire that all the codes of their respectable Kansas town demand that they suppress. When they are not on screen together, alternating scenes track them individually.

As the film begins, a subtitle informs us that it is September of 1928, and we see Deanie and Bud parked by the river, kissing and "fooling around." Shots of the beautiful waterfalls, whose torrents provide a backdrop for their passion, are interspersed until Deanie pushes Bud away, telling him she's afraid and that they "mustn't," and he angrily storms out of the car before he takes her home, where Mrs. Loomis (Audrey Christie) is waiting up. As her mother tells her that their Stamper Oil shares rose fourteen points today, Deanie, knowing that Bud doesn't care about his father's business, is preoccupied with listening to the sound of the sea in a conch shell that sits on the mantle; then, wanting to be alone, she tries to escape upstairs. Deanie's mother can see that her daughter is in love, and she follows her to her room and gives her some advice: "Boys don't respect a girl they can go all the way with. Boys want a nice girl for a wife. Wilma Dean, you and Bud haven't gone too far already have you?" Deanie tells her mother the truth, which is that they have not "gone too far," and then she asks, "Mom, is it so terrible to have those feelings about a boy?" "No nice girl does," her mother tells her, but Deanie, hugging her mother and hiding her face, presses her: "Mom, didn't you ever ... feel that way about Dad?" Mrs. Loomis' reply is important because it establishes the moral tenor of her household. She hugs Deanie back and softly confides, "Your father never laid a hand on me until we were married, and then I just gave in because a wife has to. A woman doesn't enjoy those things the way a man does. She just lets her husband ... come near her ... in order to have children." Impatient now to get her mother out of her room, Deanie pleads fatigue, and when her mother leaves, she gets in bed, stares at her Teddy bear, throws it across the room, gets back up, kisses the pictures of Bud that are taped to her vanity mirror and tacked to the wall over it, and says her prayers on her knees by the bed. Back in her own room, Mrs. Loomis admits to her husband, Del (Fred Stewart), that Bud would be "the catch of a lifetime."

We next visit Bud's house where his father, Ace Stamper (Pat Hingle), is in the kitchen throwing a party for his oil drillers to celebrate the new gusher. Ace takes Bud into the living room and begins to talk about Deanie. "You're not doing anything, boy, you're going to be ashamed of—are you?" he asks. "I've got nothing against [the Loomises], Bud, because they are poor. I'm not a snob or anything like that. The only difference between me and Del is that I got ambition. But if anything was to happen, you'd have to marry her." Bud wants to talk to Ace about some "stuff," but Ace won't listen, telling Bud about how he is going to send him to Yale and, after Stamper Oil merges with "one of those big Eastern outfits," he's going to put him "in there." "There's nothing I wouldn't do for you, Bud, if you do right. Don't disappoint me, boy.... I've got all my hopes pinned on you now," Ace tells him. Clearly out-talked, Bud goes to bed.

The next morning at breakfast, Ace is ranting about Bud's sister, Ginny (Barbara Loden). He reminds his wife (Joanna Roos) that Ginny, while at a Chicago art school, "[got] tied up with some cake eater that [got] her into trouble just so he [could] marry her," but when Ace cut off her allowance, the man "backed off." Ace vows to teach this "headstrong little flapper" some "discipline," but Ginny clearly has other plans and leaves the table. Irritated, Bud grabs some fruit and runs out, causing Mrs. Stamper to observe, "Oh dear. Neither of my children gets any real nourishment," a line that does seem to validate the complaint that Inge's screenplay "tells one what to think" (Leeson 171).

Bud picks up Deanie and they drive to school. They hold hands as they walk down the hall, and Deanie doesn't take her eyes way from his face (in exactly the same way that Blanche doesn't take her eyes away from the Doctor's face at the end of *Streetcar*). Standing in the doorway of Deanie's English class, they are interrupted by Juanita (Jan Norris), the class "bad girl," who looks at Bud as she squeezes between them and flirtingly murmurs, "*Pardonnez-moi.*" It soon becomes clear that although Bud is the "big man on campus" who could have any girl in the school, he has eyes only for Deanie. He goes to his class, slamming locker doors on his way, and Deanie, late, takes her seat. The topic for the day's lesson is written on the board—"'Morte d'Arthur'—Sir Thomas Mallory." As Miss Metcalf (Martine Bartlett) questions the class about the values that the knights of old held dear, Deanie practices writing "Mr. and Mrs. Bud Stamper" in her copybook. Juanita volunteers that the knights had "a very high regard for women" and considered them "very pure," an ironic answer that makes some of the girls snicker. The scene ends with Miss Metcalf asking, "Well, how about it, girls. Do any of you feel you're on a pedestal?"

At the afternoon's football game, Bud's team is penalized for Bud's "unnecessary roughness," and Bud attacks the referee. Arthur McClure observes that Bud's sexual "tension breeds an irrational anger.... It affects his athletic prowess and he becomes subject to puzzling outbursts of rage" (58). After the game, in the showers, the boys are kidding Allen "Toots" Tuttle (Gary Lockwood) about Juanita, whom he dates, and when Bud goes to his car where Deanie is waiting, he passes by Juanita who compliments him on his good game. Deanie feels slighted and tells Bud, "I suppose you wish I was more like Juanita Howard." Reacting defensively, he tells Deanie that it is unrealistic of her to believe that he doesn't notice girls "like that."

Back at Deanie's house, Bud confesses, "I don't know what's the matter with me lately. I always lose my temper. If it weren't for you, Deanie — I don't know." Shuman criticizes Inge for not doing "more to show the extent of some of Bud's conflicts. He does to some extent early in the film when he has Bud go down the hall of the high school slamming the locker doors and creating a great deal of noise" and again "when Bud is playing football, he tackles an opponent with what Inge describes as 'a crushing blow'" (104). Shuman, however, makes no mention of what happens next, which all by itself it would have been enough to convey Bud's frustration. Kissing Deanie and pulling her body close to his, he suddenly says, "You're nuts about me," and then, leaning against the door that leads to the store, he ignores Deanie's protests, roughly puts his hands on her shoulders, and pushes her to her knees. "At my feet, slave," he dictates. "Tell me you love me. You can't live without me. You'd do anything I ever asked you to do — anything." Deanie collapses to the floor, and to Bud's "I was just kidding. I thought you knew that," she answers, "I can't kid about these things because I am nuts about you, and I would go down on my knees to worship you if you really wanted me to. Bud, I can't get along without you, and I would do anything you'd ask me to. I would. I would. Anything." Then, almost as if Bud were no longer there, Deanie sensuously murmurs, "Oh, Bud. Bud. Bud." As McClure points out, "The game becomes all too real and they experience a still deeper glimpse of the somewhat mysterious passion that is sweeping them along" (58). When Deanie's mother comes home, the young lovers frantically go to the piano and start to play "Chopsticks." When Bud leaves, Mrs. Loomis indulges in a bit of gossip. "Ginny Stamper is too low for the dogs to bite," she tells Deanie, for evidently she had to "have one of those awful operations performed. That's what happens to girls who go wild and boy crazy," she warns.

The next scene opens with the "wild and boy crazy" Ginny playing a ukulele along with a phonograph record in such an obnoxious way that she goads Ace into ripping out the electrical cord. He summarily dismisses her from the room, saying that he wants to talk with his boy. "Dad, I want to marry Deanie. I don't want to go to Yale," Bud boldly announces. Ace urges him over and over to "trust" his advice. "I spent my whole life trying to make a place of importance for you. Trust me." Shuman suggests that "although Ace is not a leading character, he is the film's most important secondary character" (102) since he is the one who most actively discourages the marriage. Although "the economic gap between Bud and Deanie is substantial, ... the cultural gap is hardly noticeable since both come from basically simple small-town families" (100). Nonetheless, "Ace probably objects" to Bud's marrying Deanie "because he thinks Bud will soon be able to make a better marriage" (102), but Ace is too smart to object directly. Instead, he "realizes that to forbid the marriage would be to force it and that to delay it will be to destroy any chance of its taking place" (Shuman 101).

When Bud says that he can't wait, "I feel like I'm going nuts sometimes," Ace tells him that what he needs, "for the time being, ... is a different kind of girl." Ace reminds him that "there was always two kinds of girls," but Bud insists that he doesn't "want to do that" because he loves Deanie. After several moments of silent torment, he caves in to his father's pressure and agrees to go to Yale and marry Deanie "when I get out," as if attending Yale were a prison sentence.

Bud tells Deanie about his decision on a rainy Sunday at church. Predictably, Deanie vows to "wait for [him] forever." During a sermon based upon Jesus's advice to "lay not up treasures for yourself on Earth, ... for where your treasure is, there will your heart be also," the camera pans the congregation, and we see Deanie gazing into Bud's treasured face, her parents watching her gaze, Ginny clearly thinking about the minister's message, and Ace sleeping soundly. After the service, Deanie and Bud huddle under one umbrella while Del and Ace, under another, talk about stocks, and Mrs. Loomis and Mrs. Stamper, under another, talk about how each is "mighty proud" of the other's child. The Reverend Whiteman, played by Inge himself, is aloof, and we see him retreat across the churchyard, solitary under his own umbrella.

The next scene begins with Ginny frantically trying to pry open the liquor cabinet that her father has locked before his departure for New York to see about the big merger. Her date is Glenn (Sean Garrison), a slow-witted filling station attendant, obviously chosen for his good looks. When Ginny announces that she and Glenn are going out, Bud, who has promised Ace that he would "keep an eye" on his sister, says that he and Deanie will go too. They drive to what appears to be the family's second house, located in the oil fields, and while Bud builds a fire, Ginny sings a popular little tune — "Everybody's talking about Mabel," who is "willing and able, ... a cheat and a flirt, to show a guy around." When Ginny's song ends, Deanie watches her begin her seduction of Glenn with a "fill me up," and Bud, disgusted, offers to take Deanie for a walk. Before they go, however, Ginny gives Bud some advice: "You're pure and righteous.... You never do anything except what Dad tells you, isn't that right, Deanie? You've been finding that out, haven't you? He just lets things torment him inside and make him miserable and he never does anything about them. He never does anything!" Leaving Glenn and Ginny alone, Deanie and Bud go out to look over the oil fields, whose pumps are heavy-handedly mimicking what Glenn and Ginny are now doing. "All this is going to be ours someday," Bud tells Deanie.

It is Christmas. At the Loomis's house, Deanie is thrilled over the watch Bud has given her, but Mrs. Loomis is not so pleased. She wishes that it were a ring and that Bud had "a little more gumption." At Bud's house, the family uncomfortably poses for a holiday photograph while Ginny waits for her date, this time Brian Stacey (uncredited), a married bootlegger. As she is getting dressed, humming "Mabel," Bud comes into her room and scolds her about seeing Brian. She slaps Bud, hard, three times on the cheek and says what's on her mind: "If you want to listen to Dad, go ahead. One of these days you'll find out — you'll find out, and God help you."

At Ace Stamper's big New Year's Eve party, Ginny tries to get her father's attention by doing a shimmy in front of him and then giving him a New Year's kiss on the mouth. He rejects her, embarrasses her, and gives her reason to drink in earnest. When Bud tries to take her home, she slurs, "You're a nice boy. You're nice. I know what you nice boys are like — you only talk to me in the dark," and escapes into a group of men who follow her outside. Three chauffeurs look on (one of whom is played by the then-unknown Godfrey Cambridge) while Ginny's complaint of dizziness is ignored. She almost becomes the victim of a gang rape until Bud finds her and fights with the men. Badly beaten, Bud reels around the parking lot, dazed and stumbling, until Deanie finds him and they manage to get to his car. He drives her home and then, probably seeing his own behavior reflected in and magnified by the men who took advantage of his enticing but thoroughly intoxicated sister, he delivers the lines that Deanie never expected to hear: "We've got to stop all this kissing and fooling around. I don't think we ought to see each other for a while."

Three short sequences follow. Bud makes errors during basketball practice, and his important term paper receives a poor grade. Deanie, who sees him in the hall, can say only, "I miss you, Bud." In the next sequence, a basketball game, he becomes ill and passes out on the court. Dr. Smiley (John McGovern) suspects pneumonia, and at the hospital, where Deanie is waiting,

Ace offers the doctor a blank check if he will cure Bud. When the doctor declares that Bud's health depends upon the "will of God," Deanie goes to see the Reverend Whiteman. In this sequence, he tells her that God wants to hear the prayer that is in her heart, and Deanie prays, "Dear God, make him well. Make him well." Whiteman, whose body language suggests that the demands of his flock are too much for him, is part of the feckless minister tradition in American literature. What Mary E. Wilkins Freeman writes of the minister Hersey in "The Revolt of 'Mother'" could apply to Whiteman: "He had to scourge himself up to some of his pastoral duties as relentlessly as a Catholic ascetic, and then he was prostrated by the smart.... He could expound the intricacies of every character study in the Scriptures.... He could deal with primal cases, but parallel ones worsted him" (617).

After Bud's sun lamp therapy, Dr. Smiley reminds him that it is now Spring, the time for a "young man's fancy [to turn] to thoughts of love." Using this as an opening to talk to the doctor about his conflict over Deanie, Bud confides, "I love her and she loves me. But it's no fun to be in love. It hurts." Confessing that he "just can't go back to seeing her again, not like the way we were doing," he probes the doctor for some solution to the problem. He even confides that his father told him to find "another kind of girl," but Smiley, who says, "No, no," to Ace's advice, can finally only remark, "I don't know how to advise you, Bud," and then dismisses him with the promise of "another shot of iron and another sun lamp treatment" next week.

When we see Bud and Juanita sunbathing on the rocks near the falls, we worry that Ace's advice has won the day. And when, in the next shot, Bud and Juanita, stripped to their underwear, embrace under a waterfall, our worst fears are realized: Bud will not remain faithful to Deanie.

Predictably, the news that Bud has had sex with Juanita spreads throughout the high school like wildfire, and during English class Deanie's shame and trauma surface. Miss Metcalf, standing in front of the blackboard on which is now written Wordsworth's name and dates, recites from memory in a thin, wistful voice:

> What though the radiance which was once so bright
> Be now forever taken from my sight,
>   Though nothing can bring back the hour
> Of splendour in the grass, of glory in the flower;
>   We will grieve not, rather find
>   Strength in what remains behind;

Seated behind the gloating Juanita, Deanie has not been paying attention. Miss Metcalf, recognizing this and fed up with the incessant class chatter, calls on her to tell the class what Wordsworth "means by these lines." When she admits that she has not been listening, Miss Metcalf cruelly makes her stand and read the same lines aloud. On the verge of tears and with genuine emotion in her voice, Deanie reads, then explains: "When we're young, we look at things very idealistically, I guess. And I think Wordsworth means that when we grow up that we have to forget the ideals of youth and find strength...." Rapidly deteriorating, Deanie makes her way to the teacher's desk, whispers, "Miss Metcalf, may I please be ex —," and then runs into the hall. This is the beginning of what proves to be a complete emotional collapse.

In two parallel short scenes, we see, first, at school, Deanie's girlfriends promising each other that they will support Deanie by snubbing Bud and then, in a movie theater, Bud and his friends Rusty (Mark Slade) and Toots watching a film where a young woman, in a dismissive gesture, offers a man several coins as the title card reads, "*Allez vous en, M'sieur*. I shall find another teacher." The man, however, clutches her extended hand and kisses it. Toots, in a whisper, asks Bud about Deanie, and when Bud confirms that they are no longer seeing each other, Toots asks if it would be all right if he called on her. To Toots's "Any objections?" Bud replies, "I can't stop you." Shuman reads Bud's answer as "one of defeat — essentially Bud's attitude throughout the remainder of this portion of the film" (105–06). Also important to notice is the reflexive role of the silent film. Juanita, who, we recall, spoke French to Bud, had been Toots's girlfriend, and the words on the title card imply that not only has Juanita found another "teacher" in Bud, but also that Deanie will also find one in Toots, who, like the man in the film, will take advantage of her dating him.

Meanwhile, Deanie does what she can to make herself feel better. When her mother calls her, she tries to eat dinner, but as the camera pans the food-laden table, we feel Deanie's repulsion. While she toys with the heavy conglomeration of meat and potatoes and gravy and corn that her mother has piled on her plate, Mrs. Loomis does a stereotypical American Indian war dance and a bit of the Charleston to celebrate a 76⅜ point rise in Stamper stock. Finally, unable to stand it, Deanie excuses herself, whispering to her mother, "Mom, I can't eat. I can't study. I can't even face my friends anymore. I want to die. I want to die."

Upstairs, Deanie finds some relief in a hot bath, but her mother trails her into the bathroom and bluntly asks, "Is it all on account of Bud? Because he doesn't call for you anymore?" Mrs. Loomis threatens to telephone Bud, and Deanie screams at her, "Don't you dare, Mom. If you do that I'll do something desperate. I will. I will!" Her mother persists. Questioning "how serious" the relationship has become, Deanie's "shrewish, virginity-obsessed mother" (Koller 2) badgers Deanie about whether Bud has "spoiled her."

Deanie ducks under the water and then shouts at her mother, "No, Mom. I'm not spoiled. I'm not spoiled, Mom." In this "key (and censored) bathtub scene" (Koller 2), she gets out of the tub and stands naked in front of her mother, proclaiming hysterically, "I'm just as fresh and I'm virginal as the day I was born, Mom. I'm a lovely virginal creature. I'm a good little girl, Mom, a good little, good little, good little girl. I've always done everything Mommy and Daddy told me. I hate you! I hate you! I hate you!" As McClure informs us, the "original bathtub sequence depicted Deanie running naked from the tub, away from the camera. This sequence ... marked the first time that a star in an American feature film was ever viewed as nude. After much discussion and at the insistence of the censors, the studio ordered the deletion of the scene" (61). What American audiences saw is actually startling enough — Deanie, her long, dark, wet hair streaming down her wet and naked back, her arms held out to the sides so that her mother can see her unspoiled body. Female students especially recognize that Deanie is in deep emotional trouble, for few seventeen- or eighteen-year-old girls ever want their mothers to see them naked. The scene ends as Mrs. Loomis's desperate calls to Del are interrupted by Deanie, now in her bedroom, still screaming, "Leave me alone. Leave me alone. I'm not spoiled! I'm not spoiled!"

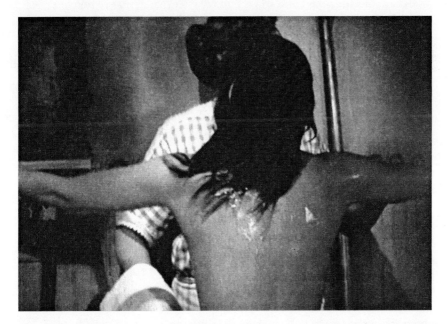

Elia Kazan and William Inge's *Splendor in the Grass* (Warner Brothers, 1961) stars Natalie Wood as Deanie, a teenager in love, who is hysterically trying to convince her mother that she is not "spoiled."

The next shot reveals Deanie, sitting at her vanity table, cutting her hair, flapper style, as her parents discuss sending her to a psychiatric hospital in Wichita. Mrs. Loomis doesn't want to sell rising stocks now, but before the conversation can continue, Toots shows up to invite Deanie to the Spring dance. Telling him that she'd "probably be an awful drip at the dance," Deanie does nonetheless agree to go.

On the night of the dance, Deanie is again at her vanity, winding spit curls. The pictures of Bud are still in place. Deanie is singing "Mabel." In her short, red satin dress with rolled stockings and high heels, she looks stunning — and wild. When her mother tells her, "Don't stay out too late," she confides to Toots, "Did you hear her? I used to think it meant something, but it doesn't mean a thing."

At the dance Deanie greets her girlfriends, and they link arms and jump up and down together, for Deanie, except for attending school, has been virtually house-bound since New Year's Eve. She sees Bud dancing with Kay (Sandy Dennis) who vowed to snub him and who asks Toots to dance with her, obviously so that Deanie can talk with Bud. Deanie does approach Bud, asking him to "come on outside for a cigarette," for she also has picked up a bad habit during their months apart. They tell each other how much they've thought about the other, and when Bud tells her that every evening after dinner he has to "force" himself to keep from calling her, Deanie puts her head on his chest and tells him to take her to his car. He does, and she immediately lies down on the seat and tries to draw his body to hers. "Take me, Bud. Take me. Here. Right here. I don't care.... I'll do anything, Bud.... I haven't had a happy moment since you stopped seeing me ... I want to stay here with you. I want you," she begs. "Stop it, Deanie. You're a nice girl," Bud reminds her, to which she replies, "I'm not. I'm not a nice girl." "Where's your pride?" he chides, and in an outburst even more violent than the one in the bathtub, she cries, "My pride! My pride! I haven't any pride. I don't care what happens. I haven't any pride! I just want to die!" As she delivers these lines, Bud slaps her face.

The first part of Shuman's analysis of the scene is excellent — "Bud, who cannot put Deanie in a class with Juanita or with his nymphomaniac sister, rejects her advances. This rejection is more than Deanie can bear"— but having based his analysis on the published screenplay of *Splendor* instead of on the finished film, his next comment is misleading — "So she bolts from the car, runs away, and plunges into the river" (106). What we actually see on the screen is more protracted. After Bud refuses her in the school parking lot, Deanie runs from Bud to Toots, who has been waiting in the shadows. Toots lifts her into his car, begins to kiss her, and, when the distraught Deanie doesn't object, he drives her to the river.

At the river, kissing Toots, Deanie moans, "Don't Bud, don't," indicating not only that she is imagining being in Bud's arms but also that she is still the "nice" girl who can't bring herself to be a Juanita or a Ginny. In response to Toots's "Bud?" Deanie runs from the car and climbs the rocks until she can enter the reservoir. The watchman sounds the alarm, and as shots of falling water take us back to the film's first scene, we know, even before we hear Deanie murmur "Bud," that she is thinking of him as she swims towards the falls, remembering their moments of bliss. Perhaps the cautionary note that Frances Ferguson interjects into her discussion of the "relationship between thought and recollection" in the Ode is appropriate here as well:

> [T]he inevitable sense of alienation of the mind from itself in exploring that relationship could raise the specter of madness. After all, just this linkage between thought and memory was taken for a symptom of Ophelia's madness: "Ophelia: There's rosemary, that's for remembrance. Pray you, love, remember. And there is pansies, that's for thought. Laertes: A document in madness, thoughts and remembrance fitted" [141–42].

A number of boys, who have abandoned their dates because of this emergency, swim after Deanie and stop her just before she reaches the brink.

Elia Kazan's comments about this scene remind us of the uncanny connection between art and life that always catches us up short with its irony:

> There is a scene in this film where the character Natalie played tries, in her desperation, to drown herself in a lake. Some days before this scene was scheduled, Natalie took me aside and explained to me that she had a terror of water, particularly dark water, and of being helpless in it. Of course, I thought how perfect for the scene she had to play, but I reassured her. The next day she told me that the fear would paralyze her in the water of the small lake I'd chosen, and she wasn't sure she could play the scene. Couldn't we do it in a studio tank? I assured her it was a very shallow lake and that her feet would always be close to the bottom. She said that even if her feet were *on* the bottom, she'd be in a panic of fear about it. So I asked my assistant, Charlie Maguire, to get into the water with her, just out of camera range, while she played the scene of struggling to save herself. This didn't entirely reassure her, but she did the scene and did it well — then clutched Charlie. "Cut!" I cried. On dry land she continued to shake with fear, then laughed hysterically, with relief.
> Years later I was to remember Natalie's problem with that scene when I read the newspaper accounts of her death. "The actress may have been panicked, missed a step and slipped into the water while trying to board the yacht's dinghy.... About midnight, a woman in a boat anchored nearby heard someone calling from the darkness, 'Help me! Somebody help me!'"
> The name of the yacht from which she'd stepped into the dark water was *The Splendour* [604].

The contradiction in Kazan's remark is puzzling. He writes first that Deanie tries "to drown herself in a lake." Later, however, he notes that she "struggl[es] to save herself." His first comment is correct: she struggles to die.

In the hospital waiting room, Mrs. Loomis tells Bud that "he's the cause of all [Deanie's] trouble" and that she doesn't "want to see [him] ever again." Ace arrives to lend his support, and Mr. Loomis determines to sell his stocks to send Deanie to Wichita. Bud has cornered Dr. Smiley: "Doc, look. I'm going to marry Deanie. I don't care what *he* says. I'm legal age." When the nurse (uncredited) comes out of Deanie's room with her dripping red dress and disappears down the hall, Bud slips in, but Deanie is not completely conscious, and Bud soon comes out, sobbing. Dr. Smiley tells him to stay away from her, and when the nurse returns to Deanie's bedside, we know that Deanie has heard Bud's voice. "Who's that? Who's there?" she asks. "It's nobody," the nurse says, but Deanie knows that "somebody was here. Somebody was here."

At Yale, Bud is certainly no student. We see him sweeping the debris from his desk with his forearm, playing Solitaire, drinking beer, smoking cigars, and tossing unopened letters from his father into a disheveled pile. His roommate (uncredited), at his own neat desk, suggests that Bud is "trying to get thrown out of school." A quick cut to the hospital in Wichita simply shows us the back of a rocking chair in which Deanie is steadily rocking.

In a pizza parlor off campus, Bud has taken up a study of "home brew." The waitress, Angelina (Zohra Lampert), tries to make him eat something — pizza. "What is pizza?" he asks her. When she asks him where his home is and he tells her Kansas, she asks, "Where is that?" Bud tells her that Kansas "is very friendly. That's what it's like. It's friendly." And when she asks if he has a sweetheart, he tells her, "I *did*."

Deanie has been hospitalized for six months when the next scene opens. She is painting a picture of a white house while Johnny (Charles Robinson), another young patient, approves. For his part, he says, "I like metal work. I can get rid of a lot of hostility this way." It becomes clear that his situation parallels Bud's when he tells Deanie that he can pretend that the metal is his "old man," who had his heart set on his son becoming a surgeon. But, Johnny says, he couldn't "make that first cut, that first cut into the flesh of another man's body." Their discussion ends when Deanie is informed that her parents have arrived. From the beginning Deanie seems strained with her mother, who chatters on about Deanie being just as normal as any of the girls she went to school with. She suggests that Deanie might even visit her chum Hazel (Crystal Field) at the university, not far from Wichita, but the look on Deanie's face prompts Mrs. Loomis to agree that it wouldn't be "suitable," a word that seems to upset Deanie even more. "There's nothing wrong with you," her mother repeats, and when her parents want to take her to dinner, Deanie's nurse helps her to gracefully escape over Mrs. Loomis's purposefully guilt-producing protests that after driving for so long, "This is all we get to see of you?"

Later, Deanie tells her psychiatrist, Dr. Judd (Ivor Francis), that she's not sure that she can "go home" again. He flatly tells her that it's useless to think that her parents will change. "You're the one that's got to change. They can't." He tells her to try to "accept them as people with a lot of faults maybe — not just Mama and Papa." He, "most assuredly," had parents too and he confides that this way of thinking worked for him. When Dr. Judd asks if she's heard from Bud, Deanie says that they have "given up writing" and that "nobody writes to me about him." She admits that it would be upsetting to hear about him. Then, her session over, Deanie runs across the hospital lawn to meet the waiting Johnny.

The shot that begins the next short scene is unusual, almost a "marked element" in Lotman's sense of the term. With the camera on the porch floor, we see Mr. and Mrs. Loomis's disembodied feet rising and falling as they rock side-by-side in matching rocking chairs. At first their rocking is not synchronized, but soon their feet are rising and falling together in a rhythm not unlike that of the oil well pumps. Mrs. Loomis is blathering on about the topics that preoccupy her: "I'll bet they've been practicing some of that Freud on her, too. Oh, I've read about him. All he's concerned about is sex, and it's costing us every blessed penny we made on our stocks. If we could've held onto those stocks, we would have made a fortune." Del gets up to turn on the radio, and we suddenly hear the terrible message — "Stock prices crashed today." As Tim Dirks points out, "The values of the business-oriented civilization — at the time of its greatest crash — coincides with the collapse of [Deanie and Bud's] tender romance" (2).

Ace goes to New Haven to check up on Bud. He's hired a private detective to find out why Bud has been "flunking every course," and Angelina, the waitress, is identified as the distraction. The sequence shifts to the Dean's office. Ace monopolizes the conversation, but when he leaves the room to take a phone call, Dean Pollard (uncredited) asks Bud what the trouble is. "I've never held the belief that everybody should go to college," he reassures Bud and observes that Ace is not a "good listener." Ace returns and announces that he's going to New York where the "whole town" is "jumping out of windows" and that he intends to take Bud with him but will have him back on Monday morning. "Don't give up on him, Dean Pollard," Ace begs the Dean. He even tells him that a woman is involved and that he had to "break up something like this once before."

In a New York nightclub, Cupie dolls still cost $50, and Ace of course buys one. The club comedienne (Phyllis Diller) jokes about having "had to dodge the bodies jumping out of windows" on her way to work. When the show girls begin their dance, Ace notices that one of them looks like Deanie (uncredited). "Listen Bud," he says. "It may be that I haven't always done the right thing by you. Anything I might have taken away I'd like to make up to you." He points to the girl who resembles Deanie: "Same damn thing, exactly. Just as pretty.... Same damn thing. You want that, boy? I'll get it for you."

When the yawning dancer knocks on Bud's hotel room door, he tells her there must be some mistake. A quick cut takes us to Ace's room, where he's looking out of the window. And when we are returned to Bud's room where's he's sleeping alone and hear the police calling him and knocking on the door, we know that Bud will be asked to identify the body in the alley. Bud tells the officers that he is going to "take him home."

Several years pass, and, in Wichita, Deanie is seeing Dr. Judd for the last time. She tells him that John, now practicing medicine in Cincinnati and "doing very well," has asked her to marry him. "Do you love John?" Dr. Judd asks. "I think so. It's different from the way I felt about Bud, but I love him," she replies. "Will you see Bud?" Dr. Judd asks her, advising her to "face her fears" before she marries John. "All right, Dr. Judd. I'll see him. I'll write to you," and with that, Deanie's cab arrives, she crosses the hospital porch where an old woman is methodically rocking, and she is on her way home.

With Deanie back in her old room, Mrs. Loomis still insists that her "little girl" was "just run down." She wants to know if John is a "New Dealer," the verbal clue that lets us know that a considerable amount of time has passed. But mostly she wants to know if "those doctors at the hospital say your mother had raised you wrong or something." She tells Deanie that she raised her "the only way [she] knew how," the way her mother raised her and the way her grandmother raised her mother. Deanie is reassuring. "I don't blame you, Mother," and "I love you, Mother," she says. As Deanie stands in front of her dressing table, we look, with her, at the mirror and the surrounding wall. Bud's pictures are now gone, and only pale rectangular shapes indicate that they were ever there. With the camera behind Deanie as she stands in front of her mirror and looks at "what remains behind" of her shrine to Bud, we hear Mrs. Loomis muse: "You know it would be nice if children could be born into this world with an absolute guarantee that they would have just the right kind of bringing up and all lead happy, normal lives. I guess when we get born we all have to take our chances." Deanie's only reply is a question: "Is he married?" Mrs. Loomis claims not to know but tells Deanie that Ginny "got killed in a car accident," that "the Stampers are almost extinct in this town now," and that the Stamper mansion has been turned into a funeral home.

June (Maria Adams) and Hazel arrive, and the three young women link arms and jump as they did at the Spring dance so long ago. When Deanie goes back upstairs to change her clothes, Mrs. Loomis lies to the girlfriends. "Keep her away from Bud Stamper," she warns, telling them that when Deanie got home she "lay down on the bed and cried and cried." The camera takes us back upstairs, and for a moment we see Deanie picking out a white dress. Back downstairs, Mrs. Loomis says, "Keep her away from him." When Deanie returns, looking beautiful in the white dress, a wide-brimmed white hat, and white gloves, her only line is "I want to see Bud now." Her friends hedge, but suddenly Mr. Loomis, who has been quietly reading the paper, says, "He's staying out at his father's old ranch." In a very touching and intimate gesture, Deanie pinches her father's cheek and kisses him and then sets off with June and Hazel.

Out at the ranch, Hazel goes looking for Bud. When she peeks into the somewhat shabby and disheveled house, we see a pregnant Angelina frying a steak at the stove. When Hazel finds Bud "around back," we learn that he and Angelina now have "forty head of cattle" and are "eating regular." And then for the first time in several years, Deanie and Bud catch sight of each other. "Long time no see," he says. "You want to meet my family?" In the kitchen Deanie observes the quiet domesticity that now characterizes Bud's life. She meets the toddler, Bud, Jr., playing under the sink with a chicken that looks comfortably habituated to being in the house. She stoops down and holds little Bud close, pressing her face to his. When Angelina, with food on her hands, declines to shake the proffered hand of the white-gloved Deanie, Deanie grasps her forearm and shakes that, a gesture that defuses some of the tension between them and makes them laugh.

"She was wonderful to me when things started to go wrong," Bud tells Deanie. Their conversation continues as Bud walks her back to the car. Deanie wants to know if Bud is happy, and he responds, "I guess so. I don't ask myself that question very often, though. How about you?" Deanie tells him that she's "getting married next month" and that she thinks that Bud "might like" the young man. When Bud wishes Deanie happiness, she answers, "I'm like you, Bud. I don't think too much about happiness either." Bud, slightly cynically, says, "What's the point? You gotta take what comes." And with that, they say goodbye.

As Deanie and her friends prepare to leave, Bud returns to the house, and Angie, who had been watching this scene from a distance, looks insecurely into Bud's face. He, reassuringly, kisses her and makes her smile. In the car, one of the girlfriends asks, "Deanie, honey, do you think you still love him?" She does not speak, but, through voice-over, we become privy to her answer:

> Though nothing can bring back the hour
> Of splendour in the grass, of glory in the flower;
> We will grieve not, rather find
> Strength in what remains behind;

As we have already noted, students have no problem talking about what happens in *Splendor in the Grass*. They can even agree with Voss that the characters' determination to "'find/Strength in what remains behind' in their lives" (194) is indeed a theme. To help them achieve a similar level of expertise with Wordsworth's Ode, we read John A. Hodgson's excellent "'The Eternal Mind': The *Intimations* Ode and the Early Books of *The Prelude*." Although it is Chapter 5 of his *Wordsworth's Philosophical Poetry, 1797–1814*, it can be read by itself with only a brief, general description of *The Prelude* as preface.

Studying in detail the changes that Wordsworth made during the composition of *The Prelude* and scrutinizing especially what he was writing in early 1804 when he resumed work on the Ode after a two-year respite, Hodgson discovers that between 1804 and late 1809 or early 1810, when Wordsworth wrote his "Essay upon Epitaphs," he believed, quite literally, in the pre-existence of "the individual soul":

> Clearly, when Wordsworth dictated the Fenwick note on the ode, and even when he wrote his first *Essay upon Epitaphs*, he believed, along philosophical lines at least close to those of orthodox Christianity, in the immortality of the individual soul. But when he wrote the ode in early 1804, I would suggest, he did not quite or exactly believe this; and the ode carefully records the tentativeness and the skepticism of his faith and speculations [105].

This is why the widespread use of the note to Isabella Fenwick as an introduction to the Ode is misleading. In this note, written in 1843, Wordsworth explains, "I took hold of the notion of pre-existence as having sufficient foundation in humanity for authorizing me to make for my purpose the best use of it I could as a Poet" (Abrams, Norton 175). The editors of *The Norton Anthology* follow up the note itself with the comment that Wordsworth "insisted that he did not intend to assert this as doctrine, but only to use it as a poetic postulate, enabling him to deal 'as a poet' with an experience to which everyone, he says, 'if he would look back, could bear testimony'" (176). As Hodgson points out, however, "in order properly to appreciate Wordsworth's special philosophical stance in this poem, we must take particular care not to confuse his ideas here anachronistically with notions prevalent in his work of a few years before or after" (104), let alone with the notions expressed in the Fenwick note of 1843. Further, Wordsworth himself, not just the anthology editors, actively contributed to the confusion that surrounds the Ode. Hodgson believes that after 1809 or 1810 Wordsworth was not only trying to retract the ideas of the Ode but that in 1804 he was attempting retroactively to credit his earlier poem [*The Prelude*] with the recognition and presentation of feelings about which it (and for that matter all of Wordsworth's poetry before 1804) in truth remained silent — or, alternatively and even more disturbingly, as if he were attributing to his earlier life feelings which in truth he had not then experienced.... There remains the striking fact that not once before 1804 does Wordsworth allude to such a remembrance or such a childhood experience [101–02].

Hodgson quarrels with "the straw man arguments of various critics" who believe that the "major interpretative crux of the Ode" is "the image of the child" (105). "The real crux," he continues, "and still a crux today despite so many assaults upon it, centers upon Wordworth's multiple tropes for the individual soul," which he pictures as "our life's Star" (105). To the two central questions — "Is its light innate or borrowed? Transient or eternal?" — Wordsworth's answer, Hodgson believes, is "Both" (105). To understand this "daring and tentative — and potentially confusing — answer," we must "understand the poetic cosmography" that informs the poem (105).

First, Hodgson notes that "just as this mortal world is illuminated by the sun, 'the light of common day' (l. 77), so is the heavenly world illuminated by God, the source of supernatural light and glory.... Man, as he passes the boundary of birth separating the heavenly world from this earthly one, simultaneously leaves God's realm of light.... But in infancy, man is still very close to God's realm, and its now indirect light remains present to him like a twilight" (106). The presence of this "twilight" state calls to mind the relationship between Lacan's Imaginary Order and Symbolic Order: "We are not repressing the Imaginary Order. Rather, the Imaginary Order continues to exist in the background of consciousness even as the Symbolic Order holds sway in the foreground" (Tyson 31). In Freudian terms,

> Originally the ego includes everything, later it separates off an external world from itself.... If we may assume that there are many people in whose mental life this primary ego-feeling has persisted to a greater or less degree, it would exist in them side by side with the narrower and more sharply demarcated ego-feeling of maturity, like a kind of counterpart to it. In that case, the ideational contents appropriate to it would be precisely those of limitlessness and of a bond with the universe ... the "oceanic" feeling [qtd. in Wolff 249].

Hodgson continues that "this celestial light, properly a feature of the transcendent, heavenly world, enters this mortal world with the newborn man as a kind of afterglow, an evanescent nimbus of glory" (106).

Second, Hodgson contends that the "Immortality which broods on the child is not his personal immortality, but the glorious aura of God, his source and home.... Here the sea is immortal; the Children, however, are not. To repeat: the immortality of which Wordsworth speaks in the ode is not the immortality of the particular individual but rather the immortality of his transcendent source" (107). Hodgson continues to maintain that "while the growing man is being gradually divested of the transcendent raiment which clothed him at birth, he is simultaneously putting on the sadly contrasting burdens of mortality — 'the inevitable yoke' (l. 125), the 'earthly freight' (l. 127), the weight of custom, 'heavy as frost, and deep almost as life!' (ll. 128–29)" (107–08). Again, sadly, the "consolations available to mortal man's 'philosophic mind' are but finite: 'the faith that looks through death' (l. 126)," which is "genuinely humanistic and even stoic, a reliance on 'the human heart by which we live' (l. 201) and 'the soothing thoughts that spring/Out of human suffering' (ll. 184–85)" (108).

Finally, for Wordsworth, "our death should be but an awakening and a remembering, and the setting of our life's star a rising into the transcendent world, a return to the celestial light which is our source and home" (109).

Why there are "so many assaults" upon "the real crux" of this reading Hodgson does not say (105). Perhaps part of the answer may lie in the poet, for, as Hodgson notes, "Wordsworth's obscuration" of what the Ode is about "in truth proved notably effective" (98). Part may lie in the poem's readers who approach it from a variety of critical perspectives. But part certainly lies in the Ode itself, in its richness. A small passage from *The Well Wrought Urn* illustrates the kind of thinking that seems to have dominated the study of the Ode. Cleanth Brooks asks, "How is it that the child is an eye among the blind?" His answer is "Because he 'yet [doth] keep/[His] heritage'; because he still dreams and remembers, for all that birth is a sleep and a forgetting; because he is still near to God, who is our home. This, I take it, is what Richards calls the '*overt* implication of ... Wordsworth's treatment'" (141–42). And Brooks continues, "But it is not so simple as this in Wordsworth's poem" (142).

Having seen the film and with Hodgson's excellent reading of the Ode at their disposal, students are ready to contemplate thematics. When pressed to define "theme," most find themselves at a bit of a loss, though a few will tentatively speculate that it is a "message" or a "moral." A comparison of two often-read handbook entries can help students understand that a theme is not simply a lesson to be learned, but an element of literature whose definition inspires a good bit of critical struggle, the kind of struggle that we explored in the chapter on *Streetcar*.

M.H. Abrams's *A Glossary of Literary Terms* is perhaps the most famous and most frequently assigned of the handbooks. In his 1957 revised edition, Abrams defines "motif" and "theme" in the same entry. "Motif," he writes, "is a term now applied to a frequently recurrent character, incident, or concept in folklore or in literature." Examples include folklore's "'loathly lady' who turns out to be a beautiful princess"; the lyric's "*ubi sunt* motif, or 'where-are' formula" that "lament[s] the vanished past"; and "*carpe diem*, or 'seize-the-day' motif" (51). He goes on to indicate that the term "'motif' is also applied to the deliberate repetition of a significant phrase in a single work, as in the operas of Richard Wagner and the novels of Thomas Mann, James Joyce, and Virginia Woolf" (52). After acknowledging that "a motif is sometimes called a theme," Abrams makes his main point:

> ... [T]he word "theme" is more usefully employed to denote the thesis or doctrine of a didactic work. The broad theme of the *Essay on Man*, for example, as Pope states it is to "Laugh where we must, be candid where we can,/But vindicate the ways of God to man."
>
> In modern criticism, the word "theme" is often used also to signify the abstract concept which is said to be embodied in the structure and imagery of a nondidactic or purely imaginative work. It has been said, for example, that the theme of Keats's "Ode to a Nightingale" is "man's inability to correlate finally the ideal and the actual aspects of existence." ... [B]ut it is not very helpful to speak of it as the "theme" of the work, and to do so can easily be misleading.... Various other abstract statements would fit Keats's poem just as well as this one [52].

At first, students are happy to recognize their own belief that a theme is a message in Abrams's assertion that "the word 'theme' is more usefully employed to denote the thesis or doctrine of a didactic work." But then some questions arise. Does Abrams think that the term "theme" is inappropriately applied to all "purely imaginative work"? Or is he quarreling with the specific proposition about Keats's poem because "[v]arious other abstract statements" could be made? In the case of "Ode to a Nightingale," would it be possible to devise an "abstract concept" that would function "like the theme of a didactic work"? The task is to help students raise questions like these. At this point in their study of literary theory, the answers are not as important as the queries.

The definition in the sixth edition of 1993 is much different. Again, "motif" and "theme" are treated together, and although little has been changed concerning "motif," Abrams significantly alters the definition of "theme":

> "Theme" is sometimes used interchangeably with "motif," but the term is more usefully applied to a general concept or doctrine, whether implicit or asserted, which an imaginative work is designed to incorporate and make persuasive to the reader. John Milton states as the explicit theme of *Paradise Lost* to "assert Eternal Providence,/And justify the ways of God to men." ... Some critics have claimed that all nontrivial works of literature, including lyric poems, involve an implicit theme which is embodied and dramatized in the evolving meanings and imagery [121].

While a theme is still a "doctrine," Abrams now clearly believes that the term can be applied to "an imaginative work." The didactic/imaginative dichotomy is gone, replaced by the "implicit or asserted" opposition. Milton has replaced Pope. Further, Abrams no longer seems to be concerned about the "whole" text supporting the theme, nor does he take issue with "some critics" who claim that "all nontrivial works of literature, including lyric poems, involve an implicit theme." He adds the idea that "meanings and imagery" are capable of "evolving." Finally, he again describes a theme as "embodied" but reinforces this idea with a revised definition — theme is that which "an imaginative work is designed to incorporate and make persuasive to the reader." While these additions and revisions do clear up some of the woolliness of the earlier entry, they also raise a new and more germane question: Where can the theme that the "imaginative work is designed to incorporate" be found? Where does it wait while the work that will "embody" it is being created?

This, as it turns out, is a question that can be answered, but we need to read further. In addition to Hodgson and the two selections from Abrams quoted above, my students and I work with Werner Sollors's introduction to his 1993 collection *The Return of Thematic Criticism* and one of its inclusions, Menachim Brinker's "Theme and Interpretation." Sollors explores the place of thematics in the postmodern, theoretical academic world by investigating "the annual bibliographies and indexes to convention programs of the Modern Language Association" (xi). He finds that topics such as "Images of the Holocaust in Fiction, Poetry, Theater, and Film" and "Heterosexism in Utopian and Dystopian Literature" are "now no longer perceived to fall under the rubric of 'Themes' and are instead listed under a variety of new categories," the most frequently used being "treatment of" (xii). This shift in nomenclature leads him to conclude that " ... while one could probably argue that, *de facto*, thematic criticism has grown enormously, few scholars now seem to be willing to approach methodological issues of thematic criticism, or to look at their own works in the context of thematics" (xii–xiii). Indeed, "'Thematic' has become a rather pejorative term in literary studies, typically coupled with the adverb 'merely.' ... Thematics is regarded so passé that it does not even seem to deserve a rationale for its undesirability.... At this moment, then, thematics may be an approach to literature that dares not speak its name" (Sollors xiii–xiv).

Within the context of Abrams's definitions and Sollors's comments — so well illustrated, as we saw in the previous chapter, by Nicholas Pagan's attack upon Thomas Adler — we turn to Brinker for an answer to our question: Where can the artist find the theme that he wishes to embody in his text? "Existing and comprehended in the intertextual space created by the partial overlapping of artistic fictional texts and other cultural texts, [themes] are rightly suspected of extraliterary origins or at least of impure (literary) blood. Yet literature is always inescapably contaminated with their existence" (30–31).

They exist in an "intertextual space," the intersection where literature and "other cultural texts" overlap. Their origins are "extraliterary." If we define "text" narrowly, we can infer that themes come from the "overlap of artistic fictional texts" and nonartistic, nonfictional texts — in other words, from all those creations into which man inscribes himself. If we agree with Derrida's assertion that "*Il n'y a pas d'hors-texte*, 'There is no outside-the-text'" (qtd. in Abrams "How to Do" 441), we can infer that themes come from the textualized world in which we live, from the "cultural texts" that surround us, in other words, from the "real" world and everything in it. While it may, on first hearing, seem shockingly postmodern, Derrida's comment is actually rather Wordsworthian. During a walking tour of Scotland in the summer of 1803, Dorothy Wordsworth wrote that she and her brother saw a little Highland boy, "Probably calling home the cattle for the night," whose "appearance ... was a text, as Wm. has since observed to me, containing in itself the whole history of the Highlander's life — his melancholy, his simplicity, his poverty, his superstition, and, above all, that visionariness which results from a communion with the unworldliness of nature" (qtd. in Gill 215).

Though the image of the artist traveling into "intertextual space" to retrieve a theme has a certain appeal, it is problematic; for while some artists may begin their work mindful of the themes around which they wish to build their texts, this is not true for all artists. In 1954, Inge responded to critics who noted "dominant themes common to most" of his plays:

> I have never written a play that had any intended theme or that tried to propound any particular idea.... I want my plays only to provide the audience with an experience which they can enjoy (and people can enjoy themselves crying as much as laughing) and which shocks them with the unexpected in human nature, with the deep inner life that exists privately behind the life that is publicly presented [qtd. in Shuman 31].

Shuman remarks that "Inge always begins his work with characters rather than themes. Once he has sketched his people, he incorporates them into a situation from which theme emerges" (31).

While some critics, as Brinker notes, define "theme as infrastructure of a story, controlling and generating all elements of fable, poetic world, and language" (23), Inge, as Shuman suggests, defines it not as generating but as generated. The next question, then, is this: Do themes "emerge" from or "control and generate" the other elements of literature? The answer must be "both." From the point of view of the artist, the question is moot. Inge's remarks notwithstanding, the act of creation is such a complex, multi-faceted, recursive, and personal process that any description of what comes first, what comes next, etc., must be largely — even if unintentionally — disingenuous. From the point of view of the reader, however, the question is pertinent. It may be that theme arises from the language of the text as it does, for example, for Helen Vendler who takes issue with Lionel Trilling's general conclusion that the Ode is, among other things, "about growing up" (131), claiming instead, through a brilliant and meticulous analysis of the poem's diction, that it is about "the capacity to make natural things into metaphors of human life" (69). For her and for those who have read her "Lionel Trilling and the *Immortality Ode*," it is perfectly obvious that the poem's theme arises from its language. It may also be true, however, that themes are not dependent upon the specific language of the text. This is the case, for example, for Bowra and other biographical critics who read the Ode with Dean Sperry as "Wordsworth's conscious farewell to his art, a dirge sung over his departing powers" (qtd. in Trilling 129). Brinker seems to side with this latter view, rejecting the "linguistic" (27) or "generative-transformational model" (23) of thematics because "it is difficult to see what kind of help we might get from linguistic attempts to identify the theme" if "the theme is not explicitly formulated in the text" (27). Because "very often in the case of fictional text none of the things mentioned will present us with its hidden or implicit theme" (27), he prefers what he calls the "philosophic model of aboutness," an adaptation of Wittgenstein's observations in *Philosophical Investigations*.

Brinker applies Wittgenstein's term "seeing as" to literature since it, like the phenomena that Wittgenstein examines, is "seen" in "more than one way." In brief, because we may be "given to, or taken by, one way of perceiving, ... we shall not be aware that our viewing is really a kind of interpretation, a case of 'seeing as'" (34). Further, as the film adaptation theorists point out, "seeing as" is not an innocent activity. Dudley Andrew, for example, takes a Marxist stance in observing that "our consciousness is not open to the world but filters the world according to the shape of its ideology" (97). Millicent Marcus urges us to resist a passive acceptance of "seeing as": "the truth that semiotics is urging upon us today," that "there is no such thing as 'innocent,' precodified reality," acts as a warning that "it is better to make a free and conscious choice of codifying systems than to leave that choice to the invisible artificers of ideology" (7). Before such choice can occur, however, we must become aware of the possibility of other ways of seeing. Then, as Brinker puts it, "we become aware simultaneously of the new aspect of the seen object and of the interpretative character of our viewing" (34). Brinker is careful, however, to stipulate that "this does not entail sheer anarchy" because

> the different ways of seeing X are partially rooted or inscribed, so to speak, in X itself. This explains the fact that though we lack a grammar for distinguishing acceptable from unacceptable moves in the game of "seeing as," it is not the case that we have to accept *every* seeing ("reading" or "understanding") [35].

In other words,

> The determinate components of the poetic world limit the freedom of the interpreter.... Poetic worlds and fictional narratives may always be open to different and incompatible thematic readings. Nonetheless, they are possessed of determinacy enough to reject some thematic interpretations as unconvincing, forced, or, at least, unnatural [33].

Always an important stipulation for students to contemplate, it becomes especially so in the case of the Ode's poetic world. The Ode may be about many different things, but it is not about all things. Moreover, Brinker's comments help explain why opinion is divided about the relationship that themes bear to other elements of the text — do themes emerge from or do they generate the others? Our answer depends upon "the way of perceiving" that we are "given to" and upon "the determinate components" that the text gives to us. It also depends upon our "aim":

> We do ... classify texts according to their themes with different aims in mind. It is this difference in aims which decides the varying degree of generality or particularity involved in the theme's formation. Theme's most common function for critics is the aid it affords in the description and interpretation of a work or a group of works. Accordingly, changes tend to occur in degree of generality vs. particularity or of abstractness vs. concreteness as scrutiny shifts from the work to a group of works (for example, a collection of short stories), to the whole corpus of an author's work, to the work of a literary group, generation, or school.... What we're getting at, rather, are the things which it is significantly or importantly about. Significance and importance may vary from one interpretive context to another, even within the same work [Brinker 22].

Trilling's "The Immortality Ode" and Vendler's response illustrate Brinker's observation. "It is hard to understand any part of the Ode," Trilling tells us, "until we first understand the whole of it," in other words, until we know what it is "chiefly about" (131). But what it is "chiefly about" for Trilling depends on his aim, which, for one thing, is to challenge the assumptions of a biographical critic like Dean Sperry. In turn, Vendler's aim is to challenge Trilling's assumptions about poetry itself.

Our working definition of themes as "loci where artistic literary texts encounter other texts" (Brinker 26) also helps us account for Brooks's New Critical urge to reject a "simple," literal reading of the Ode, the kind of reading that tells us what the text is "absolutely about." Borrowing Nelson Goodman's distinction between "absolutely about" and "relatively about," Brinker concludes that "whatever a specific text is absolutely about is ascertained by what the specific text states. Yet that which it is only relatively about is ascertained by the juxtaposition of this text with other, relevant texts (or with beliefs derived from them)" (31–32). The texts that constitute the world of the highly educated, extremely well-read critic and that shape his or her perception of relative aboutness are largely if not totally unknown to today's students. Vendler's assertion that the Ode is about the ability to make metaphor rests upon certain assumptions about poetry that she does not share with Trilling, the assumption, for example, that poetry is not "discourse" but "action" (67). This premise, only one among several upon which she bases her argument, is a very sophisticated and complex concept in itself. Harold Bloom believes that the Ode's "passionate logic of questioning, despairing, and ultimately hoping response ... is derivative, ultimately, from the prophetic portions of the Hebrew Bible" (*Visionary* 170), one of the major touchstones upon which he draws time and time again. For Abrams, in *The Mirror and the Lamp* (66), and for Bowra (83–96), Coleridge himself and his "Dejection: An Ode" (66) fill most of the intertextual space surrounding Wordsworth's poem. Goeffrey Hartman calls it "Wordsworth's *Being and Time*" and uses "Plato's myth of recollection in relation to our forgetfulness of Being" to elucidate both Wordsworth and Heidegger (202). And the survey could go on and on. My point is that because work like this is well over the heads of most of my students, well outside the range of their cultural texts, Hodgson's description of the Ode's absolute aboutness is a much better starting place than even a text-centered reading like Brooks's, preoccupied as it is with the Ode's irony and ambiguity. As Brinker reminds us, themes "depend upon our familiarity with texts that are neither necessarily artistic nor fictional and upon various beliefs held by the reader or the interpreter concerning general cultural and human issues" (31). George Steiner's observation echoes Brinker's:

> Theme and motif, which are the weave of intertextuality, demand, can only exist by virtue of, recognition. Even for privileged students and readers now, elementary biblical, classical, historical allusions and implicit motifs have become inaccessible. The books which speak and sing inside books are largely closed. Canonic texts wobble absurdly above stilts of more and more basic footnotes [299].

While I do largely agree with Steiner's position, it is sad that Sollors places Steiner's short essay last in his collection, the position of most rhetorical stress. The "situation is critical" as Steiner suggests (299), but it is not hopeless. As we have maintained throughout this book, today's students can and do read films, perhaps not as well as the professionals, but well enough, and certain of these films can become the cultural texts that provide a context for serious written literature.

What Brinker calls the "theme *in*" a text is equivalent to what Abrams calls motif. "Theme *in*" is a "specific representational component that recurs several times ... in different variations" and is "completely analogous to that of a musical theme" (21). By the end of *Splendor in the Grass*, the audience has heard Wordsworth's lines recited three times, once by Miss Metcalf and twice by Deanie, both aloud and to herself. As "theme *in*" or motif, they provide the same kind of continuity as do the film's main musical theme, which we first hear as the credits roll, and the "Mabel" song that Ginny and Deanie sing. More importantly, however, the poem's lines become the basis for an exploration of relative aboutness, of what Brinker calls "theme *of*":

> Our quest for the theme or themes *of* a [literary text] is always a quest for something that is not unique to this specific work. The theme is understood as potentially uniting different texts. Various stories and poems are written on one and the same theme, and most often so are various additional texts other than poems and stories. A theme is, therefore, the principle (or locus) of a possible grouping of texts, ... an interesting meeting point of texts [21–23].

Furthermore, these texts can be "of various kinds: artistic and nonartistic, fictional and nonfictional, and, quite often, narrational and nonnarrational" (26). To identify the themes shared by the narrative, fictional film *Splendor in the Grass* and the lyric, philosophic Ode becomes, then, a practical application of Brinker's definition.

Jonathan Ramsey's description of the Ode's fame is pertinent here: "Not only is the 'Ode: Intimations of Immortality' the most widely quoted, misquoted, praised, and parodied of Wordsworth's poems, for many readers it has also come to characterize poetry in general" (96). In light of the conflict between this appraisal and George Steiner's more pessimistic stance towards the fate of literature, one cannot help but wonder how many of the film's viewers — those who saw it on the big screen in 1961 and those who, like my students, know it only through video — were familiar with the entire poem. One suspects that lessons about Wordsworth like Miss Metcalf's were not isolated events until, perhaps, the late 1960s, a time of massive and far-reaching shifts in public school curricula. At least for some members of the film's audiences over the years, Wordsworth's lines would not have remained a disembodied fragment but would have summoned to mind the phantom text, the entire Ode, especially since Inge prods the audience's memory by identifying the lines as Wordsworth's on the blackboard and having Deanie say the poet's name. If this line of reasoning holds, then what Deanie and Miss Metcalf recite does more than announce the theme that Voss identifies — that Inge's characters must "find/Strength in what remains behind." Positioned as they are in the schoolroom scene and at the film's end, the poem's lines link what Deanie was (a teenager who knew the heights and depths and torments of first love) to what she has become (a poised, self-possessed young woman ready to marry) and thus give credence to the idea that "The Child is Father of the Man" or, in this case, Mother of the Woman. At the film's end Deanie's words, eyes, and resigned small smile (what Shakespeare called a "smilet" [xxii]) tell us that "though nothing can bring back the hour/Of splendour in the grass, of glory in the flower," the girl who knew such "splendour" and "glory" in her relationship with Bud lives on in the older, wiser, woman.

The definitions of theme that Brinker defends — "the principle (or locus) of a possible grouping of texts" (22), "an interesting meeting point of texts" (23), a "semantic point of contact between the individual text and other texts" (26), "a meeting place of texts of various kinds" (26), "loci where artistic literary texts encounter other texts" (26)— are certainly broad, but are they broad enough to allow us to consider a shared pattern of arrangement a theme? David Perkins's comments are applicable:

> Whatever we mean by literary form, themes refer to content, and cannot easily take hold of a work in its formal aspects. Of course, thematologists anticipate that this difficulty will be overcome: "The relation between *Stoff* and form is ... largely unexplored," Manfred Beller said hopefully in 1970. And Petriconi thought that a theme could be taken as a constant (though not an unchanging one) and the aesthetic realization or form of works on the theme could be viewed as a meaningful variable [116–17].

Nancy Armstrong, who studies Foucault's *Surveiller et Punir* as "the story of a theme," concludes that "what we call 'form' is simply the dominant theme of a given moment" (45). And Alexander Zholkovsky maintains that "there is no need to choose between 'formal' and 'thematic'— Structuralism has successfully integrated both" (297). In the case of the Ode, however, any theoretical quarreling over the relationship between form and theme is purely academic, for the *Stoff* and form of the Ode are inextricably entwined. So too are they in *Splendor in the Grass*. Sources such as the 6th edition of Abrams' *Glossary* or D. Myrddin Lloyd's entry in Alex Preminger's *Princeton Encyclopedia of Poetry and Poetics* provide basic information about the history of the odic form in general and include comment about Wordsworth's Ode in particular. Abrams informs us that the "prototype was established by the Greek poet Pindar, whose odes were modeled on the songs by the chorus in the Greek drama. His complex stanzas were patterned in sets of three: moving in a dance rhythm to the left, the chorus chanted the strophe; moving to the right, the antistrophe; then, standing still, the epode" (137). Lloyd, whose title is too interesting to omit, — "Keeper of Printed Books, National Library of Scotland"— adds that "the strophe, antistrophe, and epode of the classical model [are] indicated by the Eng. terms 'turn,' 'counter-turn,' and 'stand'" (586). Abrams describes the Pindaric ode as "serious in subject and treatment, elevated in style, and elaborate in its stanzaic structure" (137). Lloyd describes the Latin odes of Horace as "stanzaic and regular, ... personal rather than public, general rather than occasional, tranquil rather than intense, con-templative rather than brilliant, and intended for the reader in his library rather than for the spectator in the theatre" (585). Abrams offers Keats's "To Autumn" as a prime example of this type. Turning to Wordsworth in partic-ular, Lloyd quotes stanza 2 and notes that the poem's "varied line lengths, complex rhyme scheme, and stanzas of varying length and pattern" make it an irregular Pindaric Ode (586). Abrams does not cite actual lines but tells us that

> Romantic poets perfected the personal ode of description and passionate med-itation, which is stimulated by (and sometimes at its close refers to) an aspect of the outer scene and turns on the attempt to solve either a personal emo-tional problem or a general human one (Wordsworth's "Intimations" ode, Coleridge's "Dejection: An Ode," Shelley's "Ode to the West Wind") [137].

Students will notice that though Wordsworth's poem is irregularly structured, it shares with Keats's "To Autumn" the Horatian qualities of being "personal," "general," "tranquil," "contemplative," and "intended for the reader in his library."

How the parts of Wordsworth's Ode fit together is a disputed topic. Paul Magnuson, for example, thinks of the first four stanzas, written in 1802, as the antistrophe to the work Wordsworth had done in 1799 and 1800:

> The time of "There was a time" was not specifically childhood, which in 1802 was not clearly identified as the time of the presence of the glorious light. The time was the period of great productivity and optimism two years before, and the opening stanzas allude directly to the poetry written then, a time of mature achievement and greater promise. The opening stanzas originate in that work because they turn from it. *The Prelude* (1799) and the "Home at Grasmere" fragments precede the opening stanzas as the hopeful and perhaps highly speculative strophe to the elegiac tone of the first stanzas. The totality of Wordsworth's previous writing, not just that done in the spring of 1802, provides the context in which the opening stanzas have their full significance [284].

While Trilling and Bloom do not separate the 1802 and 1804 stanzas as Mag-nuson has done, both claim that the "despairing" second movement and the "hopeful" third are unconnected but balanced responses to the first movement. Most critics agree with Vendler, however, who describes the Ode in terms that correspond with the general information that Abrams and Lloyd pro-vide: the third movement grows from the second and is the "apotheosis or transfiguration which ... aims at the re-establishment of value" (78). For Bowra, too, the first four stanzas comprise the "crisis" (76), a movement marked by "something close to anguish," this anguish surfacing especially in the last line of stanza 1, "The things which I have seen I now can see no more," the last lines of stanza 2, "But yet I know, where'er I go,/That there hath past away a glory from the earth," and the questions which conclude stanza 4, "Whither is fled the visionary gleam?/Where is it now, the glory and the dream?" (79). What Bowra calls the "explanation" (76) consists of stanzas 5–8 and "descends," as all elegies do, "to that point of death" (Vendler 78): "Full soon thy Soul shall have her earthly freight,/and Custom lie upon thee with a weight,/Heavy as frost, and deep almost as life!" Finally, the "consolation" (Bowra 76) begins with stanza 9's "Oh Joy!" and ends with the great tribute to the "human heart." In short, the Ode's triadic form and the "turns" of its content are inseparable.

The film's movements are also odic. As *Splendor* opens, Bud and Deanie's relationship is in crisis because of the mounting tension between youthful sexual desire and long-standing social mores, between nice girl and bad girl, between unspoiled and spoiled. Both teenagers are also in a crisis situation with their parents, especially Bud with his father and Deanie with her mother. And while this first movement of the film shows the young couple doing all the things that teenagers do — going to basketball games and dances and taking rides in the car — clearly there's a tension. Yet even after the New Year's Eve dance, when Bud tells Deanie that they shouldn't "see each other for a while," the "gleam," the "glory and the dream" of the relationship, has not completely faded away. It is only after Bud becomes sexually involved with Juanita that we see in both Deanie and Bud what might properly be called "anguish." The sad situation at the end of the film's first movement is that Bud's betrayal has displaced the happiness that had suffused his and Deanie's life together, and the fact that their sense of well being has indeed "fled" is conveyed through Deanie's breakdown in the English classroom.

The film's second movement is an intensification of the first. Deanie disintegrates again, this time in the bathtub, and then, believing that relief can come only if she transforms herself into a bad girl, she cuts her hair. The trauma of Bud's rejection in the school parking lot and the shock of finding herself with Toots at the river lead to a third breakdown, the suicide attempt, and when, at the hospital, the doctor and nurse seem to conspire to keep Bud away from her, the young lovers reach "that point of death" (Vendler 78). Bud's sobbing in the hospital corridor and Deanie's certainty that "somebody was here" mark the end of this second movement. Shuman believes that "here, dramatically at least, the movie ends. Circumstance has not forced the decision toward which the film has been working, and everything that follows is anticlimactic and dramatically unnecessary" (108). But he is wrong, for — like the Ode — the film must accomplish its third movement, the consolation.

Through Dr. Judd's kindness and expertise and Johnny's friendship, Deanie is able to regenerate her shattered emotions. Through Angelina's warmth and understanding, Bud makes a similar recovery. Shuman does grant that Inge "succeeds in building toward a second climax in the final meeting between Bud and Deanie," a climax during which "everything is solved by the passage of time" and "the principals have both made the compromise which will enable them to go on living" (108–09). Hodgson makes a similar point: the consolation of the Ode "can be only tentative and partial, for certainty lies irrecoverably lost behind the veil of forgetfulness" (108), a comment that also describes what happens in the film. The audience understands that the all-too-"human suffering" that both Bud and Deanie endure must bear at least some relationship to the "soothing thoughts" with which they comfort each other and that the kind of happiness that they knew as young lovers has necessarily become less important than their ability to "take what comes" with dignity and strength.

Christopher Salvesen writes that "water and light are the two elements in which the meaning of the Ode is suspended" (123):

> Considered separately, water, ever-flowing, mover of streams and rivers, is the human principle, light the radiant principle of eternity: but they never can be entirely separate, and in this "fountain light" of memory, in which union of water and radiance, the Being, the man in time, and the Soul, are almost One [123].

It is interesting to note here that Emerson uses images of water and light in his essay "The Over-Soul," which may be the prose piece that comes closest to what Wordsworth was expressing in the Ode. Light and water also constitute the primary image pattern of *Splendor in the Grass*, but they point to different meanings. Through a kind of transposition, a rendering of these elements in a different key, light in *Splendor in the Grass* is not "the radiant principle of eternity" or, in Hodgson's words, "an evanescent nimbus of glory" (106)—it is the light of erotic love. This transposition reflects more, however, than a main-stream filmmaker's reluctance to make a movie about the human mind's consciousness of and relationship to God. As R.C. Zaehner explains,

> [The] raptures of the theistic mystic are closely akin to the transports of sexual union, the soul playing the part of the female and God appearing as the male. There is nothing surprising in this, for if man is made in the image of God, then it would be natural that God's love would be reflected in human love, and that the love of man for woman should reflect the love of God for the Soul [151].

Further, it is thoroughly appropriate that the supernatural radiance described in the Ode be transposed to the earthly radiance of the film, for "just as the human body knows no sensation comparable in sheer joyful intensity to that which the sexual act procures for a man and a woman in love, so must the mystical experience of the soul in the embrace of God be utterly beyond all other spiritual joys" (151). That Bud and Deanie's love for each other is a reflection of God's love explains why Bud's affair with Juanita is as devastating as it is:

> All the higher religions recognize the sexual act as something holy: hence their condemnation of adultery and fornication under all circumstances. These acts are not forbidden because they are demonstrably injurious on rational grounds; they are forbidden because they are a desecration of a holy thing, they are a misuse of what is most godlike in man [Zaehner 152].

Deanie's severe and protracted reaction to Bud's infidelity is a reaction, then, to a desecration of holiness. But Bud is no monster. His dilemma — to respect the fact that Deanie is a nice girl and suffer intense sexual frustration or to pursue Juanita and find sexual relief— is expressed in the Ode, and it is the Ode that provides the grounds of forgiveness. It is natural, Wordsworth tells us, to be seduced by earthly pleasures:

> Earth fills her lap with pleasures of her own;
> Yearnings she hath in her own natural kind,
> And, even with something of a Mother's mind,
>   And no unworthy aim,
>   The homely Nurse doth all she can
> To make her foster child, her Inmate Man,
>   Forget the glories he hath known,
> And that imperial palace whence he came [section 6].

In the transposed world of the film, the love that Bud feels for Deanie mimics God's imperial love. Juanita represents Earth that "doth all she can" to sway Bud towards the "pleasures of her own" and thus ensure the continuance of humankind. As Doctor Mandelet tells Edna in *The Awakening*, "It seems to be a provision of Nature; a decoy to secure mothers for the race. And Nature takes no account of moral consequences, of arbitrary conditions which we create, and which we feel obliged to maintain at any cost" (132).

In the film, then, Bud and Deanie are often in sunlight, but so are Bud and Juanita. Indeed, Juanita's seduction of Bud takes place in bright sunlight. With his shirt off, lying on the rocks, Bud seems to be continuing his sun lamp therapy, itself emblematic of his need for love. The sad situation is that just as his love for Deanie will be painful as long as he feels honor-bound to protect her nice-girl status, so is his love for Juanita painful. The purely physical is as unsatisfactory as the purely spiritual.

The first shots of *Splendor in the Grass* focus on water. As our synopsis indicates, Bud and Deanie are accustomed to parking by the reservoir, and once the camera establishes for us just what it is that they do there, it focuses, from several different angles, on the powerful white water pouring over the dam. In one shot in particular, these "cataracts [that] blow their trumpets from the steep" make a cuneiform pattern that is as highly suggestive of female sexuality as Kazan's shot of the spraying fire hose immediately following Stanley's rape of Blanche is of male sexuality. Water also enters the film when Bud is in the locker room showers, listening to his team discussing Juanita. In a shot that lasts for several full seconds, the camera is positioned at the shower head and we see Bud's handsome, young, upturned face, eyes closed, drenched in water.

The parallel scene occurs when Deanie is in the bathtub. In both, the water indicates their innocence, their freshness, but more so their desire. Deanie is still "virginal," as she tells her mother, but were it not for those "moral consequences," those "arbitrary conditions which we create, and which we feel obliged to maintain at any cost," as Mandelet tells Edna, she would be Bud's mate, married or unmarried. Natalie Wood plays Deanie as a fully passionate young woman, ripe in all senses of the word, whose body language belies her "we mustn't." For his part, Bud listens to Toots and the boys discuss Juanita's beauties as the shower water reinforces our impression that he, too, is at this point still a virgin, but the shower soon gives way to the falls under which Bud becomes sexually active with Juanita. The Sunday rain that is the setting for Bud's breaking the news to Deanie that he will go to Yale becomes an objective correlative for the dreariness of separation, but it is also associated with passion, fecundity, and new life. The umbrellas, then, under which Deanie and Bud and all the other church-goers take shelter might represent civilization — the ideologies of the church and the special brand of moral dictates of Midwestern society. What Richard McGhee in his *Guilty Pleasures: William Wordsworth's Poetry of Psychoanalysis* says of the Ode is true of the film: "the 'Ode' sadly acknowledges the need to accept those restraints [of civilization], recognizing that civilization may exact too high a price at the same time it offers compensations for lost childhood" (130).

Deanie's thwarted attempt to drown herself in the reservoir corresponds, though somewhat crudely, to the "immortal sea" of the Ode, the birthplace and, by extension, though Wordsworth doesn't say so directly, the resting place of souls. In the film's second scene, we will recall, Deanie avoids the pain of her mother's talk about money by listening to the sound of the sea in the conch shell. Writing of the shell's song in Book 5 of *The Prelude*, Hodgson identifies it as not only the song of the "eternal motion of the sea" but also as "the pulsing" of blood, and as such, it is "an intimation of mortality" (147). In the film, then, the shell could be said to foreshadow Deanie's suicide attempt by drowning. And with this scene, "the point of death," all images of water in *Splendor in the Grass* come to an abrupt end. For the remainder of the film there is not one shot of rain, waterfalls, showers, or bathtubs. Though certainly images of light continue — there could be no film otherwise — half of the film's imagery has fallen away. At the level of the film's broadest setting, its macrocosm, as it were, this is highly appropriate since the beginning of the Dust Bowl in Kansas is at hand. At the personal level, the microcosm, Deanie's and Bud's psychic landscapes are dry — he, bent on flunking out of Yale, she, rocking in the hospital in Wichita. But even with their emphasis, in Kazan's words, on "memories and desires that are unfulfilled" (Schickel), Ode and film are not like "The Waste Land" with its "empty cisterns and exhausted wells." Rather, both texts remind us that "The Child is Father of the Man," a concept that students, familiar as they are with the current psychological talk about "the inner child," do understand. The Deanie and Bud that were once capable of great love survive. Shuman's assessment, therefore, that "Bud will never know real love again" and that Deanie "has experienced the one all-consuming love in her life, and she will never relive it" (109) is perhaps not entirely correct. The enthusiastic way in which Deanie runs across the hospital lawn to the waiting Johnny after a session with Dr. Judd and the reassuring kiss that Bud gives Angie to calm her fears after she has come face to face with his remarkably beautiful and kind first love tell us that their futures are not as bleak, not as dry, as Shuman would have them.

While Deanie's attempted suicide in the reservoir is part of the film's water imagery, it also points to a theme recognized by the psychoanalytic critics. As Wolff makes clear in her analysis of Edna's death by drowning, the sea is the symbol of the "bond with the infinite" that Freud calls the "oceanic feeling" (250–51). Wordsworth's image of the "immortal sea" is absolutely, literally about the unborn souls, the Children, who "sport upon the shore" of those "mighty waters rolling evermore." In psychoanalytic terms, it is thematically about the "totality," to appropriate Wolff's words, that can come only with the "annihilation of the ego" (250). In the Ode, man's journey through linear time is pictured spatially, as a movement further away from his Source, a movement further and further "inland." Only in a "season of calm weather" can the embodied soul, not stranded "far" inland, "have sight," through intimation, of the "immortal sea." In the film, Deanie's sense of separation, of aloneness, is so acute — she is so far inland — that death by water, with its promise of ego dissolution, seems the perfect solution. We cannot lose sight of the transposition, however. Deanie is not thinking about God as she swims toward the dam. She wants to fuse with Bud, to be lost with him in a sea of love.

McGhee hypothesizes that light in the Ode represents the "oceanic feeling":

> In the unconscious regions that constitute infancy ... "sense and outward
> things" are brought into question; there reality falls away and vanishes before

the power of "high instincts" that make up the central core of psychic being. In that core is a power without consciousness, without identity — as close to the instincts of rainbows, roses, birds, and lambs as human being can be. It is the source of all that is human, although it may not be in itself distinctly human. It is, paradoxically, the "fountain light of all our day," "a master light of all our seeing," because those first affections are Wordsworth's conception of what Freud called the id [131].

Seen in this way, the Ode is what McGhee calls a "family romance" (130). It is, as Trilling proclaimed, a poem about "growing up." As McGhee puts it,

Instinct as a "light" is a center without circumference and blind to itself. Certainly, to instinct itself, any imposition of limits will seem threatening, but those limits must and will be imposed by the process of maturation, until "at length the Man perceives [the light] die away,/And fade into the light of common day." Both naturalization and domestication, or acculturation, are enemies to the light of instinct, which seeks immediate gratification as its only rationale for being [81].

As the film transposes God's love into the key of erotic love, it also transposes infancy into adolescence. And the instinct that surfaces during adolescence is sexual. The balance, according to McGhee, that Wordsworth strikes in the Ode is what Inge is also after in *Splendor in the Grass*:

Naturalization requires that instincts be made subordinate to the authority of parents for survival and gratification, while acculturation requires separation from parental authority as well as continuous self-control and sublimation of desire. Wordsworth's poem does not condemn these processes of human development, for condemnation would be a foolish denial of reality.... [H]owever, [w]hen a person spends his entire life in "endless imitation" of human life, he will inevitably fall beneath the weight of its "earthly freight." This death of self occurs when "custom" bears down heavy as frost and nearly extinguishes the instincts of self-gratification [82].

These "failures of mind and spirit" (82) happen to Bud and Deanie. Caught between her urge for self-gratification and the subordination of that urge championed by her mother, Deanie will learn from Dr. Judd that she must "separat[e] from parental authority" by changing herself. Bud, who is allowed by society's double standard to have sex with "another kind of girl," has also fallen victim to parental authority, for, we must recall, he never wanted anything more than to marry Deanie. It is only after the suicide attempt, when Dr. Smiley tells him that Deanie can't possibly marry, that he gives up. What both need to do, in current psychoanalytic parlance, is nurture the inner child so that it can be Father to the Man. As McGhee describes, "Recovering those buried instincts, making conscious the sources of childhood energy even as the fantasies of childhood, is the task of the healthy ego, battling as it must to keep its independence from the authority of culture as well as the authority of nature and parents" (82). Deanie's return to Bud at the end of the film signals the completion of this recovery: "They, like Wordsworth, are no longer acted upon but act.... [Wordsworth] is more actor than acted upon, declared by the force of his statement that 'I again am strong'" (McGhee 81). Though it comes too late to keep them together, Deanie and Bud also become actors and have acquired what Mrs. Loomis calls "gumption," the kind of "self-direction," as opposed to parental and cultural direction, "which instincts insist upon" (McGhee 83).

Meeting as they do at the intertextual spot devoted to family romance, it is not surprising that the Ode and the film share a vision of parents. The "six years' Darling" of the poem is "Fretted by sallies of his mother's kisses" and is bathed in the "light ... from his father's eyes." He plays at life with his "little plan or chart" and will eventually "fit his tongue/To dialogues of business, love, or strife." Wordsworth urges the child to slow down, to not be so eager to grow up, for "The years [will] bring the inevitable yoke" and "Full soon thy Soul shall have her earthly freight." But as McGhee points out, the parents too bear responsibility for the pace of this process. "To be healthy as well as successful, this conditioning must be wary of accelerating the process of maturation, as Stanza Seven warns" (131). In *Splendor in the Grass*, the problem is not so much one of acceleration as it is of retardation. The strange, inaccurate advice about female sexuality that Mrs. Loomis gives Deanie and Ace Stamper's prolongation of Bud's dependent status through further schooling inflict their own sorts of damage.

That the adults in *Splendor* are painted with such a broadly unpleasant brush led Stanley Kauffmann to comment in *New Republic* that Inge is "preaching the dangers, not of sex, but of abstinence" (Leeson 19) and Dwight Macdonald, in *Esquire*, to accuse "Inge of exaggeration, because it was hard to believe that Kansas parents in 1928 were 'stupid to the point of villainy'" (Voss 196). Students, however, especially freshmen who are still Deanie and Bud's age, do not read the film in these ways. They do not blame Deanie's "silly, meddling mother" (Crowther 1), Bud's heavy-handed father, the passive Reverend Whiteman, the side-stepping Dr. Smiley, and the unnamed, misguided nurse. Deanie loves her mother, and we can see that before she fell in love with Bud the mother/daughter relationship must have been very close. Likewise, Ace's repeated attempts at horse-play with Bud indicate that in past years he was no stranger to his son. One can easily imagine that Ace came home from the oil fields and threw a football to his little Bud and that Bud loved him. My students are right — these parents are not villainous, and abstinence is not dangerous. But it is time for Deanie and Bud to make a life together, time for the kind of self-direction that is denied them.

When the day is not seized, it is lost. And the sense of loss that *Splendor in the Grass* conveys is the same sort conveyed by the Ode. Regret itself becomes a theme. Writing of Wordsworth's lines 51–53, " — But there's a Tree, of many, one,/A single Field which I have looked upon,/Both of them speak of something that is gone," Salvesen indicates that

> this sense of loss, of regret for time past, becomes, on occasion one of the most radical forms of Wordsworth's memory: it is a regret which is all the more tormenting and more forceful because its object does not seem to be absolutely lost, but lingers in the form of fitful "gleams" and "shadowy recollections" — because the object is an emotion, a state of mind which seems to be palpably, though dimly and intermittently, still present in a memory of which it is part. And yet, this kind of regret is almost a paradox of memory; for it is akin also to human grief, the sorrow for something absolutely gone, completely inaccessible — which yet, because it had all the reality of a human life, continues to exist in memory, and, almost, in time [110].

Bud and Deanie are not dead, and yet they are "absolutely gone, completely inaccessible" to each other. Because Bud now has a family, their intense feelings for each other are reduced to "shadowy recollections" just as the pictures of Bud that surrounded Deanie's vanity mirror have left behind mere pale, shadowy shapes on the wall, shapes that "speak of something that is gone." Keith Cohen, drawing on Roland Barthes's "*Rhetorique de l'image*," tells us that "in the photograph, an illogical conjunction is produced between the *here* and the *bygone*.... Its reality is that of the *having-been-there*...." (66). The shapes on the wall, then, as the *having-been-there* of a *having-been-there*, are analogous to the Ode as an expression of a memory of a memory, a haunting by the "intimations of [a] haunting" (Hodgson 109).

Our study of a very different sort of theme through which the Ode and the film come together requires us to visit that spot where biography has insinuated itself into the intertextual web, into the "meeting place of texts of various kinds" (Brinker 26). As we have already seen, Inge abandoned his teaching career in 1950 when *Come Back, Little Sheba* opened on Broadway. The 1953 *Picnic*, which earned him a Pulitzer Prize, was followed in 1955 by *Bus Stop* and in 1957 by *The Dark at the Top of the Stairs*, which ran for 469 performances (Leeson 11). All four plays also became successful films. But when *A Loss of Roses*, which, as Voss puts it, "limped into New York for its November 28 [1959] opening," Inge was nowhere in sight. Voss speculates that "perhaps he ventured into the darkened theater alone this time, and thus was alone, characteristically, when he sensed his first Broadway failure" (189).

His only successes of the 1960s were movies. After the production of *Splendor in the Grass*, which was actually filmed on Long Island so that Kazan could be near his ill father, Inge moved to Hollywood "to write more screenplays and continue to search for a new, relevant voice that would find an audience on Broadway. It was a voice he never found" (Leeson 13). The sad fact is that "on Academy Award night in 1962 he was standing in the bright light of national celebrity for the last time" (Voss 201). He did, however, successfully adapt James Leo Herlihy's *All Fall Down*, which went to Cannes in 1963. Inge wrote, "Jim Herlihy's novel was irresistible to me. I relished the characters, a mixed assortment of mixed-up Midwesterners who seemed to demand that I take them off the printed page and put them into a movie" (McClure 63). Yet, when he refashioned his early one-act play *Bus Riley's Back in Town* for the screen in 1965, "there were so many production problems ... that he refused to accept the screenplay credit and had his name removed. The writer of record became 'Walter Gage,' a pseudonym for William Inge" (McClure 63).

In 1968, Inge returned to teaching at the University of California at Irvine. He was by all accounts, according to McClure, a "wonderful teacher when his health was good," "modest about his own accomplishments," "indulgent with his students," "never harsh," and "very complimentary about their work." But, as McClure further notes, "[H]e was by this time of his life simply not always able to deal with people" and "at the beginning of an academic term, he would phone in and say that he could not teach" (63). On June 1, 1973, suffering from alcoholism, Valium addiction, generalized despair, and the "pain and difficulty" of his homosexuality, Inge attempted suicide by "taking a drug overdose" and "succeeded, finally, in his Hollywood garage on June 10 ... by breathing carbon monoxide from his car's exhaust" (Leeson 13).

In 1995, Kazan remarked that "Bill was a man that was always on the verge of suicide, and he didn't know where he stood with men or where he stood with women and where in the world he wanted to be. And he was a great hit and then he suddenly dropped. All the critics were making fun of him" (Schickel). Writing of *Splendor*, Kazan was even more forthright:

> What I like about this ending is its bittersweet ambivalence, full of what Bill had learned from his own life: that you have to accept limited happiness, because all happiness is limited, and that to expect perfection is the most neurotic thing of all; you must live with the sadness as well as with the joy. Perhaps this theme rings so true because Bill himself had come to a point where he had settled for less, a place not in the first rank of playwrights along with O'Neill, Williams, and Miller but on an honorable sub-platform where — damn the praise, damn their prizes — the work would be its own reward; he realized that he'd find peace only if he sought goals within the reach of what talent he had and didn't hope for miracles.
> Or am I talking about myself? [602].

As it had been for Inge, 1950 was a pivotal year for Elia Kazan. By then he had become "the dominant creative force in American theater and was becoming so in American movies" (Schickel). His theater credits included *A Streetcar Named Desire* (1947) and *Death of a Salesman* (1949). He had done his homework, first by co-founding, in 1931, the Group Theatre, "dedicated to bringing work by new, socially conscious writers to the fore," and then, in 1947, by forming with "fellow Group alumni" the "Actors Studio, which was dedicated to the Method, an acting technique that concentrated on the psychological motivations and emotions of the performers" (Hornaday 1E).

His first feature film, the 1943 *A Tree Grows in Brooklyn*, was a hit. Kazan attributed its success to his feeling that directors, as "desperate people," had the license to wring realistic emotional response from their actors by using somewhat underhanded methods. The child actress who played the "little girl who loved her father absolutely despite all" (Kazan 245) was in real life the daughter of a fighter pilot, and when Kazan whispered to her something about her real father, something that he was loathe to reveal, he made her cry for hours on end, lending a reality to the scene where she, her film father having died, must assist her mother in childbirth. Later, Kazan capitalized upon the very different acting styles and very real animosity, even hatred, between James Dean and Raymond Massey in his creation of the father/son relationship in *East of Eden*. In *A Streetcar Named Desire*, he used Vivien Leigh's rocky marriage to Laurence Olivier to the film's advantage: "She was very upset in her own personal life, and I think it worked out well" (Schickel). And he did nothing to dissuade Natalie Wood and Warren Beatty from having an affair during the filming of *Splendor*, even though Robert Wagner, Wood's well-liked husband, was publicly humiliated (Kazan 603).

The 1950s brought *A Streetcar Named Desire, East of Eden, Baby Doll, A Face in the Crowd, On the Waterfront,* and *Panic in the Streets* to the screen and *Cat on a Hot Tin Roof* and *Dark at the Top of the Stairs* to the stage. According to Thomas Pauly, however, Kazan's heyday ended in 1960 when, "several months before he began filming *Splendor in the Grass*," he announced that he would not direct "Williams's upcoming play, *Period of Adjustment*" (234). He was evidently "not just breaking with Williams—he was fed up with Broadway and wanted to get away" from what had become "intolerable conditions"—"shows either closed quickly or enjoyed long lucrative runs" (234). He agreed to serve as co-director, with Robert Whitehead, of the new Lincoln Center's Repertory Theatre, which would offer

> a combination of "best new plays," modern American classics, and traditional masterpieces. When a skeptic challenged these plans with the charge "You can't be everything to everybody," Kazan wrote that he and Whitehead were moved to respond "why not?" Such was their logic. Compromises were not to be made; they were to be transcended. It did not take long for Kazan's grand scheme to develop worrisome cracks [Pauly 236].

In April, 1963, Arthur Miller's autobiographical *After the Fall* opened at Lincoln Center. It was not, as Pauly notes, "an acclaimed masterpiece and Kazan's direction went largely unnoticed" (237), but it did draw audiences. The next two plays, however, Sam Behrman's *But for Whom Charlie* and Thomas Middleton's classic *The Changeling* were disasters. The *Newsweek* review of *The Changeling* read as follows: "When an audience literally cringes in embarrassment, when it can scarcely muster even the conventional rounds of applause, when it laughs at a play whose implacable terror is unmatched in all dramatic literature — then we are in the presence of a cultural disaster" (qtd. in Pauly 237).

At the same time, Kazan's filmmaking took a new direction. He wanted "to do a picture about immigration which has never really been done before," a picture about his own origins. As Pauly recounts, *America America* "opens with a dark screen and Kazan is heard saying, 'My name is Elia Kazan. I am a Greek by blood, a Turk by birth, and an American because my uncle made the journey'" (239). Always uncomfortable with Technicolor, Kazan returned to the "black-and-white documentary styling, which was an almost obsolete brand of moviemaking in 1964" (Pauly 241). And, though Pauly notes that Kazan "achieved an eloquence and virtuosity that had been lacking in his recent films," the audiences rejected *America America* as "an overblown piece of self-indulgence" (241). Richard Schickel called it "a great director's last great film."

When Hollywood "lost interest in his kind of filmmaking," Kazan turned to writing (Schickel). Before his death in 2003, he had published seven novels and an autobiography. His being awarded a lifetime achievement Oscar on March 21, 1999, was sullied by protests over his testimony in 1952 before the House Un-American Activities Committee. The decision to bestow the award was the result of a "tortured calculus" that weighed "a body of work [that] surpasses anything that could have been made by those he named — as well as the dozens of blacklisted filmmakers who were unable to work during and long after the plague years" — against the fact "that Kazan's lifetime achievement was built on the backs of those whose achievements — and sometimes even lifetimes — were abridged or ended outright by his actions" (Hornaday 3E). While nothing can detract from Kazan's excellent and ground-breaking films like *East of Eden* and *On the Waterfront*, the man himself invited the kind of scrutiny that can be unforgiving.

Professionally, Inge and Kazan reached their peaks in the 1950s. Personally, both were wrestling with serious problems and both underwent psychotherapy. A quick critical survey reveals that it is not as easy to be that precise about Wordsworth. Magnuson, as we have seen, theorizes that the first four stanzas of the Ode, written in 1802, tell that Wordsworth's time of "meaningful and responsive utterance" was over and thus act as antistrophe to the "total-ity of Wordsworth's previous writing" (284). Salvesen sets a somewhat later date: "Wordsworth ... felt memory to be working for him as a kind of con-tinuous creative energy: and he seems further to have sensed, at least by 1804, that this virtue might become exhausted" (109). *Merriam Webster's Encyclo-pedia of Literature* teaches that early work for *The Prelude*, the 1798 and 1800 editions of *Lyrical Ballads*, and the "brilliant lyrics that were assembled in Wordsworth's second verse collection, *Poems, in Two Volumes* (1807), help to make up what is now recognized as his great decade, stretching from his meet-ing with Coleridge in 1797 until 1808" (1214). Similarly, Stephen Gill identifies 1807 as the year of decline: "In 1805 all of the Wordsworths were to rely on each other in the first great grief of their adult lives [the death at sea of brother John]. Two years after that Wordsworth was to discover how lavishly he could draw on Mary for strength and encouragement when he had to face the fact that he appeared to be failing in his poetic mission" (213). Gill notes that "the reviews of *Poems, in Two Volumes* were devastating"— reviewers used phrases like "namby-pamby," "miserable trash," "a very paradigm of silliness and affec-tation," and "quintessence of unmeaningness." Even the Ode was accused of being "a wilderness of sublimity, tenderness, bombast and absurdity" (266). Finally, Gill suggests that "the most significant thing about the poems of 1817 was that they had been written at all, for Wordsworth had been harassed throughout the previous year by unproductive worry" (325). While these poems do testify to "Wordsworth's vigour, ... their tone suggests a poet aware that a movement in his imaginative life is coming to a close. The ebullience of earlier lyrics is missing, the energy that suggested the limitless possibili-ties for poetry in the play of the imagination upon the everyday" (325).

Trilling is more vague about chronology: "After the composition of the Ode," there was "a great falling off in his genius," though "it was not so sharp as is commonly held," and "it did not occur immediately or even soon after the composition of the first four stanzas with their statement that the vision-ary gleam had gone" (152–53). Trilling believes that Wordsworth was impelled to create "a new poetic subject matter" that would exercise his "new poetic powers of sensitivity and responsiveness," the powers that provide consola-tion for the loss of the "visionary gleam" (152). The new subject would be tragedy, for "thoughts that lie too deep for tears are ideally the thoughts which are brought to mind by tragedy" (152). The "tragic mode," however, "could not be Wordsworth's," for

> he did not have the "negative capability" which Keats believed to be the
> source of Shakespeare's power, the gift of being able to be "content with half-
> knowledge," to give up the "irritable reaching after fact and reason," to
> remain "in uncertainties, mysteries, doubts." In this he was at one with all the

poets of the Romantic Movement and after—negative capability was impossible for them to come by and tragedy was not for them [Trilling 152].

But even if Wordsworth had been able to write tragedy,

> ... what mattered most in him was gone—the creative imagination which carried him beyond the bounds of space and time into some vast order of things, where, in almost losing his individuality, he saw in impassioned vision the power which sustains the universe and gives meaning to life. And when he lost this, it was not long before he lost his secondary but hardly less remarkable gift of feeling himself so close to nature that in its presence he was able to understand the tenderer movements of the human heart and to enter into full sympathy with them [Bowra 102].

In terms of what Wordsworth himself said about tragedy, Gill quotes Charles Lamb's comment made on February 26, 1808:

> Wordsworth the great poet is coming to town. He is to have apartments in the Mansion House. He says he does not see much difficulty in writing like Shakespeare, if he had a mind to try it. It is clear then nothing is wanting but the mind. Even Coleridge a little checked [sic] at this hardihood of assertion [266].

Vendler, too, who fights so hard with Trilling on a number of other issues, is not being sarcastic when she assents to the fact that "Wordsworth's original impulse—which everyone will agree was to lament those departed powers—still begins the Ode and sets an unforgettable tone" (81). Bowra, while he is adamant that "there was in Wordsworth something tough and bellicose which Coleridge lacked" and thus the Immortality Ode is not "Dejection: An Ode" (87), maintains that with the loss of the "old raptures, [Wordsworth's] whole outlook was affected" (102).

Finally, Carlos Baker drives home the point:

> Too much has probably been made of the alleged shrinkage of power in Wordsworth, as if, after forty, his stature had suddenly declined to that of a dwarf. We read of how his genius decays, of how "tragically" he is carried off the stage on the double shield of religious orthodoxy and political conservatism. This is a "despondency" about Wordsworth that needs to be corrected, and a number of modern critics have undertaken the task of correction. "Some think," wrote the poet, "I have lost that poetic ardour and fire 'tis said I once had—the fact is perhaps I have: but instead of that I hope I shall substitute a more thoughtful and quiet power." The poet speaking here is not Wordsworth; the sentences come from a letter by John Keats. Yet it is a clear statement of what happened to Wordsworth. His powers ripened gradually, reached a peak in his middle and late thirties, and thereafter very gradually declined. In that development and decline, as in so many other respects, the giant Wordsworth is one of us: the epitome of the normal man [109].

Brinker's concept of theme is broad enough to subsume other literary elements. The intersection where the Ode's and the film's intertextualities overlap is crowded with details concerning the lives of the authors, the form and structure of the texts themselves, the imagery that gives substance to idea, and the approaches taken by critics (their own special kinds of "seeing as"). In focusing on these various thematic elements, we have been content to attend to the trees at the expense of the forest. From a more distanced perspective, however, it becomes obvious that each individual theme, each of these spots where intertextualities intersect, informs us that "there was a time," a golden time that is no more. Each points toward a consolation that, however partial, must be accepted in order for life to continue. Each reinforces the truth, as Ruskin tells it, that "imperfection is in some sort essential to all that we know of life.... Nothing that lives is, or can be, rigidly perfect" (qtd. in Sitterson 35). Perfection is a haunting from a far-removed place, a memory of a memory. Further, the perspective that brings this super-theme into focus — a super-theme that involves, in Robert Frost's words, "what to make of a diminished thing" — affords us deeper insight into the nature of the relationship between Ode and film. And it is a strange relationship indeed.

First of all, we can see that the Ode is the source text of *Splendor in the Grass*, for our exploration of Inge's literary and personal background can leave no doubt that he had a feeling for Wordsworth's poem, was most certainly haunted by it, and was eventually able to transpose its themes into a key that would play well on the screen. But if the Ode is the film's thematic source, it is also part of the film's story. As such, it functions somewhat like a *mise-en-abyme*.

> The term *mise-en-abyme* was used by André Gide to describe novels such as *Paludes* and *Les fauxmonnayeurs*, which contain within themselves a replica of their own stories. Metz's translator [of his "mirror Construction in Fellini's *8½*" in *Film Language*] proposes the English equivalents "mirror construction" and "inescutcheon construction," since Gide's original term was a metaphor drawn on the presence in heraldic shields of a small shield duplicating the containing shield [Chatman 231, note 37].

Of course, the Ode is not a true *mise-en-abyme*, for it is not a duplication in miniature of *Splendor in the Grass*. A more obvious example of a filmic *mise-en-abyme* is Atom Egoyan's adaptation of Russell Banks's novel *The Sweet Hereafter*:

> In his poem ["The Pied Piper of Hamelin" written in 1842], Browning includes a lame boy who arrives too late to join the others. The lame child resembles Nicole Burnell, a survivor of the bus accident and babysitter of two of the drowned children, who listened to her reading the Pied Piper poem. Nicole becomes a paraplegic and, appropriately, recites the tale in significant scenes.... Thus, the poem serves as a *mise-en-abyme* or microcosm of the town's tragedy [Landwehr 221].

"The Pied Piper of Hamelin" is a narrative poem, thus making its transition to film, itself a narrative, a relatively clear-cut matter. In *Splendor in the Grass*, the Ode cannot be exactly a "microcosm" of the film. Rather, it functions as a thematic *mise-en-abyme*, for the themes of the Ode make up the "small" picture that mirrors the themes of the big picture — the "containing" film. The strangeness lies in the fact that the *mise-en-abyme*, the Ode, is at the same time the source of the themes of the big picture. In other words, the Ode is inside the film (as *mise-en-abyme*) but also outside (as source). It is contained within that which is derived from it. It mirrors its own themes.

Two images, both consummately appropriate in terms of the work of this chapter, capture the nature of the Ode's relationship to the film. Both are somewhat, but not absolutely, Platonic. First, we can imagine a pool of water into which we sink a heavy, opaque cup so that it lies in an overturned position, rim down, on the pool's bottom — next, a window hung with curtains that are partially translucent. A little fish trapped in the water under the cup can no longer see the greater pool. A man locked in the dimly lit room cannot see the sun. Yet, when the cup is pushed to its side, the curtains opened, it becomes immediately apparent that what had appeared separate is really part and parcel of the greater source. Similarly, the Ode within *Splendor in the Grass* — its *mise-en-abyme* — would be immediately recognized as the source itself (not a Platonic shadow of it) if the film's elements that do not share intertextual space with the Ode — its distracting cups or curtains — were withdrawn.

In the Ode, Wordsworth's images of light and water lay before us a vision of spiritual connectedness. Stanza 5 suggests, with its light imagery, that the soul, "trailing clouds of glory ... /From God, who is our home," gradually loses sight of its Source as the boundaries that make material life possible — boundaries of body, of ego, of ideologies, of civilization — thicken and obscure spiritual vision. And yet, the man's "seeing as," his perception of its gradual dying away, in no way negates its existence. Similarly, in Stanza 9, Wordsworth suggests that in "a season of calm weather," during a visionary moment, "Our Souls have sight of that immortal sea/Which brought us hither." While the analogy seems to break down — for "the Children," the souls yet to be born, "sport upon the shore" of the immortal sea and are not pictured as being one with it — perhaps we could dare to suggest that, in fact, the analogy does hold. Those souls on the shore have already begun to cross over the boundary that separates the material and spiritual worlds. They have already become individuated from the immortal sea and are just on the cusp of experiencing the confining cup, the dimly lit room of materiality. If the logic of these images holds, then Wordsworth's belief in the pre-existence of souls is not the only heretical element in the Ode, for not only do "we *come*/From God" — we *are* God, our true nature hidden from us except through glimpses or the recognition of traces.

Brinker's expanded definition of "theme" has allowed us to indulge in these somewhat wild and heady observations. At the end of this chapter, however, we can rest in a more conservative definition. Theodore R. Hovet hypothesizes that Harriet Beecher Stowe, in writing *Uncle Tom's Cabin*, "worked within a tradition of religious writing in which the function of the narrator was not to hold a mirror up to life, as William Dean Howells would advocate, but to order events according to a pre-existent narrative which would disclose the meaning hidden in the seemingly random events of daily life" (7). Hovet cites Fredric Jameson's description of this way of telling a story: "A sequence of historical events or texts and artifacts is rewritten in terms of some deeper, underlying, and more 'fundamental' narrative, of a hidden master narrative which is the allegorical key or figural content of the first sequence of empirical materials" (7). Brinker discusses this "hidden master narrative" in thematic terms — as a "traditional thematic 'deep' formula" (25). In *Splendor in the Grass*, it expresses itself through the triadic movements — crisis/death/consolation — that we have described. But this "formula" rivals a different, more compelling one, the one which underlies and shines through the diegetical events of *Uncle Tom's Cabin*, the one that chronicles the journey of the soul from an original spiritual center, a state of Oneness, to the material circumference where it becomes part of "masculine exile/division/dominance (patriarchy)," to, finally, a redemptive surrender to "feminine return/union/liberation (matriarchy)" (Hovet 8). Such an enlightenment experience, however, if it comes at all, comes only in that rare "season of calm weather" that lasts only for a moment. Although Uncle Tom experiences this moment of incredible peace and happiness immediately before the death of his body, he does experience it. Most of us, however, like Wordsworth, Inge, Kazan, Deanie, and Bud, have to settle for something less, a remnant, something that "remains behind," something that will carry us across the stretch of our years, a diminishment that makes our days on Earth no longer glorious but nonetheless worth living.

PART II. TEACHING LITERARY AND ADAPTATION THEORY

4. Classifying Adaptations Through Image Patterns

Film-literature criticism [is] not for those who cannot live in a messy house. — Charles Eidsvik ["Soft Edges" 21]

I have gone straight to the noisiest corners of that discourse and have sought to make sense of the yelling and the whispers overheard there. — Dudley Andrew [vii]

Whenever we teach a film adaptation — whenever we watch an adaptation as an adaptation — we treat it as an intertext designed to be looked through, like a window on the source text. — Thomas Leitch [17]

Insofar as I view the craggy terrain of adaptation through a limiting window — my perspective is rhetorical and restricted to three films directed by one person — I must concede that none of my findings assumes the form of a universal law. — Greg Jenkins [3]

Eidsvik, Andrew, Leitch, and Jenkins use the image of a house to describe the condition of literature/film discourse. It is a large and "messy house" partly because it subsumes so many topics over which there is much debate. Adaptation theory is just one of these topics, just the "corners" of a more general discourse. In such a large house, however, there are many windows through which to gaze and corners where the most noise, whether "yelling" or "whispers," manages to collect.

That these writers create such metaphors is typical of adaptation theorists in general. Many of those cited here also rely upon figurative language to describe the overall state of adaptation studies and to explain how this process works, and those who don't can often be better understood when their work is associated with the appropriate image. Moreover, we can capitalize on the fact that students enjoy working with imagery. It makes abstract ideas much easier to absorb and remember. In Shklovsky's words, it is a "means of reinforcing an impression" (23).

Although adaptation terminology becomes more sophisticated as the years pass, especially after the mid–1980s (lagging about a decade behind the rise of a more complicated vocabulary in literary criticism and theory), the basic tenets of adaptation theory remain the same. For instance, what George Bluestone says in 1957 about "characters and incidents which have somehow detached themselves from language" (62) is echoed in McFarlane's 1996 use of Roland Barthes's "cardinal functions," the "irreducible bare bones of the narrative" which are "transferable" from one medium to another (14). This example is a model-in-miniature of what the historical sweep of adaptation theory looks like. The earliest, and most fundamental, ideas are present in later discussions, but they may well be cloaked in a sometimes not-so-thin disguise, a disguise of words. This is not necessarily a drawback, however. As those who love masquerades well know, a disguise is a sign that teases its reader into figuring out the identity beneath. In semiotic terms, the signifier (the disguise) points to many signifieds (the identities). Likewise, the more complex language of contemporary dialogue — when it is not excessively abstruse — both encourages and accommodates an ongoing refinement of thought.

Perhaps the most negative image comes from filmmaker Alain Resnais, who, in trying to express the relationship between the source text and its adaptation, "has said that for him adapting a novel for one of this own films would seem — since the writer of the book has already 'completely expressed himself' — 'a little like re-heating a meal'" (Beja 79). In other words, the adaptation is a left-over. Left-overs provide a respite from the work of cooking, but nobody wants a steady diet of them. They are, after all, just one step away from being garbage. Implied in Resnais's dismissive simile is the idea that the filmmaker has nothing new to bring to the source text, can do nothing to give it new life, and has taken the easy way out, merely putting a diminished form of the original on the screen.

In "Toward a *'Politique des Adaptations,'*" confessing that he "habitually sneer[s] at adaptations and quote[s] Resnais to the effect that they are 'warmed-over meals'" (28), Eidsvik appropriately introduces another image of food. "Second-hand is not the same thing as second-rate. Second-hand has to be judged by what it is that is second-hand. There is much difference between a second-hand Rolls Royce in good shape and a second-hand sandwich" (30). Because "a second-hand sandwich" has by definition previously belonged to someone else who may or may not have already taken a bite, half of Eidsvik's image appears to be even more negative than Resnais's. Eidsvik, though, balances the sandwich with the Rolls Royce. The adaptation itself is not necessarily poor, though by virtue of its very nature it always seems second-hand. Factors having to do with strictly cinematic qualities (casting, camera angles, pacing, etc.) notwithstanding, the adaptation's quality surely depends at least partly on the quality of its source, the "first-hand" text.

Joy Boyum, using the language of New Criticism, makes a similar point: "All things being equal, of course a movie based on a work with greater thematic density and larger human significance will be more rewarding than a movie that remains tied in concept to a literary work whose materials are comparably thinner" (65), "thinner" being yet another word associated with food. Further, Robert Stam, noting that "adaptation theory has available a rich constellation of terms and tropes," also uses a rather unsettling word that relates to food — "cannibalization," an image echoed by Simone Murray when she notes that "newer media do cannibalize the content of older media" (9). The word implies that there is extreme violence associated with the adapted film, which "eats" its source text.

For example, while conceding that Roland Joffe's adaptation of *The Scarlet Letter* is a "loosely adapted version," James Welsh still deems Hawthorne to have been "corrupted beyond endurance and almost beyond recognition" (299–300). The source text — "a superior American classic," "an important novel," a text with "thematic density" and "human significance" — could give any director much to work with and deserves better than the "abomination" Joffe has created. On the other hand, even if Johnny Depp's portrayal of Hunter Thompson had not been amusing — some would even call it inspired — no one would have cried "abomination" when the "thinner" novel, *Fear and Loathing in Las Vegas,* came to the screen.

Gerald Mast sees the adaptation/source relationship in terms of a compass: "Although the filming of a literary work has been called 'adaptation' by some and 'translation' by others, both terms imply (indeed demand) a respect for the original text as the fixed foot of a compass around which the film version must revolve" (280). In the next sentence, however, Mast seems to want to dismiss or qualify what his image implies: "If one terms the film work an 'interpretation' of the original text, ... the burden for artists becomes the wholeness and integrity of their artistic interpretations, not their loyalty to the original" (280). This said, however, what the compass image represents — the idea of "loyalty," "respect," or, as most writers call it, "fidelity" to the original — looms large in the discussion of adaptation theory.

In writing about the movie *Wuthering Heights,* Bluestone concludes that "it is not Emily Brontë as we know her that endows the film with substance" (113). Retaining only "spare situational remnants ... left over from the novel," the filmmakers altered characterization, plot, and theme (113–14). Nonetheless, the movie was a critical and financial success. Bluestone first speculates about why the radical changes did not especially matter to the critics or to the public:

How can we account for this success in spite of the consequences which follow from the film's deletions, alterations, and additions? ... One can, if he wishes, argue with alterations which change the novelist's intention and meaning. But the final standard, the one to which we must always revert, is whether, regardless of thematic, formal, and medial mutations, the film stands up as an autonomous work of art. Not whether the film-maker has respected his model, but whether he has respected his own vision [110–11].

Putting aside the fact that the circumference of the filmed version of *Wuthering Heights* is far from the fixed foot, Bluestone admits that it stands up *"qua* film"* (111). But he continues to ruminate about the film's lack of fidelity to its source:

> The film-makers still talk about "faithful" and "unfaithful" adaptations without ever realizing that they are really talking about successful and unsuccessful films. Whenever a film becomes a financial or even a critical success, the question of "faithfulness" is given hardly any thought. If the film succeeds on its own merits, it ceases to be problematic. The film-makers are content with the assumption that they have mysteriously captured the "spirit" of the book. The issue goes no farther [114].

Into these two brief excerpts from his pioneering work, Bluestone packs several concepts that are related both synchronically and diachronically to other adaptation studies as well as to literary theory. Of particular concern here are those concepts associated with fidelity: intentionality, meaning, and "spirit."

In 1954, W. K. Wimsatt ushered the term "intentional fallacy" into the formalist discourse. In *The Verbal Icon: Studies in the Meaning of Poetry*, he maintains that the poem is not the critic's own and not the author's (it is detached from the author at its "birth" and goes about the world beyond his power to "intend" or to control it). The poem belongs to its readers. It is embedded in language (as critics following Derrida assert that everything, all ideologies, are thus embedded), and it is about the human being, also embedded in language fraught with ideology. Because Wimsatt's book predates Bluestone's by three years, it is somewhat surprising that Bluestone regards the "novelist's intention and meaning" as fixed, knowable entities.

In 1975, Dean Wilson Hartley, attempting to list "ideal" adaptations, reiterates Bluestone when he rejects, on one hand, those that "merely repeat the story of the literary work with a camera instead of a pen" and, on the other, those that "fail to adhere to the literal or figurative levels of the literary work at all." Ultimately, for Hartley, "ideal" adaptations are "essentially if not literally faithful to the intentions of the authors; that is, these films recognize and recreate the totality of meaning of authorial intention in the literary works" (68). In 1988, commenting on his agreement to bring *To Kill A Mockingbird* to the screen, Horton Foote confesses that "when you try to get inside the world of another writer, you're under constant tension not to vio-late this person's vision" (7). And as recently as 1995, Jacqueline Bobo cites the work of Deborah McDowell, who "contends that Alice Walker's intended audience [for *The Color Purple*] comprises mainly 'Walker's sisters,' other black women" (89). Bobo takes Steven Spielberg to task for "[wanting] to make the story available to a wider audience" (74) and then "manufacturing" his film "in line with [his own] experiences, cultural background, and social and political world view" (76), in other words for failing to discern and honor Walker's intentions. It seems that some scholars are still occasionally seized by a need to measure the worth of film adaptations by a criterion that has been roundly invalidated by others. However, neither Walker's novel nor Spielberg's film has been studied in the context of new historicism, where an author's intentions are published and studied as part of "the developing his-tory" of a text (McGann 24). To return to Mast's image, intentionality can become a sort of pesky phantom toe on the fixed foot of the compass.

Especially when it is thought to inhere in the author or in the work itself, meaning, like intentionality, has become increasingly suspect as the years pass. As early as 1925, however, in language that anticipates reader-response the-ory, I. A. Richards counsels that "we continually talk as though things pos-sess qualities, when what we ought to say is that they cause effects in us of one kind or another" (21). Writing about *The Shining* in 1992, John Brown both echoes and updates Richards:

> Contemporary literary theory tells us, I think rightly, that the text does not "possess" a single meaning which exists independently of the reader or viewer. Instead, meaning consists of a complicated process of production which occurs through a specific interaction of forces within and upon the text — forces such as the formal organization of the text, the skills of the reader/viewer and the social and ideological context in which the act of read-ing/viewing as well as the act of writing/film-making, takes place [115].

In other words, there is no one "meaning" for the adaptor or the viewer to discover, no fixed spot for the compass's foot to rest.

If Bluestone's belief in the availability of "the novelist's intention and meaning" dates his work, his placing quotation marks around the word "spirit" seems surprisingly contemporary, as does the way in which he uses it. To review, "if the film succeeds on its own merits, it ceases to be problematic. The film-makers are content with the assumptions that they have mysteri-ously captured the 'spirit' of the book. The issue goes no farther" (114). Forty years later, what Brian McFarlane says about "spirit" not only glosses Blue-stone but also returns us to Mast who, as we should recall, follows up his compass image with a very different idea — that adaptation is an "interpreta-tion of the original text." Working from Christian Metz's statement that the reader "will not always find *his* film, since what he has before him in the actual film is now somebody else's phastasy," McFarlane suggests that

> fidelity criticism depends on a notion of the text as having and rendering up to the (intelligent) reader a single, correct "meaning" which the film-maker has either adhered to or in some sense violated or tampered with. There will often be a distinction between being faithful to the "letter," an approach which the more sophisticated writer may suggest is no way to ensure a "successful" adaptation, and to the "spirit" or "essence" of the work.

This "essence" is

> very much more difficult to determine since it involves not merely a parallelism between novel and film but between two or more readings of a novel, since any given film version is able only to aim at reproducing the film-maker's reading of the original and to hope that it will coincide with that of many other readers/viewers.

McFarlane thus concludes that

> since such coincidence is unlikely, the fidelity approach seems a doomed enterprise and fidelity criticism unilluminating. That is, the critic who quibbles at failures of fidelity is really saying no more than: "This reading of the original does not tally with mine in these and these ways" [7, 8–9].

Like McFarlane, Neil Sinyard also identifies adaptation as interpretation, as "an activity of literary criticism, ... a critical essay" which "selects some episodes, excludes others, offers preferred alternatives. It focuses on specific areas of the novel, expands or contracts detail, and has imaginative flights about some characters. In the process, like the best criticism, it can throw new light on the original" (117).

In short, the notions of authorial intention, of meaning that resides in the text, and of an identifiable "spirit" of the source have been intensely scrutinized on a theoretical level. "Interpretation" has become the key word — except, of course, when a favorite book comes to the screen. Then is becomes all too clear that the image of the compass is still alive and well. Indeed, if professional critics (as we have seen) cannot overcome their desire that the film-maker be faithful to the author's intentions and if, with a sense of indignation, they resurrect the "old-fashioned" fidelity discourse, then it is no wonder that students, too, attest to the truth of Morris Beja's statement that "most readers and most movie-goers agree that books and films with the same title ought to be virtually identical, and that if they are not, then something unclean has to have happened along the way" (88). In a film adaptation course where adaptation theory was much discussed, my students nonetheless mimicked Bobo's heated criticism and ignored Walker's positive comments about Spielberg's *The Color Purple*. One student wrote that "the whole idea of film adaptation is to portray the novel the same way on film and at the most change some of the details, never the theme." Another suggested that "the film has been successful in its own way as its own story, but it has failed to tell the story Walker set out to tell." And a third asks what she calls "the real question": "Did Spielberg's film stay true to the text of Alice Walker's novel?" When critics and students alike look to the author and his or her text as "the unquestioned master code" (Mayne 25) which the film-maker must read and respect, they firmly fix the compass's point and fail to confront the more contemporary theoretical position: "This reading of the original does not tally with mine..." (McFarlane 9).

In describing his second "mode" of adaptation, the *commentary*, "where an original is taken and either purposely or inadvertently altered in some respect" (223), Wagner uses the metaphor of the footnote. Admitting that it "seems to represent ... an infringement on the work of another" Wagner nevertheless defends the commentary. "Film," he says, "can make authentic reconstructions in the spirit of so many cinematic footnotes to the original" (223), citing, for example, a change in the "essential motivation" of a character or the addition of a new scene, like the "celebrated meal" in *Tom Jones* that is "fully in Fielding's spirit" (224). Unlike Bluestone and McFarlane, Wagner uses the word "spirit" in a straightforward, unquestioning way. Like Bluestone, however, Wagner believes that if the film is successful, these footnotes "[cease] to be problematic" (Bluestone 114). While the footnote image recognizes that adaptation is interpretation (footnotes, after all, interpret and annotate), it also minimizes the film's status (footnotes often appear in small print and are, by definition, placed at the bottom of the page). Later theories will deny a difference in value between the primary (book) and secondary (adaptation) sources and object to any "privileging" of the book over the film.

Like Wagner, Bordwell and Thompson, Desmond and Hawkes, and Cahir (whose categories are described in the Introduction), Dudley Andrew also proposes categories: *fidelity of transformation, intersection, and borrowing* (98). It is the middle term, "intersection," to which he pays the most attention and for which he conjures up an image. He refers to André Bazin's comparison of "the original artwork ... to a crystal chandelier whose formal beauty is a product of its intricate but fully artificial arrangement of parts" (99). In the adaptation process, Andrew imagines the source text as a chandelier and the new text, the film, as a flashlight. He analyzes Robert Bresson's adaptation of Bernanos's *Diary of a Country Priest* in those terms:

> ... The cinema would be a crude flashlight interesting not for its own shape or the quality of its light but for what it makes appear in this or that dark corner. The intersection of Bresson's flashlight and the chandelier of Bernanos's novel produces an experience of the original modulated by the peculiar beam

of the cinema. Naturally a great deal of Bernanos fails to be lit up, but what is lit up is only Bernanos, Bernanos however as seen by the cinema [99].

Andrew goes on to argue that "the modern cinema is increasingly interested in just this sort of intersecting" (99) because, first, it "insists that the analyst attend to the *specificity* of the original within the *specificity* of the cinema" (100) and, further, that "the disjunct experience such intersecting promotes is consonant with the aesthetics of modernism in all the arts" (100). For Andrew, this "disjunct experience" arises from the "dialectical interplay between the aesthetic forms of one period [the source text's] with the cinematic forms of our own period" (100). What he says about this middle category, lying between tight and loose adaptations, roughly coincides with Wagner's definition of *commentary* or Cahir's definition of *traditional translation*. In shining the flashlight of cinema upon the chandelier of written literature, the adaptor "purposely" (even inevitably) alters our perception of the original. Further, in his use of the phrase "dark corner," Andrew joins the cluster of critics who in some way liken film adaptation to a house.

Andrew's image calls to mind both new historicism and Russian formalism. His emphasis on "the *specificity* of the original" with its "aesthetic forms of one period" contrasted to "the *specificity* of the cinema" with its "cinematic forms of our own period" echoes new historicism's "awareness of discontinuities" (Gossman 26) and its interest in "the always particularized interchange of a present with a past" (McCann 5). Further, when Andrew declares that our experience of the original is rendered "disjunct" or "modulated" by its film adaptation, he is saying, in essence, that the adaptation "defamiliarizes" its source. For Shklovsky, the defamiliarizing function of art rejuvenates both observation and criticism: "after we see an object several times, we begin to recognize it. The object is in front of us and we know about it, but we do not see it — hence we cannot say anything significant about it" (24). By extension, when a literary work becomes so familiar that "we do not see it" anymore, adapting a text becomes a revitalizing act.

Lorne Buchman also suggests an image that he explicitly identifies with Russian formalism — "the tramp [of *Modern Times*], diligently working on the assembly line ... and end[ing] up in the great modern machine itself, processed through its gears and wheels" (3). "Part of the power of the image of the human being and the machine lies in the shock of seeing those two elements juxtaposed in that particular way..." (11). Calling Chaplin's tramp "a potent illustration ... of defamiliarization ... because of the new relationship it opens, a relationship that sheds new light on the individual and the technical environment as well," Buchman wonders if "this same process of revitalizing the familiar [could] occur in the specific instance of a Shakespeare play viewed in the strange context of the cinema" (11). The answer, of course, is yes — not only for Shakespeare but for any other source text as well. Is it not the case that seeing an adaptation — even a poor one — of a text we know well sparks a whole array of new thoughts, inspires a new dialogue, and makes the familiar wonderfully strange again? One might venture that even Joffe's poor version of *The Scarlet Letter* inspired Welsh not only to mount the gleeful attack of the righteously indignant but also to think about Hawthorne's classic in new ways or in ways he may have put aside.

When words like Welsh's "corrupted" and "abomination" find their way into the discourse, a new problem presents itself. Certainly, looking at the process of adaptation in terms of categories or as a critical act protects us to some extent from the siren-song of fidelity criticism. However, we are still left with the very real issue of how to evaluate the quality of the adaptation — how to choose the better flashlight or the better second-hand Rolls Royce, how to know that the commentary in a footnote is trustworthy.

This problem regularly arises in the classroom. Given that students have been taught that a "good" text will open itself to many different readings, it's often hard for them to understand why some of their interpretations are more satisfactory than others. They may not yet have grasped the idea, as Menachim Brinker points out, that "the determinate components of the poetic world limit the freedom of the interpreter" (33), or they may still be what Umberto Eco calls "empirical readers": "The empirical reader is you, me, anyone, when we read a text. Empirical readers can read in many ways, and there is no law that tells them how to read, because they often use the text as a container for their own passions, which may come from outside the text or which the text may arouse by chance" (8). The empirical reader, however, needs to become a "model reader" — "a sort of ideal type whom the text not only foresees as a collaborator but also tries to create" (9). Until this transformation occurs, students will not be "interpreting a text but rather *using* it" (10).

This issue involves both primary and secondary sources. In the latter case, students often assume that everything they have gathered is of equal value (from articles published in scholarly journals to random comments launched into cyberspace). They can't always locate the boundary that separates a possible reading from an impossible one, a strong one from a weak. The scope of the problem has become especially clear in terms of the Internet, and the need to address it has opened up a new genre, new possibilities for publishing — especially for university librarians like UCLA's Esther Grassian, whose 1997 online guide, "Thinking Critically about World Wide Web Resources," poses such questions as "What are the date(s) of coverage of the site and site-specific documents?" and "How valuable is the information provided in the

Web Page (intrinsic value)?" Although the first question is easy to answer, the second only returns us to the problem at hand.

Critics, too, make value judgments when they are faced with the job of commenting upon adaptations. Regarding stage and film adaptations of Shakespeare, for example, Buchman writes, "I do not mean to suggest that 'anything goes.' There are many ways to distort the plays and to use them for one's own peculiar cause, often with no relevance to anything in the text or, at least, nothing major in it" (4). In her "Teen Scenes: Recognizing Shakespeare in Teen Film," Ariane M. Balizet recognizes the worth of adaptations that are "almost Shakespeare" and uses the image of a jewel to describe *Get Over It!*, Tommy O'Haver's adaptation of *A Midsummer Night's Dream*: "O'Haver's jewel is this idealized manifestation of adolescent bliss, and the frame of 'Shakespeare' acts to prove that jewel is precious, indeed" (132). While admitting that "one cannot direct Shakespeare's plays (or any play for that matter) without a concept, without something to say," Buchman insists that this concept "must come from careful thought and deliberation by all the artists involved, both individually and collectively. Performance relies on rigorous interpretation" (4). Though this rings true and no one would deny the value of rigor, even in adaptations like *Get Over It!*, the vagueness of Buchman's remarks certainly inspires a different version of the same basic question: Just what is "rigorous interpretation"?

Boyum, returning largely to the New Critical method of close reading, offers some answers. She lists "the most basic principles at work in determining validity": "that an interpretation must be consistent with the facts of any given text; that it must not break with linguistic conventions and must take account of the denotations and connotations of words and the total context that determines them; that it must be capable of support with evidence from the text itself" (72). These criteria are relatively clear-cut. As Boyum notes, the student who reads Blake's "The Tyger" and sees it "as a celebration of the gentleness, friendliness, and warmth of the animal" has failed to reasonably interpret the text. Like Brinker, Boyum goes on to claim that "any work carries within it certain implicit clues as to how we are to take it" (72). Again, as teachers know, students often misread these clues, for instance when they fail to detect irony and sarcasm, taking the words at face value, or, as in Boyum's example, when their own wishes about what the text *should* say override what it, in fact, does say. In Eco's terms, they have "superimposed" their own "expectations" on the "expectations that the author wanted" from model readers (10). Moreover, because we "tend to conceive of substantial literary works, at least, as displaying a certain degree of complexity, a certain richness and suggestiveness, ... a valid reading in turn then would be one that reflected a recognition of this quality, that was sensitive to such riches and nuances, and that was somehow nuanced itself" (Boyum 72–73). In addition, "a work's patterns, its point of view, its genre" must also be considered. Finally, Boyum maintains that "we expect a responsible reading to deal with the work as a totality," to indicate a consciousness of "the text's own logic" (73). The professional critic, the student-as-critic, and the film-maker-as-critic, then, are "subject to many of the same criteria as those we've cited: consistency and coherence, sensitivity and nuance" (73).

We should note once again that even the most learned and respected critics, like Eco, still yearn for an interpretation in line with the "expectations that the author wanted." The concept of the "intentional fallacy" and the concept of the reader/viewer as "collaborator" are very different things. And while some of what Boyum proposes is fairly easy to accomplish, some opens up new problems that are not so easily solved and concepts that are not so easily taught. Still more complex is the situation of those in the audience when they think about and evaluate their responses to the film. What they are doing, in fact, is creating "not just an interpretation, but an interpretation of an interpretation, the film itself" (Boyum 71). It is not hard to see why there is a very real temptation to fall back into fidelity criticism, to wish for a fixed foot.

In "Literary Commentary as Literature," Geoffrey Hartman theorizes that "the commentator's discourse ... cannot be neatly or methodically separated from that of the author: the relation is contaminating and chiastic; source text and secondary text, though separable, enter into a mutually supportive, mutually dominating relation." He admits that "it is hard to find the right analogy, the right figure, for this relation" (354). Perhaps he would approve, however, of Boyum's proposing the palimpsest to describe just this "mutually supportive, mutually dominating relation":

> ... [A]n adaptation is by its very nature both work of art and palimpsest. Comprehensible without reference to the literary work on which it's based, it nevertheless stands in indissoluble relation to it, much in the manner of any reworking of preexistent materials — whether it's Marcel Duchamp's moustachioed and bearded version of the *Mona Lisa* or a jazz musician's arrangement of themes by Mozart or Bach [64].

Not only does the image strengthen Boyum's general claim that adaptation is interpretation and satisfy Hartman's requirement that its elements be both "separable" and not "neatly or methodically separated," but also her examples of the "reworking of preexistent materials" — the postmodern *Mona Lisa* and the Bach jazz arrangement — illustrate the idea that adaptation entails defamiliarization. In Andrew's terms, Duchamp and the jazz musician are shining their unique flashlights on these masterpieces, causing us to rethink them in light of their strange new forms.

In Buchman's terms, these masterpieces have been caught in Duchamp's and the jazz musician's gears. However, there is an important difference. While the image of the human being in the gears defamiliarizes through a kind of collision of unlike elements, with one element at the mercy of the other, the image of a chandelier glowing through the flashlight's beam defamiliarizes because of the structure of the palimpsest. What lies on top of this "ubiquitous palimpsestic form" (Hutcheon 139) does not victimize or destroy what lies under it. The source text continues to be visible, even if only sporadically or duskily so, and makes its presence felt. Hartman's adjectives — "contaminating and chiastic ... mutually supportive, mutually dominating" — provoke us into thinking even more deeply about how elements of the palimpsest relate to each other. In *Palimpsestes*, Gérard Genette proposes the term *hypertextuality* to relate the adaptation, the "'hypertext,' to an anterior text, or 'hypotext,' which the former transforms, modifies, elaborates, or extends" (qtd. in Stam, "Beyond Fidelity" 65). Genette also contends that "quotation, plagiarism, and allusion" (65) are images that describe the relationship between hypotext and hypertext (66). Martin Esslin writes about performance — whether on stage or on screen — in similar terms, but he offers a different metaphor. Echoing Marshall McLuhan's dictum that "the medium is the message," Esslin remarks that the "message" of the source "put onto stage or screen has undergone a sea-change" (124), another word (like "smilet") coined by Shakespeare (*Sonnets* xxii). The original is still there, but it is altered. It simultaneously is and is not its former self. In a broader usage, Simone Murray suggests that the entire field of adaptation is "ripe for a sea change in theoretical and methodological paradigms" (4).

The faintly unreal nature of these images — the ghostly traces visible in the palimpsest and the smoothing out and morphing that occur during a sea-change — allows us to connect adaptation-as-interpretation to dreams. Stanley Cavell maintains that photographs — and, by extension, films — have the reality of dreams:

> We are not accustomed to seeing things that are invisible, or not present to us, not present with us; or we are not accustomed to acknowledging that we do (except for dreams). Yet this seems, ontologically, to be what is happening when we look at a photograph: we see things that are not present [18].

Even more relevant to adaptation theory, Boris Eikhenbaum, writing in 1926, connects novel and film and dream. A film is "something analogous to a dream: a person approaches; now you see only the eyes, now the hands — then everything disappears — another person — a window — a street, and so on. Just as if, having read a novel, you saw it in a dream" (qtd. in Mayne 28). With these thoughts before us, we can turn again to Sinyard's description of how an adaptation interprets and therefore inevitably distorts its source: "It focuses on specific areas of the novel, expands or contracts detail, and has imaginative flights about some characters. In the process, like the best criticism, it can throw new light on the original" (117). As a dream distorts and defamiliarizes reality but is always connected to it (indeed, we try to read our dreams in terms of our realities), so an adaptation distorts its source while remaining "in indissoluble relation" with it (Boyum 64). As a dream sometimes gives us insight into our conscious lives, so does an adaptation "throw new light on the original." In fact, the adaptation is even more palimpsestic, more dreamlike than other films, for it not only possesses the peculiarities of the film medium in general (for Stanley Cavell, its mysterious quality, "seeing things that are invisible" [18] or for Eikhenbaum, its cinematic techniques such as close-ups and cuts) but it also has the specific peculiarities of an adaptation: to "[focus] on a specific area," to "[expand] or [contract] detail," to indulge in "imaginative flights" (Sinyard 117).

Actual, everyday viewers do, in fact, experience films not only as dreams but also as memories. This is borne out by "Morgan," an otherwise unidentified participant in the "interpretive community" that Bobo assembled to study how black women read Spielberg's *The Color Purple*:

> When I watched the movie for the first time, it's like if you had some favorite song from when you were a kid and heard it again many, many years later, something that you associated with something very special. Reading the book was like that for me. With the book, it was an original event, and the movie was like kind of a reminder, of revisiting or reliving it [121].

Her description is uncannily similar to John Ellis's insight that "adaptation into another medium becomes a means of prolonging the pleasure of the original representation, and repeating the production of a memory" (4):

> The adaptation trades upon the memory of the novel, a memory that can derive from actual reading, or, as is more likely with a classic of literature, a generally circulated cultural memory. The adaptation consumes this memory, aiming to efface it with the presence of its own images. The successful adaptation is one that is able to replace the memory of the novel with the process of a filmic or televisual representation [3].

Adaptation, then, is "a massive investment (financial and psychic) in the desire to repeat particular acts of consumption" (Ellis 4). While we might not want to read the same book twice, we are willing — in fact, eager — to see it brought to the screen.

The "indissoluble relation" between and among layers of the palimpsest and its strangeness as a whole require that we see not only the adaptation as a dream or memory of its source but also see the source too as a dream remembered in spite of the crush of everyday consciousness. The source, then, is also like a memory.

In terms of our images, the successful adaptation as flashlight has distracted us from the chandelier; as top layer of the palimpsest it may have turned our attention away from all the texts that have preceded and lie beneath it; as sea-change it has made us forget what the original object might have looked like; as dream it displaces conscious thought. Ellis can then go on to redefine fidelity criticism: "the faithfulness of the adaptation is the degree to which it can rework and replace a memory" (4). In other words, if our particular memory has been replaced, then we conclude that the adaptation has been faithful to its source. Of course, different members of the audience will reach different conclusions because, as the reader-response critics would put it, "the generation of a memory from a reading of a text will involve associations of a contingent and personal nature as well as more culturally pervasive ones" (Ellis 4).

Like Ellis, John Brown also writes of the source text as a memory. He borrows an image from the art world to make his meaning clear. Defining "*bricolage*" as "the procedure in contemporary avant-garde art ... in which fragments of existing artefacts are re-worked and placed together to form a new artefact in itself," he hypothesizes that "Kubrick's [*The Shining*] functions like a bricolage based upon King's novel" (118) and offers two examples in support:

> A key moment occurs in the novel when Jack finds a mysterious scrapbook (itself a kind of bricolage) which contains the hotel's history. This doesn't happen in the film, but Kubrick places the scrapbook open on the table beside Jack's typewriter; it can only just be seen in the corner of the screen and no reference is made to it. Similarly, Danny's vision of the word "redrum" which occurs in the novel, building up a small mystery of its own, is omitted from the film, except for Danny's sudden (and in terms of the film inexplicable) scrawling of the word on the bathroom door, the reflection of which Wendy sees ("murder") as Jack's axe comes crashing through the outside door [118].

Brown then speculates that "[t]hese moments serve as fleeting memories of the book"; and indirectly acknowledging the dreamlike quality of adaptations, he suggests that they are like "glimpses of an alternative version made by another director" (118). The novel has been so defamiliarized by the film as a whole, so "re-worked," that these very concrete yet elliptical remnants seem to emanate from a ghostly "alternative version" made by a ghostly director. It is interesting to note here that Derrida uses the term "*bricolage*" to refer to the slippery quality of language that "doesn't have the solidity and stability we have assumed it has, and we can therefore improvise with it, stretch it to fit new modes of thinking" (Tyson 253). His usage might very well be applied to film adaptations that can be "stretch[ed]" past the concept of fidelity criticism into "new artefact[s]" like the *commentary*, as we saw in Kazan's *A Streetcar Named Desire*, or like the *analogy*, as we saw in his *Splendor in the Grass*. Further, the "fleeting memories of the book" can be likened to Derrida's notion of "trace." As Tyson points out, "What we take to be meaning is really only the mental *trace* left behind by the play of signifiers. And that trace consists of the differences by which we define a word." For example, "the word *red* carries with it the trace of all the signifiers it is not (for it is in contrast to other signifiers that we define it)" (253). In the discourse of film adaptation, we might say that the source text is what it is because it is not something else, and its adaptation or adaptations are what they are because they are not something else. *Grand Isle* is *Grand Isle* because it is not *The End of August*, but both adaptations evoke "fleeting memories of the book" which, in this case, leaves a very strong trace in that both film versions of Chopin's novel are *transpositions*. On the other hand, the trace of Wordsworth's Ode in *Splendor* is superficially (but only superficially) not strong since its adaptation is an *analogy*. It is also important to note that these types of adaptations carry no value judgments. They are simply different.

Robert B. Ray writes that "'film and literature' has always meant film and the novel or film and drama, never film and poetry, unless the poetry under consideration tells a story" (38). Although the Ode, unlike "The Pied Piper of Hamelin," is not a narrative, our analysis of Wordsworth's lyric poem and Inge and Kazan's film does uncover two images that undergird both texts: an image of autumn and an image of stillness. As we have seen, Trilling believes that Wordsworth could not write in the "tragic mode" because, like the other Romantic poets, "negative capability was impossible" (152). However, for Northrop Frye, both poem and film would be considered "tragic": "Tragedy involves a movement from the ideal world to the real world, from innocence to experience, from the mythos of summer to the mythos of winter, and therefore Frye calls tragedy the *mythos of autumn*" (Tyson 222). Both the poem and film begin in innocence, the ideal world, the mythos of summer. In the poem the child "is trailing clouds of glory"; in the film Bud and Deanie are experiencing romantic love. Both texts then move their characters and readers into the world of experience, the real world, the world of loss, the mythos of winter. The child grows up; Bud and Deanie lose each other. But in both cases, the mythos of autumn contains a third movement: though the human being is left primarily with "Strength in what remains behind," there is the possibility of "intimations of immortality," fleeting moments of cosmic splendor. Sadly, for both Bud and Deanie, "what remains behind" is a life far "inland," a life that is not ecstatic, not even particularly happy (we should recall that neither thinks very much about happiness at the film's end), but both are able to go on with their lives — Bud with Angie, pregnant with their second child, and Deanie marrying the young man, John, whom she meets in the psychiatric hospital and whom she thinks Bud "would like." Second, as Murray Abrams observes, the Pindaric ode was "patterned in sets of three: moving in a dance rhythm to the left, the chorus chanted the strophe; moving to the right, the antistrophe; then standing still, the epode" (137). In the stillness of the epode, we leave the persona of the Ode waiting for a "season of calm weather" and Bud and Deanie settling for marriages which will last for the rest of their lives.

Images of the palimpsest, the sea-change, and the *bricolage*; notions that adaptations are like dreams or memories; and the nearly identical phrasings of John Brown ("fragments of existing artefacts are re-worked" [118]) and Boyum ("reworking of preexistent materials" [64]) are evidence that the concept of intertextuality, so important in literary theory, has also found its way into adaptation theory. Writing about literature, Hartman actually uses the phrase "intertextual *bricolage*" to describe Derrida's *Glas*. Comparing it to *Finnegans Wake*, Hartman is "convinced" that *Glas* "introduces our consciousness to a dimension it will not forget, and perhaps not forgive." He goes on to try to identify its genre—"criticism," "philosophy," or "literature"?—and concludes that "it is hard to affirm it is a book. *Glas* raises the specter of texts so tangled, contaminated, displaced, deceptive that the idea of a single or original author fades, like virginity itself, into the charged Joycean phrase: 'Jungfraud's messonge book'" ("Literary" 353). "Does it amount to more," he asks, "than a dignifying of *bricolage*?" (353). In their footnote, Adams and Searle inform us that "*bricolage* is a term brought into theory by Claude Lévi-Strauss, characterizing the work of a handyman who uses the tools at hand. Lévi-Strauss applies it to the logic of myth" (353). Hartman's "specter of texts so tangled," Lévi-Strauss's "tools at hand," Brown's "fragments of existing artefacts," and Boyum's "reworking of preexistent material"—all organized by "the logic of myth"—are the materials of intertextuality.

M.H. Abrams helps us connect the term "intertextuality" to Derrida's "axial proposition" in *Of Grammatology*: "*Il n'y a pas d'hors-texte*, 'There is no outside-the-text'" (441). Abrams assigns it a double meaning: first and most simply, "it says we can't get outside the written text we are reading." More pertinent to intertextuality, however, is Abrams's second reading:

> *Il n'y a pas d'hors-texte* ... says that there is nothing in the world which is not itself a text, since we never experience a "thing itself," but only as it is interpreted. In this inclusive rendering, then, all the world's a text, and men and women merely readers—except that the readers, according to Derrida, as "subjects," "egos," "cogitos," are themselves effects which are engendered by an interpretation; so that in the process of undoing texts, we undo our textual selves [441].

Abrams calls this an "apocalyptic glimpse ... of a totally textual universe whose reading is a mode of intertextuality whereby a subject-vortex engages with an object-abyss in infinite regressions of deferred significations" (441). Murray Krieger writes in much the same key as he contrasts the New Critical with the deconstructive stance: "For what we have taken to be the self-fulfilling and self-sealing poem is, like all discourse, mere vacancy, acknowledging an absence of substance, fleeing all presence as it leads us down the lines moving outward to the intertextual forces which become the code ... [only] of writing itself" (539–40). Derrida himself, using the image of childbirth, echoes such language as he describes the birth of a "kind of question" that is as yet "unnamable" and "proclaim[s] itself ... only under the species of the nonspecies, in the formless, mute, infant, and terrifying form of monstrosity" (94).

Encountering this strange and different — perhaps even apocalyptic — way of thinking that seems to be based on the "logic of myth," this vortical abyss of thought that paradoxically generates centrifugal energy propelling us out into "intertextual forces," is like reading "a catalogue of wavering intimations and half-joined ideas" (Geertz 522). We can take comfort, though, in the humanistic last words of Adams and Searle's anthology: "Intertextuality and the proliferation of choices need not present added weight to wearied minds but an invitation to consider the claims of reason as coextensive with the pleasure of imagination, both of which seek the good" (872).

How Peter Donaldson reconciles the old methods of humanistic, text-centered criticism with the new ideas of poststructuralism perhaps exemplifies the state of mind that Adams and Searle advocate:

> *Shakespearean Films/Shakespearean Directors* will focus on individual works of art and individual filmmakers and honor them. Yet, with Foucault, I do not believe in authors — or cinematic *auteurs*— in quite the old sense and have learned to value dissonance, irresolution, and contradiction in ways that exceed the old new critical, ultimately Coleridgean aesthetic of opposition and tension within organic unity. Texts are, in principle, open to a play of meaning both essential to the experience of art and impossible to constrict, foreclose, or prevision. Authors and *auteurs* cannot foresee the uses and misuses their words or images will subserve, and in fact live only in and through such wayward and secondary acts of reconstitution, performed by adaptors, translators, critics, students, readers [xiii–xiv].

In the first sentence of this paragraph, Donaldson pronounces his intention to "honor" individual texts and filmmakers. Then he modifies it by citing some of the key terms of poststructuralism: "dissonance, irresolution, and contradiction," "play of meaning." Finally, he acknowledges that the adaptor "reconstitutes" the text, the adaptor being, in fact, a translator, a critic, a student, and — at bottom line — a model reader. The structure of the paragraph, which mimics the chronology of Donaldson's professional life, works as a sort of palimpsest — the "old new critical" methods on the bottom, the newer ways of thinking on top, so that the first is not lost but rather colors and is colored by what has superseded it.

The pattern that Donaldson details also appears in Adams and Searle's introduction to J. Hillis Miller, where they summarize the "progression of Miller's work, from formalism through phenomenology to deconstruction." Using Miller's metaphor of the parasite and the host, Adams and Searle observe that "each succeeding stage of critical practice effects the conversion of the parasite into the host, as the formalism of the New Criticism hosts phenomenology and structuralism as parasites, which in turn become the hosts for deconstruction." They build upon Miller's metaphor by adding that "the genetic identity of these symbiotic couples persists." Specifically, "the frustrated search of New Critics for some adequate principle to differentiate literary art from other forms of discourse ... persists through its *unheimlich* transformations, to appear in this instance as intertextuality and indeterminacy, subject to the 'uneasy joy of interpretation'" (451). It is just these "*unheimlich* transformations," these strange colors in the palimpsest of the history of criticism, that interest us here. Like the adaptation's source text, New Criticism does not die (the parasite does not kill the host, for it needs it to live) but "persists," dimly perhaps, but nonetheless distinguishable. Similarly, Derrida connects not only art but "critical language itself" to *bricolage* when he quotes Gérard Genette: "The analysis of *bricolage* could 'be applied almost word for word' to criticism, and especially to 'literary criticism'" (Adams and Searle 88).

For Esslin, the written play or screenplay is a "blueprint" to be interpreted. He envisions a chain of readings extending from blueprint to spectator as a multi-layered "'thickness' of the texture of what is presented to the recipients of the communication." This thick texture, this palimpsest of readings, as it were, becomes an image of the process of interpretation:

> But this first interpretative reading of the text in turn becomes, at the second
> stage, the basic "text" for each individual spectator, who now has to "read"
> and "interpret" the "performance text," which again is open to a further
> infinite number of "readings" and "interpretations" within the parameters that
> have been drawn by the performers' reading of the original blueprint they
> have interpreted [124].

Esslin's interest in poststructuralism and semiotics is apparent. His assertion that an "infinite number of 'readings' and 'interpretations'" is possible rephrases the semiotician's "infinite regressions of deferred significations" (Abrams 331) into the language of drama. Andrew also describes this phenomenon. As he puts it, "Verbal and cinematic signs share a common fate: that of being condemned to connotation. This is especially true in their fictional use where every signifier identifies a signified but also elicits a chain reaction of other relations which permits the elaboration of the fictional world" (103).

Not every theorist would agree, however, with Andrew's use of the phrase "cinematic signs." John Fell, for example, finds no evidence that film has "second articulation": there is no "meaning unit" in film which "breaks through and becomes a sign" (220). This is precisely why, he argues, Christian Metz "has difficulty locating [film's] minimal meaning unit — the equivalent to the linguist's 'phoneme,' which Metz calls (for film study) a 'taxeme'" (220). For James Monaco, film has "almost" no "second articulation" because "the signifier and the signified are almost identical: the sign of cinema is a short-circuit sign" (127), not symbolic but iconic and indexical. Mast agrees. Whereas language functions through a "double articulation system," phonemic and morphemic, "films usually manipulate only a single articulation system, the filmed image itself" (298). He also argues that "whereas verbal language operates according to clearly established paradigmatic and syntagmatic codes, film 'language' seems to lack any paradigmatic codes, and those syntagmatic codes that have been identified in film fail to explain much and have failed to convince many" (299).

As Mast explains, the problem with a true semiotics of film is that shots, the smallest units in film, are "not equivalent or even analogous to the words," for shots vary in length from "a single frame ... to thousands of frames" and "convey an immense amount of information simultaneously" (299). Thus, "shots cannot be compared paradigmatically" because "it is probably impossible to construct a shot that is absolutely identical to another" while, "in a functional paradigmatic system, it is necessary that a rose first be a rose if it is to be meaningfully compared with a carnation" (299). His example is an interesting one:

> The black and white hats of western films have been suggested as one paradigmatic code, ... [but] the code holds truer of cheap westerns (of the Ken Maynard and Hoot Gibson variety) than of major ones (John Wayne and Montgomery Clift wear various hats of varying shades in *Red River*), suggesting that the hats are less a code than an easy and stale metaphor [299].

As far as syntagmatic relationships are concerned, Mast asserts that Metz's attempt to "identify the 'grand syntagma' of narrative construction — the various temporal and causal connections between two shots" — is flawed because these "syntagmas are not codes at all but mere analyses of structural patterns that underlie only certain kinds of films — narrative feature films of the 'classic Hollywood' style" (300). Further, it is not the "encoded operation of the syntagma" but "our understanding of the whole narrative" that allows us to connect shots when no "relevant temporal connection could possibly exist" (300). In brief, "the single syntagmatic law of cinema is that two successive shots are *somehow* related," a law which "surrealists exploit, for in their films our minds search for a connection between shots without success. (This exploitation does not violate the syntagmatic necessity of connection: it is simply an alternative principle of connection — a deliberately nonconnected connection)" (300). The major difference, therefore, between film and literary "languages" is that "all sources of meaning in a film — with the exception of words (either uttered or written) and, possibly, of certain syntagmas of editing — are 'codes' of the color and shot sort rather than of the linguistic sort" (301). Thus "the audience must perpetually make fresh sense" of what it is that "most creative 'speakers' of cinema" create when they "refuse to rest on their syntagmas and insist on perpetually casting for fresh ones" (302). However, film and literary "languages" are similar in that both are

> additive (individual signs are added to one another), cumulative (each addition progressively increases and specifies meaning and understanding), progressive (the direction of its progressive meaning cannot be reversed; previously established significances cannot be erased), and therefore, temporal (the signification process unfolds over a period of time and requires time for its operation) [298].

Fell ends his own discussion of syntagma with a reference to metonymy, for it, not metaphor, is associated with the syntagmatic plane: "Semiotics is an exciting, challenging new weapon in the arsenal of film study, but the number of problems it has yet to face is enough to make the semioticist wring his metonymies in despair" (22). Words like "weapon" and "arsenal" belong to an image cluster focused on war and will be discussed later.

No matter which couples are being scrutinized — Hartman's author/commentator or source text/secondary text; Abrams's subject-vortex/object-abyss; Donaldson's words/reconstitutions of words; Miller's parasite/host; Esslin's performer/spectator; Derrida's species/nonspecies; Adams and Searle's claims of reason/pleasure of imagination; or any semiotician's signifier/signified and syntagmatic/paradigmatic plane — the "genetic identity of these symbiotic couples" remains even as they travel along a never-ending chain, sustaining "*unheimlich* transformations," exchanging places and colliding with other "intertextual forces," until finally all opposition collapses into play, play which not only disrupts presence but "must be conceived of before the alternative of presence and absence" (Derrida 93). Andrew's remark that audiences enjoy "basking in a certain pre-established presence" when they watch adaptations (98) seems to point to the old order of things, where the only chain was the Great Chain of Being which led to God, to pure Presence.

Of the four images that help us envision adaptation as intertextuality (palimpsest, sea-change, *bricolage*, and blueprint), the blueprint is slightly different in kind. While the palimpsest is made of layers from first to last, from bottom to top (much like the packets of papers that students in a composition class will submit, with the first draft on the bottom and the final copy on top); while the sea-changed driftwood, for example, is still the original wood (the first step) but in a sort of disguise (the last); and while a *bricolage* incorporates and reworks "existing artefacts," the blueprint is not incorporated into the building. It remains separate even as it sparks a chain reaction of interconnectedness. It is like the image that Margaret Kennedy uses to describe screen writing — a "recipe for a pudding" (qtd. in Bluestone 35). The recipe may be necessary, but it never becomes part of the pudding. Though different, the blueprint image is important, for it illustrates what Millicent Marcus calls "the typology of adaptation." The blueprint, the source, is like the Old Testament; the adaptation, like the New. In this image, the adaptation does not really incorporate the source, as the New Testament does not exactly incorporate the Old. Rather, it is a "typological fulfillment of an earlier textual promise" (Marcus 31).

Looked at from Marcus's point of view, the adaptation does more than interpret or defamiliarize: it fulfills or completes its source. What Luchino Visconti says about his adaptation of di Lampedusa's *The Leopard* illustrates the adaptation's "typological fulfillment" of the novel: "I don't think that I've added anything to the ideas of di Lampedusa; I have only enlarged on some themes which interested him less and are just hinted at in the novel, although hinted at with great clarity" (qtd. in Marcus 47). It is only a small step to conclude, too, that the adaptation might not only extend but also actually improve upon its source. In a newspaper review of *This Wild Darkness: The Story of My Death*, for example, Brenda Becker hypothesizes that a film adaptation might save this story from its distracting excesses:

> It has the making of a minor but affecting Woody Allen movie: A New York literary lion, famously afflicted by ego, self-doubt, erotic angst, and writer's block, dies slowly of AIDS while penning a torrent of wry introspection and observation. If the option were available, I'd choose the movie over the book. While Harold Brodkey's *This Wild Darkness: The Story of My Death* is not without flashes of mordant humor and breathtaking insight, much of it would play better on screen, where good acting could take the place of long and self-indulgent stretches of the author's much-touted mystical prose [5F].

Though he offers no examples, Dean Wilson Hartley also suggests that a "film version [can] remedy internal structural flaws in the original work or telescope digressive material for the sake of unifying the tone or style of the work of literature" (68). Finally, Ezra Pound's observation — that "a film may make better use [than a book] of 60 percent of all narrative dramatic material"

(76)—finds its contemporary analogy in Beja, who grants that an adaptation might be "perhaps something more" than its source. When we see a film and judge it to be "more" than the book (as my students often do), Marcus's insight that adaptation can function as typology may explain what has happened and why. For example, in our students' eyes, the difficult language of the source may have prevented it from fulfilling its promise to its new readers. As one student writes of the adaptation of William Faulkner's "Barn Burning,"

> It assists the viewers in ironing out any difficulties they may have had while reading the story, and at the same time, it brings the characters to life. We can see and hear the characters and gain a feel for them more so than we could with this piece of literature. The music, which the literature cannot provide, also creates an interest to the movie. It creates an intense moment for the viewer.

Clearly, in this student's eyes, the adaptation not only manages to redeem the short story but becomes, in Anthony Burgess's words, "the true fulfillment — the verbal shadow turned into light, the word made flesh" (qtd. in McFarlane 7).

These images of intertextuality found in adaptation theory (palimpsest, sea-change, *bricolage*, and blueprint) and in literary theory (parasites and hosts, vortices and abysses, and undulating chains of mutating elements spiraling outward) are not the only ones to explore. Several other images also enrich our understanding of intertextuality.

Eric Rentschler rather pleasantly calls adaptation "a dialogue with tradition, a reworking of certain modes of expression, a play with various cultural givens" (Introduction 3). When he envisions a dialogue among many equals and cautions against "privileg[ing] the literary source as the primary determining factor" and thus "overlook[ing] vast reaches of intertextual space to be found between any film and its source(s)" (3), he echoes some of Derrida's remarks about *bricolage*. "The mythopoetical virtue of *bricolage*," says Derrida, is "the stated abandonment of all reference to a *center*, to a *subject*, to a privileged *reference*, to an *origin*, or to an absolute *archia*" (88). Using an image similar to Rentschler's, Judith Mayne calls "the relationship between two texts, one literary and one cinematic, ... a dynamic encounter rather than a static rendering of a story line from one medium to another" (25). She advocates exploring the intertextual relationship between source and adaptation diachronically, from an "historical perspective." The questions that interest her reflect this orientation: "why certain kinds of works were adapted at certain periods in film history, for example, or how the turn to literary sources was often an attempt to attract middle-class audiences to movie theaters, thus giving the cinema a certain legitimacy" (25).

In a slightly more complicated image which draws heavily not only on Barthes but on Derrida, Christopher Orr thinks of the adaptation process as "the privileging or underlining of certain quotations within the film's inter-textual space" (72). Citing Barthes's contention that every text is "a multi-dimensional space in which a variety of writings, none of them original, blend and clash" and "a tissue of quotations drawn from the innumerable centres of culture" whose origins are "anonymous, undiscoverable, and nevertheless already read," Orr describes "the literary source as one of a series of pre-texts," some of which "share some of the same narrative conventions as the film adap-tation" and some of which are "codes specific to the institution of the cinema as well as codes that reflect the cultural conditions under which the film was produced" (72). Thus, for Orr, fidelity criticism is dangerous because it "impoverishes the film's intertextuality either by ignoring the other codes that make the filmic text intelligible or by making those codes subservient to the code of a single precursor text" (72). A possible use, however, of the fidelity approach is that "lapses of fidelity ... provide clues to the ideology embed-ded in the text" (73). Orr insists that adaptation be approached "from an ide-ological perspective. That is, a film adaptation is a product of the culture that created it and thus an expression of the ideological forces operative in that culture at a specific historical moment" (73). In Bordwell and Thompson's terms, Orr wants us to focus our attention on *symptomatic meaning.*

Barthes's blending and clashing, again suggesting, at least in part, a play of opposites, reinforces the idea that the adaptation process, on some level, involves collision. Eidsvik borrows from Sergei Eisenstein the construction of such an image:

> Eisenstein tells us that "A" plus "B" can (if the two collide hard enough) equal "C." ... [T]he result is a third entity with properties not contained in either original. The process of adaptation is, like the process of Eisensteinian mon-tage, a matter of bisociation. As Arthur Koestler points out, bisociation is the core process in both humor and creativity.... I disagree with conventional bisociation theory, however, in my assessment of the effects of collision. The originals are altered, at least after a time: films and books have a social and historical dimension ["Toward" 31].

Christopher Orr might argue here that since film and literature "share some of the same narrative conventions," they can hardly be thought of as "two rad-ically disparate entities." Some semioticians would retort, however, that since film and literature operate within two very different sign systems, they may very well be considered "radically disparate entities." Putting these arguments aside for the moment, what is worth our immediate attention is Eidsvik's interesting statement that "the originals are altered, at least after a time." If, indeed, he is using Eisenstein's famous montage equation as an analogy for the adaptation process, as his discussion as a whole seems to suggest, then his use of "originals"—plural—is puzzling. Writing about George Garrett's humorous anecdote that concerns Peter Lorre's giving his studio boss a one-page synopsis of *Crime and Punishment,* Eidsvik certainly wants us to see the novel as an "original." What, though, is the *other* original? Early in his article, Eidsvik presents evidence which suggests that he is thinking of film in general here. As we may recall, even though he confesses to agreeing with Resnais that adaptations are "warmed-over meals," he admits that "adaptations frequently provide major advances in the art of film" (28). The other original, then, must be the art of film. Reminiscent of T.S. Eliot's observation "that the past should be altered by the present as much as the present is directed by the past" (50), Eidsvik's conclusion is that "after a time," the "social and historical" context in which these originals are read alters them. Though the text here is not the "mere vacancy" that Krieger decries (539), it is certainly not a static entity.

Further, time collides with time when book meets film. Keith Cohen reminds us that "each shot in a movie seems to be given in the present tense: in spite of the effects of flash-backs and jumps forward in time, it is inscribed in the here and now that seems capable of being brought back at a moment's notice" (66). Cohen cites Barthes's work in "*Rhetorique de l'image*" to reinforce what he considers to be a major difference between photograph and film: "In the photograph, an illogical conjunction is produced between the *here* and the *bygone*.... Its reality is that of the *having-been-there*.... It would not do to consider the cinema as animated photography; here the *having-been-there* gives way to a *being-there* of the thing" (66). (In this regard, one might consider the title of Jerzy Kosinski's intriguing novel *Being There* and its film adaptation.) Robert Giddings, Keith Selby, and Chris Wensley make a similar point about film and literature. "Film is now, as you see it," while literature is characterized by a "shifting, imprecise chronology" which "works against the tendency of moving film.... In translating literature into moving pictures, once-upon-a time collides with here-and-now" (xiii). To borrow Eidsvik's phrase, the collision of media that are "radically disparate" in terms of how they express the passing of time could result in "major advances in the art of film" as the adaptor struggles to translate the complex past and future tenses of literature into the cinematic present.

Since, as Harold Bloom reminds us, the word "'text' goes back to the root *teks,* meaning 'to weave,' and also 'to fabricate'" ("Poetry" 331), it is certainly fitting that Jenkins calls adaptation "a presence that is woven into the very fabric of film culture. To engage with cinema is to ponder adaptation. Yet it represents such a dark and enigmatic thread that it has elicited disparate and sometimes diametric opinions" (8). Robbie Robertson also pictures intertextuality as weaving, but perhaps more interesting is his use of "prey," a word that can be grouped with "arsenal" and "weapon," images of war.

Since the origins of any text, including film text, lies in borrowings from earlier experiences, often unconscious but sometimes deliberate, then it is well to recognize the complexity of this process. As films prey on written texts for their inspiration so, now, print preys upon film as in the past it preyed on oral narratives. Films increasingly prey also on other moving and photographic images, films, television, broadcast news, comics and advertising. These, in turn, prey on each other. Such intertextual weavings are fascinating to observe, and intriguing to deconstruct. In essence, however, they are little different from the kinds of borrowings which have been part of the normal currency of literature and living since, one imagines, communication began [171–72].

In the spirit of Derrida's "*Il n'y a pas d'hors-texte*," Robertson recognizes that humankind has always lived in what Rentschler calls the "texted realities that surround us" (Introduction 12). More specifically, Robertson points out the incredibly complex "weavings" among pop culture media. It is John Izod, however, who writes most fully about this subject. His thesis — "In the capitalist world the adaptation of literature into film is almost always a commercial enterprise" — is borne out through a description of the "interlocking of the media" by way of "cross-media marketing":

> ... Now the executives of media corporations will consider not only the exploitation of film, stage play and novel, but will also think of entering an array of coordinated markets with pre-recorded video-cassettes, cable television, the tv series, sound-track albums and audio cassette tapes, video and computer games, and a whole range of marketable tie ins from vests through shoelaces to ice-cream and horrible toys. Thus toy shops, newsagents and bookshops are implicated in the marketing programme for movie blockbusters. Cinemas sell books, record albums and video-cassettes [102–03].

Anyone with even brief experience with children knows how very true this is. Mel Brooks says it best in *Spaceballs*, where, instead of "the force," he speaks of "the Schwartz": "Merchandising. Merchandising. Where the real money from the movie is made" and which keeps the budget in "the black."

We should recall that Bluestone, too, was certainly not blind to the connection between film adaptation and commodification. He notes that our judgment of a filmmaker's success in "captur[ing] the 'spirit' of the book" hinges upon whether or not the film is "a financial or even a critical success" (114). He pragmatically observes, at least of Hollywood films, that "the question of 'faithfulness' is given hardly any thought" if the film is successful. Like Christopher Orr, who insists that fidelity criticism "impoverishes the film's intertextuality" (72), McFarlane argues that "the insistence on fidelity has led to a suppression of potentially more rewarding approaches to the phenomenon of adaptation.... It marginalizes those production determinants which have nothing to do with the novel but may be powerfully influential upon the film" (10). One such "production determinant," for example, is the whole decision-making process involved in casting, a process that John Orr discusses in terms of Victor Schlondorff's choice of Jeremy Irons to play Swann in *Swann in Love*: "The film as a commodified vehicle also forsakes fidelity of appearance to film stardom. Jeremy Irons is a photogenic Keatsian hero, not the carrot-haired eczematic Jew whom Proust describes in the novel" (Introduction 7). Bluestone would agree with these more contemporary critics that the "success" of this film would ride not on fidelity to Proust's description of Swann but on Irons being photogenic, "pale and melancholy, at times desperate, at times diffuse, always passively haunted" (J. Orr. Introduction 7). Because mainstream audiences generally want their film heroes to be good-looking, Schlondorff's's/Irons's Swann must supplant Proust's.

To return to Robertson's image, one strand of these "intertextual weavings" that has special meaning for literature/film students is the one that he has labeled "print preys upon film." It is a subject that Robert Richardson treats either explicitly or implicitly in each chapter of his 1969 *Literature and Film*. As often cited and as "classic" as Bluestone's *Novels into Film*, *Literature and Film* undertakes a plan

> ... as simple as its double subject and double interest will permit. After a sketch of the subject, there are two chapters which look for literary backgrounds and influences in the film during its rise. Chapters four and five take up some of the important ways in which film and literature are actually alike, and chapter six tries to suggest something of the impact of the film upon modern literature. The final three chapters are concerned largely with poetry and film and with the argument that these two forms have, between them, high significance for us [4].

In chapter six, "Film and Modern Fiction," Richardson concentrates on "the influence of film form" upon literary technique. His examples include "the rapid prose, the swiftly alternated scenes, the emphasis on visible detail" of Nathanael West's *The Day of the Locust* (81); the "movie-like collages called 'Newsreels'" and the "stream-of-consciousness" of John Dos Passos's *U.S.A.* (82); and "the film's proclivity for detail and external surfaces" and the "drifting cinemism" of Alain Robbe-Grillet's *The Voyeur* (88).

Predictably, later critics become, in Miller's terms, the "parasites" that feed upon Bluestone and Richardson (the earlier "hosts"), some even directly attacking them. Keith Cohen, for example, accuses Bluestone of "skirt[ing] the theoretical problems at stake" and "insisting, without further investigation, on the notion of a strict, unalterable *difference* of communication in novel and film" and Richardson of outlining "superficial similarities" (3). Boyum chastises Bluestone for his "crucial assumption that words, rather than images, make for the superior medium" (9), and Eidsvik points out that "Bluestone is wrong" when he concludes that the "world perceived on film" exists out-side of the "universe of significations" that governs our understanding of lan-guage ("Soft" 19). Mast takes Richardson to task for calling *To Have and Have Not* "a perfectly ordinary vehicle for Humphrey Bogart" and thus failing to "understand the power of such archetypal presences" (284). Such criticism notwithstanding, these two early works still have much to say. Further, the fact that Miller, then at Johns Hopkins, read Bluestone's manuscript is just one more interesting piece of the intertextual puzzle of literature/film theory.

Two new works that treat the idea that "print preys upon film" are genre studies. Laurence Goldstein's 1995 *The American Poet at the Movies: A Criti-cal History* devotes 290 pages to "a certain type of poem ... that speaks about some favorite movie, or movie star, or the movies in general" (v), and Gavriel Moses's 1995 *The Nickel Was for the Movies: Film in the Novel from Pirandello to Puig* explores "the film novel as literary genre," focusing especially on the works of Nabokov and Pirandello and including, as does Richardson, mini-chapters on Isherwood, Fitzgerald, West, and Percy.

Robertson's repetition of the verb "prey," a verb that appropriately reflects the content of his article "The narrative sources of Ridley Scott's *Alien*," deserves even more attention. As we have suggested, it evokes the parasite/host relationship that Miller "interrogates" in "The Critic as Host" and which we applied, following Adams and Searle, to the relationship among early and recent adaptation critics. However, whereas Miller interjects an ambiguity — "The host feeds the parasite and makes its life possible, but at the same time is killed by it.... Or can host and parasite live happily together, ... feeding each other or sharing the food?" (452) — the word "prey" usually and unam-biguously points toward an approaching death. Though Izod tames his use of "prey" by making it appear synonymous with "[develop] a particular inter-est in" ("Nor did the film industry restrict its activities to preying on litera-ture. It had also developed a particular interest in Broadway theatrical productions" [97–98]), Virginia Woolf evokes an image of bloodshed when she describes books as the "'prey' and 'unfortunate victim'" of film "and the movie audience itself (presumably in contrast to the audience for books) as 'the savages of the twentieth century'" (Boyum 6). Where Woolf metaphorizes, Bluestone mythologizes, using even stronger language drawn from the same lexical field: "It is almost as if the film-maker must destroy the old medium in order to catch its essence in the new" (68) and again, of *Pride and Preju-dice*, " ... [W]e can see how the screen writers and director, by taking liber-ties with Jane Austen's text, by imagining what she has not told them, have managed to render her meanings, almost as if destroying the book were a pre-condition for its faithful resurrection" (140).

In the world of literary theory, it is Bloom's work that epitomizes such diction. His 1973 "Manifesto for Antithetical Criticism" in *The Anxiety of Influence* describes his brand of intertextualty: " ... we deny that there is, was or ever can be a poet as poet — to a reader. Just as we can never embrace (sexually or otherwise) a single person, but embrace the whole of her or his family romance, so we can never read a poet without reading the whole of his or her family romance as poet" (94). In his 1976 "Poetry, Revisionism, Repression," he refutes Derrida's "*Il n'y a pas d'hors-texte*": "The strong word and stance issue only from a strict will, a will that dares the error of reading all of reality as a text..." (331) and defines the poetic "text" as "a psychic battlefield upon which authentic forces struggle for the only victory worth winning, the divinating triumph over oblivion..." (332). It is this language of the battlefield (we should recall here that Fell termed semiotics a "new weapon in the arsenal of film studies" [222]), coupled with what Donald E. Pease calls Bloom's "psychopoetics" (95), that exemplifies Bloom's work during this stage of his career. The young or "belated" poet engages in an Oedipal struggle with his poetic father, his "precursor," and if he wins, his poetry will be "strong." "Strong poetry is strong only by virtue of a kind of textual usurpation that is analogous to what Marxism encompasses as its social usurpation or Freudianism as its psychic usurpation" ("Poetry" 333).

Thus, when Marcus "takes as [her] subject the adaptational techniques of a group of filmmakers who not only rely on literary sources, but who do so quite self-consciously, and who dramatize that self-consciousness throughout their work" (x) and writes that "such filmmakers find it useful, indeed necessary, to define their own authorial task in relation to that of a literary precursor" (x), she echoes Bloom's language. When she says that she "will thus include in [her] study of adaptations the scene or scenes in which the filmmaker acknowledges the literary ancestry of the work" (x) and later says that these "umbilical scenes ... teach us how to read their cinematic rewriting of literary sources" (xi), she stands in the shadow of his notion of "family romance." And when she warns us that if we do not choose "codifying systems," then the "invisible artificers of ideology" will (7), she adds a Marxist twist to Bloom's assertion that "the quest for interpretative models is a necessary obsession for the reader who would be strong, since to refuse models explicitly is only to accept other models, however unknowingly" ("Poetry" 337).

Bloom's cosmology can even accommodate the fact that Bluestone was writing about the destruction and resurrection of *Pride and Prejudice* years before *The Anxiety of Influence* appeared. The sixth "revisionary ratio" (the ratios being steps in the new poet's struggle with his precursor) is *apophrades*, or the return of the dead:

> The *apophrades*, the dismal or unlucky days upon which the dead return to inhabit their former houses, come to the strongest poets, but with the very

strongest there is a grand and final revisionary movement that purifies even
this last influx. Yeats and Stevens, the strongest poets of our century, and
Browning and Dickinson, the strongest of the later nineteenth century, can
give us vivid instances of this most cunning of revisionary ratios. For all of
them achieve a style that captures and oddly retains priority over their precursors, so that the tyranny of time almost is overturned, and one can believe, for
startled moments, they are being *imitated by their ancestors* [141].

When we read Bluestone in light of Bloom, it sounds as if "the later poet himself [Bloom] had written the precursor's [Bluestone's] characteristic work," or
at least some of it, and it "produces the illusion of [Bloom's] having fathered
[his] own fathers" ("Poetry" 340).

    Likewise, although Donaldson directly credits Althusser and Foucault,
he evokes Bloom's *apophrades* at the end of the following passage:

> Mine is a heuristic auteurism, a skeptical bardolatry. If the ego is not even
> master of its own house, and if Althusser is right (he can be only partly right)
> that the impression of vivid, individual, lived experience is a sure sign of the
> workings of ideology, then Foucault's question (which is also Samuel Beck-
> ett's) may be asked of Shakespeare film: "Who is speaking?" Who is speaking,
> for instance, when Laurence Olivier utters Hamlet's lines (or those of the
> ghost of Hamlet's father)? "Shakespeare" is one answer, "Hamlet" another.
> But if the displacements this book attempts are successful, it will become as
> appropriate to answer "Freud" or "Ernest Jones," to cite two undoubted
> influences on Olivier's interpretation, or, in keeping with the more radical
> reversals of sequence and priority I hope for, to hear later voices, those of
> revisionist psychoanalysts and perhaps that of my own commentary, in Ham-
> let's wish to be remembered [xiv].

These "radical reversals of sequence and priority" are exactly what Bloom
names *apophrades*. Moreover, the idea that secondary sources, thinkers like
Freud, might be considered "influences on Olivier's interpretation" is stated
in Bloom's "Manifesto": "For just as a poet must be found by the opening in
a precursor poet, so must the critic. The difference is that a critic has more
parents. His precursors are poets and critics. But — in truth — so are a poet's
precursors, often and more often as history lengthens" (*Anxiety* 95). Whether
we regard Olivier as actor-artist or as adaptor-critic, he will have many "parents," uncannily both preceding and following him.

    Other images also reinforce the Bloomian worldview in the work of the
adaptation theorists, two of which belong to Charles Eidsvik, who certainly
deserves mention as the writer who has contributed the most images to this
survey. In "Soft Edges," Eidsvik claims that "the job of a critic of film-literature relationships is ... to discover on whose shoulders a film rests, that is,
to ask which traditions illuminate a particular film" (21). When film is imagined
to be standing on the shoulders of traditions, these traditions are anthropo-

morphized into a precursor who is perhaps suffering from the weight of the filmic "son," a son who has become not only stronger than the weighted-down precursor but also necessarily taller. Then, in "Toward a 'Politique des adaptations,'" Eidsvik writes about the problem of fidelity in terms of a marriage: "to be unfaithful is to be a heel and to be faithful, dull" (30). Later in the essay, he at first reminds us of our discussion of *bricolage,* with its "logic of myth," and then again takes up the marriage metaphor, noting that the "marriage of literature and film has nothing to do with logic as philosophy departments teach it; rather, it has to do with the irrational logics of economics, art history, and the processes of creation" (34). After he acknowledges the intertextual nature of the art world, Eidsvik's trope becomes Bloomian as he envisions the participants of this "lousy marriage" meeting on the battleground of adaptation. Out of this battleworn, love/hate bond, however, come "offspring strong enough and violent enough to create new directions in evolution," to "[attempt] original solutions" (28) to the problems inherent in the adaptation process. In the "family romance" of this "lousy marriage," the strong and violent child with his "strict will" ("Poetry" 331) is able to "consume" and "efface" (in Ellis's very Bloomian words) the memory of the parents. Along these lines, Stephanie Harrison begins her book *Adaptations: From Short Story to Big Screen* by stating, "Reading the story that inspired a beloved movie is a little like meeting your mother-in-law for the first time: It's never less than a revelation. Included here are several movies with strong — you might even say overwhelming — parental personalities" (xv).

As we have seen, the line of descent in Bloom's family romance includes critics as well as poets: "Poets' misinterpretations or poems are more drastic than critics' misinterpretations or criticism, but this is only a difference in degree and not at all in kind. There are no interpretations but only misinterpretations, and so all criticism is prose poetry" (*Anxiety* 94–95). Thus, this strong, violent, strict-willed child, the film adaptation-as-criticism, has succeeded in usurping its parents and has become writ large. Norman Holland quotes Wolfenstein and Leites to describe the psychology of watching "the big people on the screen," an image that exemplifies the adaptation's power:

> What novels could tell, movies can show. Walls drop away before the advancing camera. No character need disappear by going off-stage. The face of the heroine and the kiss of lovers are magnified for close inspection. The primal situation of excited and terrified looking, that of the child trying to see what happens at night, is re-created in the theater; the related wish to see everything is more nearly granted by the movies than by the stage. The movie audience is moreover insured against reaction or reproof from those whom they watch because the actors are incapable of seeing them. The onlooker becomes invisible [qtd. in Harrington 344].

As Holland comments, "[W]e are powerless, as we were when we were children, to change the doings of the 'big people.' Now, though, we are immune, the giants on the screen cannot affect us, either. Our regression is safe, secure, and highly pleasurable" (344). From a psychological standpoint, this may very well be true. However, changing the context a bit, we might suggest that in this audience of "children" sits the film adaptation theorist, who, in his "safe, secure, and highly pleasurable" position is saving up strength to make his move as the newest son, the grandson, the one who will stand on the shoulders of the adaptation, his father, and interpret the interpretation that is the film. We can again cite Adams and Searle's suggestion, compatible with Bloom's notion of family romance, that "the genetic identity of these symbiotic couples [father/son, artist/critic] persists" (451). In short, "The business of adapting a novel is something like the business of being a parent. You have to be stern with the child but you have to love him constantly and be aware that your function is to cater to his needs and not vice versa" (Jerry Wald, qtd. in Jenkins 21).

Obviously, one of the key words that have dominated this conversation is "text." As literary theorists like Bloom, Barthes, and Derrida propose different definitions of "text," so, too, do the adaptation theorists. Eidsvik, for example, writing in 1974 before the mass marketing of video cassettes, cautions against confusing a text with an artifact and reviews the New Critical position:

> The fact that books are artifacts which lose nothing in duplication makes print virtually the only medium which can fare well in an aesthetic which values immortality. The artifact-based aesthetic reached its most monopolistic point with New Criticism's demand that a critic must "go to the text." The only kind of texts a critic can go to easily are those embodied in print form ["Soft" 18].

Similarly, Donaldson, again beginning his passage by paying homage to the New Critics, focuses on the quality of repeatability:

> Film may be regarded as performance retextualized. Having a text means that what is written, inscribed, or recorded can be repeated and reexperienced in the modes that repetition makes possible. Surface meanings, manifest drifts of design may be resisted. Textualization, which might be thought of as *stabilizing* meaning, actually opens meaning to an uncircumscribable play of possibilities [xiii].

Even though it is true that "video and DVD have increased the shelf-life of classic adaptations" (Cartmell and Whelehan 6) and in this way have become more book-like, and even though an adaptation has been repeatable since the early 1980s, Donaldson, writing in 1990, ends his argument with the poststructuralist position that stability is an illusion and suggests that it is the ever-shifting intertextual universe that fosters an "uncircumscribable play of possibilities." Woven into this universe is the intertextuality of the reader. Esslin cautions us to be ever mindful of "the individual's own personal intertextuality: his or her previous experience of, for instance, performances of the same play by different actors, or individual actors' performances in other plays or films." Even more specific and personal are

> factors inherent in his or her own personality: his or her visual sense and taste, say in clothes and furniture, personal preferences for certain physical types among the actors, or, indeed, specific personal interests.... A performance may contain signs that are obtrusive and pregnant with meaning to an individual spectator of which the originators of the performance themselves may have been totally unaware and which will remain unperceived by the rest of the audience [149].

As Brinker would put it, "seeing as" is certainly at work here, for "no form of life can supply us with rules or criteria for deciding the 'correct' way of seeing" (35).

In the language of semiotics, "'text' does not merely denote the verbal element of the drama but the entire 'texture' of interacting sign systems" (Esslin 143). Esslin cites Walter Ong's distinction between "text" and "utterance," a distinction that highlights the bond between semiotics and reader-response criticism: a text "can be made into an utterance only by a code that is existing and functioning in a living person's mind" (139). Like Robertson, Esslin uses an image of weaving to further refine the concept: "The skill of the creators of any dramatic performance in issuing and weaving together their multifarious structures of signs can have its impact only if the spectators exposed to [these signs] know what they stand for" (139). Eco's metaphoric definition epitomizes Esslin's position: the text is "a lazy machine asking the reader to do some of its work" (3).

Further, Esslin makes use of Barthes's definition of "text" as "a tissue of quotations drawn from the innumerable centres of culture" when he lists some of the elements that constitute this "'texture' of interacting sign systems": "gestures, visual patterns, in the cinema 'quotation' of classical models of *mise-en-scène*, camera angles and editing" (143). Miller's question — "What happens when a critical essay extracts a 'passage' and 'cites' it?" (452) — is germane here. If Miller can ask of the microcosm of the essay, "Is a citation an alien parasite within the body of the main text, or is the interpretive text the parasite which surrounds and strangles the citation which is its host?" then perhaps we can ask the same question of the macrocosm of intertextuality. Is Barthes's text, his "tissue of quotations," a parasite within the body of culture, or is the culture the parasite "which surrounds and strangles" the text? And further, on the level of a specific film, does the film prey upon its "classical models" or do these models "surround and strangle" the film, "which is [their] host?" Simone Murray uses the image of an "ecosystem — with all the dynamism, symbiosis, and competition characteristic of ecosystems" (7) to suggest a complexity that involves "cross pollination" (5).

Jerome McGann's discussion of the textuality of a poem summarizes how ways of perceiving and defining the text have changed. What he says about poetry and poems could be equally applied to film and films:

> The poem, like all human utterances, is a social act which locates a complex of related human ideas and attitudes. Unlike non-aesthetic utterance, however, poetry's social evaluations are offered to the reader *under the sign of completion*. That sign of completion is what the formalists recognized as their object of study; i.e. the integral language construction of the poem, or what is called "the text." But this "text" is not what we should understand as a "poem." Rather, what we ought to see is that "text" is the linguistic state of the "poem's" existence. No poem can exist outside of a textual state any more than a human being can exist outside of a human biological organism. But just as a person is not identical to a particular human body, so neither is a poem equal to its text [21–22].

As McGann relates the difference between "poem" and "text" to "what Coleridge and Shelley were trying to articulate when they distinguished between 'poetry' and 'a poem'" (22), so might we relate the same kind of difference to "story" and "discourse." And this distinction is a narratological one.

The least complex image among those that can be associated with narratology comes from John Orr, who uses "picture-book" as an appositive for "adaptation" throughout his entire article: "... the adaptation, the 'picture-book' as we shall call it..." (1–2). On one hand, this appellation is unfortunate. A picture-book is just that — a book that tells its story through pictures that either replace words altogether or illustrate them. A movie, even an adaptation, is not a book at all. Orr's image, however, does call to mind old movies that explicitly try to connect themselves to their literary sources by actually showing us the books:

> Back in the thirties and forties, adaptations (at least of classic works) had a habit of beginning with a picture of the book itself: there was the book's cover, a process shot of the pages being flipped, a close-up of a line or two of the text ... and then ... another close-up of one of the book's illustrations ... that shortly was transformed into the movie's establishing shot. In this way, the film declared itself the equivalent of the book, or at the very least, an illustrated version of it [Boyum 68].

This opening technique conjures up memories of a parent or teacher reading to us and perhaps even alludes to the "reader" in a silent movie theater. On the other hand, even if we quibble with John Orr's phrase and point out that it's been a very long time since film was defined by just pictures (and even then there were titles to read and music to hear), his point is that film (picture) and fiction (book)

> have two things in common. They are both narrative forms, and both are referential. Both produce stories which work through temporal succession. Both refer to, or connote, pre-existent materials. Fiction works through a pre-existent language, film through the raw data of the physical world which its cameras record [2].

In this brief passage, Orr identifies a key concept of narratology and of semiotics, of which it is a "subset" (Prince 524): the difference between story, "which work[s] through temporal succession," and discourse, the embodiment of story in the "pre-existent materials" of "language" and "the raw data of the physical world." As Gerald Prince explains, the narratologist/semiotician regards these embodiments as "rule-governed ways in which human beings (re)fashion their universe" and attempts both to "isolate [their] necessary and optional components" and to "characterize the modes of their articulation" (524).

Bela Balázs pictures the difference between these "necessary and optional components," between those belonging to story and those belonging to discourse, when he describes "the existing work of art merely as raw material" and urges the filmmaker to

> regard it from the specific angle of his own art form as if it were raw reality, and pay no attention to the form once already given to the material. The playwright, Shakespeare, reading a story by Bandello, saw in it not the artistic form of a masterpiece of story-telling but merely the naked event narrated in it [qtd. in Bluestone 63].

Eidsvik, too, calls literature the "raw material for film" ("Toward" 33). In line with his rather sharp comment that "books are almost the only source of intelligence to be found in Los Angeles County" (33), he pragmatically observes that "film is an industrial institution with raw-material needs far beyond the native resources of Hollywood. Literature is a source of high-grade ore which can be cheaply turned into 'product'" (33). Finally, Linda Seger contributes to this image pattern when she describes adaptation as a "reconceptualizing" process:

> By its very nature, adaptation is a transition, a conversion, from one medium to another. All original material will put up a bit of a fight, almost as if it were saying, "Take me as I am." Yet adapting implies change. It implies a process that demands rethinking, reconceptualizing, and understanding how the nature of drama is intrinsically different from the nature of all other literature [2].

The "high-grade ore," "raw reality," and "naked event" are all ways of talking about what most simply has been called story. "The form ... given to the material" is discourse or what Balázs calls "content": "Success [in the adaptation process] is possible because, while 'the subject, or story, of both works is identical, their content is nevertheless different. It is this different content that is adequately expressed in the changed form resulting from the adaptation'" (Bluestone 62).

Linda Seger also pictures this "naked event" as the "story spine," "the backbone" of the story. Similarly, Andrew likens it to a skeleton. It is the "something essential" that can be reproduced. "The skeleton of the original can, more or less thoroughly, become the skeleton of a film" because

> it includes aspects of fiction generally elaborated in any film script: the characters and their inter-relation, the geographical, sociological, and cultural information providing the fiction's context, and the basic narrational aspects that determine the point of view of the narrator (tense, degree of participation and knowledge of the story-teller, and so on) [100].

Jenkins begins his study of the films of Stanley Kubrick by citing Richard Corliss: "Adapting a best-seller for the movies is like carving flesh down to the bone.... You keep the skeleton, then apply rouge and silicone until the creature looks human" (1).

George Linden also uses the phrase "narrative skeleton" to refer to the story that the script outlines:

> As Trevor Howard has remarked, the second *Mutiny on the Bounty* might not have been quite the disaster it was if the actors had known what they were doing and where they were going. As he said dryly, "It helps, at least, to have a script." When there is no script from the outset, the director and the actors have no narrative skeleton around which they may improvise. Without a skeleton, nothing holds; everything becomes an amorphous mess [161].

The same certainly holds true when the script is constantly changing or is incomplete. *Apocalypse Now* has become, perhaps, the most famous example of such a disaster, although, through a kind of synthesis of genius and serendipity, the final product managed to rise well above the "amorphous mess" of its production.

It is McFarlane, however, who most fully explores the importance of isolating these "basic narrational aspects." Indebted to Levi-Strauss's *Structural Anthropology* (1972) and Barthes's "Introduction to the Structural Analysis of Narratives" (1966), which is itself indebted to V. Propp's *Morphology of the Folktale* (1927), McFarlane offers an image identical to Andrew's skeleton. He associates the "irreducible bare bones of the narrative" with Barthes's cardinal functions, with Propp's character functions ("villain," "helper," etc.) (25), and with Levi-Strauss's "mythic elements" that are "preserved even through the worst translation" (25).

In his Preface, McFarlane states that

> the aim of this book is to offer and test a methodology for studying the process of transposition from novel to film, with a view not to evaluating one in relation to the other but to establishing the *kind* of relation a film might bear to the novel it is based on. In pursuing this goal, I shall set up procedures for distinguishing between that which can be transferred from one medium to another (essentially, narrative) and that which, being dependent on different signifying systems, cannot be transferred (essentially, enunciation) [vii].

Enunciation — or adaptation, as he more frequently calls it — involves those "processes by which other ... elements must find quite different equivalences in the film medium, when such equivalences are sought or are available at all" (13).

The elements that can be transferred are what Barthes calls the distributional functions. Like the syntagmatic or diachronic axes, they are "'horizontal' in nature" and they involve "doing" (13). The most important of these are the cardinal functions (or what Seymour Chatman, in *Story and Discourse: Narrative Structure in Fiction and Film* [1978], calls the kernels). They are the "hinge-points" of the narrative and create its "risky" moments (13). Because they are so easily transferable from one medium to another, a film that has not been faithful to the cardinal functions of its source "is apt to occasion critical outrage and popular disaffection" when "a major cardinal function is deleted or altered ... (e.g. to provide a happy rather than a sombre ending)" (14). McFarlane also argues that what Barthes calls catalysers — another subset of the distributional functions (or what Chatman calls satellites) — are powerful enough to "deform" the cardinal functions. The role of the catalysers is to "root the cardinal functions in a particular kind of reality, to enrich the texture of those functions.... They account for the moment-to-moment minutiae of narrative" and "denote small actions (e.g. the laying of the table for a meal which may in turn give rise to action of cardinal importance to the story)" (14). Catalysers, like cardinal functions, are transferable.

Integrational functions, however, are different. Like the paradigmatic or synchronic axes, they are "'vertical' in nature" and refer to "being." Like the distributional, the integrational functions can be subdivided into two kinds: indices proper, which relate to "concepts such as character and atmosphere," and informants, which are, in Barthes's words, "'pure data with immediate signification,' ... 'ready-made knowledge,' such as names, ages, and professions of characters, certain details of the physical setting" (McFarlane 14). Only the informants are transferable — the indices proper must be adapted.

Although Seger may be paying tribute to a bit of Barthes's terminology when she refers to "hinge scenes" (86), most adaptation theorists use less technical terms and fewer categories to deal with the issue of what can be transferred to the screen and what cannot. In a passage that prefigures McFarlane's use of the cardinal functions and certainly echoes Propp, Bluestone notes that the adaptor

> looks ... to characters and incidents which have somehow detached themselves from language and, like the heroes of folk legends, have achieved a mythic life of their own. Because this is possible, we often find that the film adapter has not even read the book, that he had depended instead on a paraphrase by his secretary or his screen writer [62].

Bluestone even addresses the non-transferability of the indices proper when he worries about how the "texture of the narrative prose" of Liam O'Flaherty's *The Informer*, with its "internal monologue and literary figures of speech," might be "rendered in cinematic equivalents" (80). He concludes that John Ford has, indeed, successfully "solved this problem by devising an elaborate set of symbols which function on both literal and analogical levels" (81).

Similarly, but stated in language not available to Bluestone, Andrew agrees that "it would appear that one must presume the global signified of the original to be separable from its text if one believes it can be approximated by other sign clusters" (101). This "global signified of the original" is, in essence, the set of cardinal functions. Regarding how the indices proper might be captured on film, Andrew claims that

> the strident and often futile arguments over these issues can be made sharper and more consequential in the language of E. H. Gombrich or even more systematic language of semiotics. Gombrich finds that all discussion of adaptation introduces the category of "matching." First of all, like Bazin he feels one cannot dismiss adaptation since it is a fact of human practice. We can and do correctly match items from different systems all the time: a tuba sound is more like a rock than like a piece of string; it is more like a bear than like a bird; more like a romanesque church than a baroque one. We are able to make these distinctions and insist on their public character because we are matching equivalents [101–02].

Sometimes this "matching" is difficult indeed. For example, Emily Dickinson, writing about the end of summer, surprisingly shifts the tenor of her metaphor (usually an unknown or abstract concept) to a concrete occurrence ("The Summer lapsed away — ") and the vehicle (usually known or concrete) to an abstract one ("As imperceptibly as Grief"). A little more than a century later, Joni Mitchell sings of summer as falling "to the sidewalk like string and brown paper." Although the end of summer could certainly be captured by the quality of light seen on the screen, a sort of *Light in August*, as it were, the beauty and freshness of Dickinson's and Mitchell's language would indeed be lost. However, the "matching [of] equivalents" can and does occur "all the time." As every school child who has taken a field trip to the symphony hall to listen to "Peter and the Wolf" knows, it is entirely possible to achieve, even for the indices proper, "equivalent narrative units in ... absolutely different semiotic systems" (102). What we have seen, however, is that not all theorists would grant that music and film are true semiotic systems.

Boyum, too, discusses the issue but does so in terms of style: "If style is, as some would claim, the expression of an artist's individuality (and thus resistant to adaptation, where another artist's individuality intercedes), style is also often the expression of quite the opposite: of an artist's tie with other artists, of his link with an entire period" (122). She argues that "if we can find analogous stylistic features and analogous techniques," not only in "the general style of any given period" but also in the "individual style of any particular artist," then we can effect the kind of brilliant transfer achieved in Tony Richardson's *Tom Jones*, where not only "the global elements of Fielding's style —... his loose episodic structure, his pervasive strategy of characterization by caricature —" are captured, but also captured is his verbal style, with its "hyperbole and apostrophe and personification" and the film's "wipes and freezes and pans" (123). Andrew makes the same point: "Adaptation analysis ultimately leads to an investigation of film styles and periods in relation to literary styles of different periods" (103).

First, the opposition — that the indices proper cannot be rendered in a "different semiotic system"— is represented from the *auteur's* point of view, by Ingmar Bergman:

> ... We should avoid making films out of books. The irrational dimension of a literary work, the germ of its existence, is often untranslatable into visual terms — and it, in turn, destroys the special, irrational dimension of the film. If, despite this, we wish to translate something literary into film terms, we must make an infinite number of complicated adjustments which often bear little or no fruit in proportion to the effort expended [226].

Almost as extreme is Horton Foote's remark about his adaptation of Flannery O'Connor's "The Displaced Person": "What often eluded me here was the mystic, visionary aspects of the story. Qualities that almost defy dramatization" (8). Evidently, however, Foote was able to make the "infinite number of complicated adjustments" necessary, as the word "almost" suggests.

Second, from the semiotician's point of view, Christopher Orr succinctly reminds us of the problem that has underlain this entire discussion — the problem of interpretation. He points out that those who believe that "the final signified of a verbal sign cluster" can find its equivalent in "the final signified of an audiovisual sign or sign cluster" have forgotten that "it is impossible to prove that one's reading of the audiovisual sign cluster would have been the same had one been unfamiliar with the film's literary source" (3). There is, of course, a catch: if we have not previously read the book, we don't look for equivalences at all. If we have read it, we necessarily read the film in terms of the book. As Morgan, the participant in Bobo's study of *The Color Purple*, so simply states, "I couldn't watch this movie in the state of mind of a person who hadn't read the book" (121).

Marcus beautifully summarizes the debate between those who argue that "there exists a universal, nonspecific code of narrativity which transcends its embodiment in any one particular signifying system" and those who hold that "meaning is indivisibly bound to the concrete material terms of its realization in art and that it is absurd to posit a significance separable from, and equally available to, a plurality of discursive systems" (14). The first group is represented by "Paul Ricoeur, Roland Barthes, and A. J. Greimas in France, Angelo Moscariello and Gianfranco Bettetini in Italy, and Seymour Chatman on this side of the Atlantic" and the second by "Jean Mitry and Gérard Genette in France, Luigi Chiarini, Emilio Garroni, and Galvano della Volpe in Italy" (14). Marcus herself contributes a third position so filled with common sense and elegance that one wonders why it has not previously been explored. Quite simply, she

> would suggest that the separability of story and discourse is a useful, indeed a necessary, assumption for the adapter, who must posit the existence of a narrativity that lends itself to cinematic as well as literary form. The distinction is not tenable ... for the public reception of the two media, whose psychological and sociological consequences are so intimately bound to their medium-specific languages that to distinguish between them becomes an exercise in academic frivolity [14].

Her explanation — and the triangular image that she eventually uses — are perhaps derived from the "triangle" of the artistic experience that Monaco draws:

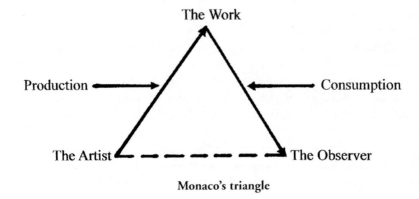

Monaco's triangle

He notes that "examination of the relationship between the artist and the work yields theories of the production of art, while analysis of the relationship between the work and the observer gives us theories of consumption. (The third leg of the triangle, artist_ _ _ _ _ _ _observer, is potential rather than actual)" (11–12).

Marcus's ability to see the problem in terms of production (the adaptor) and consumption (the film going public) is no doubt attributable to her more general dialectical critical stance. As Monaco tells us, "[D]ialectical criticism analyzes the direct relationships between the work, the artist, and the observer as they are expressed in terms of economic and political structures" (14). It is worth repeating that Marcus, looking through the lens of Marxism, warns that "the invisible artificers of ideology" will choose for us if we do not choose a "codifying system" for ourselves (7). She puts the same idea a slightly different way when she recalls to us "the fact that all perception is mediated by codes that organize and filter our cognitive input" and, therefore, "the world's apparently innocent speech [is] the inevitable conduit of ideology" (20). In terms of practical applications, this stance allows her to see that "the addition and subtraction of scenes [in *The Leopard*] thus amounts to a deliberate politicizing strategy on Visconti's part" (47). Marcus, of course, is not the only adaptation theorist who sees her subject from this particular point of view.

Andrew writes that

> if we take seriously the arguments of Marxist and other social theorists that our consciousness is not open to the world but filters the world according to the shape of its ideology, then every cinematic rendering will exist in relation to some prior whole lodged unquestioned in the personal or public system of experience [97].

Esslin, too, suggests that because

> even the shallowest play, film, soap opera or situation comedy portrays and implicitly establishes patterns of cultural values, ... all drama is a purveyor of ideological and political messages, whether it openly questions the values of its society, or, what is so much more frequently the case, particularly in cinema and television, tacitly accepts and serves to reinforce them [158].

To help Rick Instrell make his point that *Blade Runner* "can be seen as largely reflecting in its own time the dominant ideologies of Reagan's America and Thatcher's Britain" (169), he quotes Murdock and Golding: "In seeking to maximise the market, products must draw on the most widely legitimated core values while rejecting the dissenting voice or the incompatible objection to a ruling myth" (161). Also using an image of food as do Resnais and Eidsvik, Barry Brummett colorfully states, "Ideological influence in our society is anything but open and discursive, it is larded throughout the meat of everyday living," such "meat," including, of course, the everyday fare of film and television. Finally, David Lodge uses Russian formalist terms "fabula" and "sjuzet" in his discussion of his work as both novelist and screen writer. He also notes that the embodiment of the fabula (story) in the sjuzet (discourse) is not an ideologically innocent activity: "The sjuzet is always a motivated deformation of the fabula. That is to say, its selections, exclusions, rearrangements, and repetitions of the raw material of the fabula are what determine its meaning or import" (208).

If such "motivated deformation" is kept always in mind, it becomes possible to see Marcus's image of adaptation in its proper context. First, she reviews the adaptation process. The adaptor infers from the source text the fabula, or what she calls the "pre-literary idea," "prototext," or "story"—the skeleton. Then she describes her image. Both the source text and its adaptation can be called "discourse" and both come from the "story." There is no direct connection between them. Thus the base of her triangular image is a broken line.

The concept of discourse, of sjuzet, again comes into play when adaptation theorists consider the definition of "masterpiece." Perhaps it is the conviction that someone will always be proclaiming that "an important novel"—a Rolls Royce—deserves a better adaptation that causes, in Margaret Kennedy's words, "most screen writers [to] prefer to work on an ill-written, second-rate book, towards which they have no conscience, but which has some situation or character which has caught the imagination" (qtd. in Bluestone 90). She defines "a great work of art" as one in which "the medium is so wedded to the subject that it becomes impossible to think of them apart.... If any story has been perfectly told in one medium, what motive can there be for retelling it in another?" (qtd. in Bluestone 90). Like Kennedy, Anthony Burgess remarks that "the brilliant adaptations are nearly always of fiction of the second or third class" (qtd. in Beja 85). And like Resnais and the reheated meal, Truffaut believes that "a masterpiece is something that has already found its perfection of form, its definitive form" (qtd. in Beja 85), implying that an adaptation of a masterpiece has no chance to be anything but second-rate.

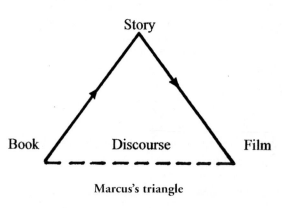

Marcus's triangle

Eidsvik, however, defines "masterpiece" differently. He suggests, after Picasso — and, I would add, Bloom — that masterpieces

> are seldom very original; truly original works are seldom well enough done to be masterpieces. Masterpieces are (after our critical rhetoric is exhausted) no more or less than works so successful that they transcend or make us forgive their limitations. But originality and success are rare bedfellows ["Toward" 27].

He makes the point that because "our expectations [are] higher for adaptations," especially if the source is "well known and highly regarded," we tend to expect the film to be a masterpiece and "thus overlook its originality" ("Toward" 27). As we will recall, even flawed adaptations advance film art, says Eidsvik, because "the attempt to adapt a work which is not 'cinematically-conceived' into 'cinematic terms' forces film-makers into attempting original solutions" ("Toward" 28). According to Walter Metz, such a solution is epitomized by Martin Ritt's 1959 adaptation of *The Sound and the Fury*, which Metz manages to single-handedly resurrect from the grave of universal disdain. He sees the film as a "deconstructive adaptation" which "refuses" the novel's "stylistically aggressive technique and its misogynist content" (22). His interesting article certainly not only makes one want to reconsider a prior judgment, but it also answers Kennedy's question: "If any story has been perfectly told in one medium, what motive can there be for retelling it in another?" As this study has shown, the "retelling" of a story in film form might very well be an interpretation just as valid as any critical essay.

Conclusion

... [W]hat we have loved,
Others will love, and we may teach them how;
Instruct them how the mind of man becomes
A thousand times more beautiful than the earth
On which he dwells, above this frame of things
(Which, 'mid all revolutions in the hopes
And fears of men, doth still remain unchanged)
In beauty exalted, as it is itself
Of quality and fabric more divine.—[*The Prelude*, 14.448–56]

In "What's a Critic to Do?: Critical Theory in the Age of Hypertext," George P. Landow describes the relationship between "hypertext, an information technology consisting of individual blocks of text, or lexias, and the electronic links that join them," and "recent literary and critical theory":

> Like most recent work by poststructuralists ... hypertext reconceives conventional, long-held assumptions about authors and readers and the texts they write and read. Electronic linking, ... one of the defining features of hypertext, also embodies ... notions of intertextuality. The very idea of hypertextuality seems to have taken form at approximately the same time that poststructuralism developed.... [B]oth grow out of dissatisfaction with the related phenomena of the printed book and hierarchical thought [1].

In *Hamlet on the Holodeck*, Janet Murray anticipates a "new kind of storyteller, one who is half hacker, half bard":

> The spirit of the hacker is one of the great creative wellsprings of our time, causing the inanimate circuits to sing with ever more individualized and quirky voices; the spirit of the bard is eternal and irreplaceable, telling us what we are doing here and what we mean to one another [9].

A project at Loyola College in Baltimore illustrates Murray's point. Graphic designer Diana Samet and four poets in the Department of Writing and Media created a CD-ROM, called "Installations & Conversations," that "explore[s]

189

poetic concepts through sound, hypertext, graphics, text and animation." Cyber-text, which allows the student to "look at things in layers and to be stimulated visually" (Shapiro 1E), gave the poets the chance to write poems that "shimmied, changed shape, or employed sound effects." It opened up "an opportunity for another way of teaching," for with its "profusion of links," observes poet Ned Balbo, a student can do "what it takes many cumbersome handouts and other materials to accomplish in a classroom" (qtd. in Shapiro 8E). Samet's com-ment about books is reassuring: "'I was suggesting that this is just another genre.' ... It didn't mean 'books are going to fade away and die. I love books. When I'm not on the computer, I am reading a book. But you have to look at this as an opportunity for another way of teaching'" (Shapiro 8E).

While the cyberbards who participated in this project have not aban-doned written text, Landow, whose insight into hypertext's "instantiation" of poststructuralism is certainly insightful, worries that future cyberbards will. The abandonment of "alphanumeric text," with "its ability economically to stand in for something else," would cause us to "lose the ability to formulate abstract or physical descriptions" ("Twenty minutes" 234), just as text-mes-saging has done. Laura Miller raises other issues relating to cybernovels. She argues, for example, that "meandering through the lexias of hypertext works," works whose agenda is to "liberate" readers from "linear narrative and the author" by making readers co-writers, is "a listless task, a matter of inces-santly having to choose among alternatives, each of which ... is no more impor-tant than any other" (43). Furthermore, she challenges the benefits of non-hierarchical thought:

> If any decision is as good as any other, why bother? Hypertext is sometimes said to mimic real life, with its myriad opportunities and surprising outcomes, but I already have a life, thank you very much, and it is hard enough putting that in order without the chore of organizing someone else's novel [43].

Miller obviously finds it still true that people want to be readers when they read, not writers, and what readers seek is literature that can "transport and humanize" (43). She echoes that "unregenerate reader" Sven Birkerts, who "still believes that language and not technology is the true evolutionary miracle." Birkerts insists that

> the experience of literature offers a kind of wisdom that cannot be discovered elsewhere; that there is profundity in the verbal encounter itself, never mind what further profundities the author has to offer; and that for a host of rea-sons the bound book is the ideal vehicle for the written word [6].

Unlike Murray, Samet, and Balbo, Birkerts does not hold out much hope that the cyberbard will tell us "what we are doing here and what we mean to one another."

This disagreement over what the future holds for literature, over what we stand to lose and to gain, is also present when we turn to theory. Laura Demanski makes the point that "most mainstream academics understand 'theory' as simply what happens when one thinks abstractly about reading and writing — for example, when one pauses, while reading a novel, to ruminate on what it means to enjoy literature" ("Arts"), in other words, to construct a reader-response statement. Beyond this, perhaps the greatest strengths of contemporary theory are its rejection of the insulation of Formalism inherent in its narrow focus on the text itself and, concomitantly, its embrace of theory's function to connect with the larger society. As Brinker would put it, in making us aware of "the interpretative character" (34) of our reading of literature and, by extension, of our reading of the world, theory teaches us about how constructed what we call "reality" really is, about the hegemony that perpetuates such construction, and about the importance of resistance. Barry Brummett's axiom is that theory — especially rhetorical theory — is a serious business, for it can "teach people how to expand their repertoires for making experience and ... show that the awareness that expanded repertoires must entail is subversive" (xxiii). Theory can destroy complacency and invite people to participate in "struggles over who they are and how the world will be made," rather than encouraging them to "simply [sit] in front of the 'tube'" (xxi). In other words, to echo Richard Macksey, literary theory has the power to direct us outwards to the larger world.

A recent case in point involves the rewriting of the scripts used in Louisiana plantation tours. Until a few years ago, tour scripts had been typically written for visitors who had "'Gone with the Wind' expectations in mind," for those who wished to romanticize slavery. This has since changed, however, largely through the efforts of Mike Hawkins, who was at that time a doctoral student in geography and anthropology at Louisiana State University and co-author, with Jean Rahier, of "*Gone With the Wind* Versus the Holocaust Metaphor," a study of "how slavery is overlooked on plantation tours." Now manager of The Madewood Plantation Home in Napoleonville, Louisiana, Hawkins has rewritten the tour narration. "The hardest thing about changing the narratives," he maintains, "is getting both guides and tourists to focus on the historical, social and economic contexts in which these magnificent piles were built and run, rather than being focused entirely on the material objects" (Reynolds 7R). The connection between Hawkins's work and literary theory is obvious: to focus "entirely on the material objects" is the hallmark of Formalism; "to focus on the historical, social and economic contexts" is a fair appraisal of the poststructuralist position. As we have previously noted, Greenblatt might comment that Hawkins's "subversion [has been] both generated and contained by the dominant ideology" (Newton

125). However, it would seem as if he has indeed managed, at least in one small location, to buck the "invisible artificers of ideology," to change "how the world will be made."

The irony is that while contemporary theory rebels against the text-centered critic whose ivory tower protects him from the social hubbub, it has itself made the ivory tower taller and the walls thicker. As Christian suggests, the culprit is not what the new theory expresses but "the way in which it is written" (246). Butler's award-winning obscure sentence, quoted in the Introduction could pass for parody, and several passages of semiotic jargon in Hulley's "The Fate of the Symbolic in *A Streetcar Named Desire*" are quite opaque. There is no excuse for such writing. Demanski is right to suggest that "literary theory would ... attract less hostility if it eased off jaw-breaking jargon that restricts its audience to a hyper-educated elite. We need more public intellectuals who write for the mainstream press" and who would share their "ideas and discoveries with an interested public that will otherwise soon go the way of the theory-phobes. And understandably so." The wonderful metaphor that Francis-Noel Thomas and Mark Turner draw in *Clear and Simple as the Truth: Writing Classic Prose* is one way of picturing what has gone wrong:

> To the classic writer, the difference between thinking and writing is as wide as the difference between cooking and serving. In every great restaurant there is a kitchen, where the work is done, and a dining room, where the result is presented. The dining room is serene, and the presentation suggests that perfection is routine and effortless, no matter how hectic things get in the kitchen. Naturally the kitchen and the dining room are in constant and intimate contact, but it is part of the protocol of a great restaurant to treat them as if they existed on different planets. The cooks do not sit down and relax in the dining room and the guests do not observe the work of the kitchen [64–65].

Even if we reject the conventions of classic style, one of which is its insistence that thought be presented only in its final shape, the power of the metaphor remains: the trouble with too much theoretical writing is that it has prematurely emerged from the kitchen. Its ideas are cast into a style that seems to pride itself on how hard it has worked, and it expects its readers to work just as hard. Literary theorists might do well to study some of the masters of classic style that Thomas and Turner praise: Euclid, Madame de Lafayette, Bernard Shaw, Mark Twain, James Watson, and Frederick Crews. Thomas and Turner's comments on Crews's *The Critics Bear It Away* perfectly reinforce the point:

> This book, mainly a collection of review articles from *The New York Review of Books*, aims at making academic disputes accessible to any intelligent reader and connects those disputes to larger political ideas and temperaments. It is

not polemical in the sense that Pascal's *Lettres provinciales* are, but it shares Pascal's conviction that academic questions can be made accessible to a general audience and can have broad cultural relevance [201–02].

We cannot expect theoretical language to be plain or simplistic, but it does need to be clear. What seems to be missing from some theorists' conceptions of writing is a recognition of the fact that without accessibility, all relevance is lost.

Reading literary theory at its best, however, can be a fascinating, mind-expanding experience, perhaps not as satisfying as reading literature itself, but satisfying nonetheless. Both literature and theory can produce what James Anderson Winn calls "serious pleasure" (qtd. in Demanski). But while Hartman's point that the critic's discourse "cannot be neatly or methodically separated from that of the author" (354) does ring true, there is a categorical difference. We can tolerate the difficulty inherent in the fiction of James Joyce, for example, much more readily than we can in the work of, say, Barthes. The subject matter does matter. Theory, even in the most creative hands, is not fiction. It is part of a great tradition of non-fiction prose and should live up to the achievements of its classic ancestors.

The works of Wolff, Dressler, Pagan, Kleb, Hodgson, Brinker, and Boyum, to name just a few of the critics cited here, are models of such achievement. In each case, the language is only as complex as it needs to be; in no case is it so complex that it excludes the willing reader. Further, these critical texts work well together, for each — as an example of poststructural criticism — identifies a particular arena of struggle in the literary text with which it works, or, in Brinker's case, in thematic discourse in general. Students can begin to see additional connections and apply the critical approach through which we viewed one text to the others — a practicum in "seeing as."

One obvious example is the applicability of psychoanalytical criticism not only to *Grand Isle* but also to *Streetcar* and *Splendor*, for each text tells the Freudian story of the struggle between individuation and fusion, about the joys and perils of blending into something larger, about the accommodations that must be made else everyday life cannot continue. Edna is unable to put aside her "journey into the underworld of instinctual impulses" and "be brought into relationship with the demands of the adult world" (Sullivan and Smith 230). At age 16, Blanche's betrayal by her young homosexual husband, her guilt over his death, Mitch's rejecting her, and Stanley's raping her send her down a spiral that eventually leads to a break with reality. Deanie wants to fuse with Bud, and his betrayal results in her having a mental meltdown.

Second, all three films illustrate the idea that "the moment a child, a self, is brought into the world, it enters representation" (Dressler 72). Edna is represented in the male gaze of the ideology of her time, and each of the three men in her life represents her differently. Léonce expects her to be a "mother-woman." Robert may love her, but she is Mrs. Pontellier to him, and his statement in reply to her chastising him for representing her thus is the reply of another Créole male: "His face grew a little white. 'What do you mean?' he asked" (129; ch. XXXVI). And Alcée represents her as a lover. When she wonders "what character of a woman" she is, he responds, "Why should you bother thinking about it when I can tell you what manner of woman you are" (103; ch. XXVI). Deanie tries to represent herself as a "bad girl," but Bud refuses to accept her representation, maintaining instead that she's a "good girl," unlike the sexually active, seductive Juanita. And Stanley finally represents Blanche as the fallen woman, disposable, cast out.

We can also see *Splendor* and *Grand Isle*, like *Streetcar*, through Foucault's eyes. It is the Same that fixes Edna in her particular historical spot, a spot into which she has been othered. Deanie, on the other hand, wants to be othered, but to no avail. Blanche, of course, wants to belong to the Same but is thrown into otherness by Allan Grey, numerous one-night stands, Mitch, and finally Stanley.

In the language of thematics, *The Awakening*, *Streetcar*, and *Splendor* meet in an intersection of intertextualities that we could label "living with diminishment." Edna cannot accept such a life and commits suicide. Blanche makes a valiant attempt to reclaim her life, but the result, as it is with Deanie, is at least temporary madness. As D. H. Lawrence proclaims, "The central law of all organic life is that each organism is intrinsically isolate and single in itself" (71). Unfortunately, for these three women "living with diminishment" implies living "isolate and single," but it is fusion, not isolation, that Edna, Blanche, and Deanie desire. It is sad that in each case being solitary is viewed as a negative state. Alice Koller paints a much more optimistic picture: "Being solitary is being alone well: being alone luxuriously immersed in doings of your own choice, aware of the fullness of your own presence, rather than of the absence of others." In *The Awakening*, Edna begins to be "immersed in doings of [her] own choice," but she cannot sustain this kind of immersion.

When theoretical writing is effective, it brings students closer to the literature itself, and this is what ultimately counts the most. Good literature speaks to the human condition, to what Faulkner so eloquently called in his Nobel speech "the problems of the human heart in conflict with itself." And good literature, far from being the intimidating stumbling block that students sometimes perceive it to be, is still a source of "serious pleasure." In Eva Brann's words,

Reading makes for delight. When we enter the world of a good novel or savor the words of a fine poem, we receive a singularly unalloyed pleasure. Let me make a bold claim at this point: people who have steady sources of such delight make better neighbors. People who take pleasure in imaginative worlds are better able to give pleasure in the real world. The reason is that they have in mind glowing scenes and images that protect them against the exasperations and catastrophes of life and show them how things might be.

When Deanie recites the lines from Wordsworth's Ode at the end of *Splendor*, we see Brann's claim in action. During her catastrophe, when she sees the person who was once everything to her and confirms for herself that there is no chance for a life with him, Deanie is sustained by the Ode. She can situate herself within its lines and find meaning there. And while this therapeutic, sustaining function of literature is by no means its only function, it is quite real and quite marvelous for students to witness, even if it happens in a movie.

In 1979, Dean J. Champion, a professor of sociology at The University of Tennessee, Knoxville, began to compare student grades in his traditional courses with those in an experimental course that would be "focused almost entirely around motion pictures" (43). For example, he used *Hell in the Pacific*, with Lee Marvin and Toshiro Mifune, to teach concepts of "socialization, comparative sociology, definition of the situation, body language, para-language, territoriality, symbolic interaction, values, culture, norm of reciprocity, prejudice" (45). The results of his study are most supportive of the work of this book:

> Did the films make a difference in student performance on exams and comprehension of sociology subject matter? While a causal relation between student grades and style of course presentation is difficult to demonstrate empirically, the data I compiled over the next four years provided convincing evidence of the fact that the film courses I offered were yielding substantially higher grades on the average compared with the non-film courses. And this general finding was consistent for all years [45].

Though I cannot say with Champion's certainty that students in classes who saw *Grand Isle*, *The End of August*, *A Streetcar Named Desire*, and *Splendor in the Grass* understood more about theoretical approaches than those who read the critical articles without the support of the films, I suspect that this is indeed so. I do know that they seem to remember the work of the semester longer — and that in itself is a good thing if they can carry what they learned into subsequent courses.

Even though we live with a "finely filamented electronic scrim [that] has slipped between ourselves and the so-called 'outside world'" (Birkerts 3), even though a cybertext bard has not yet appeared, even though we are habituated to the lightning speed and antiseptic quality of the travel that advanced technology affords, even though our brightest graduate students may be seduced by the dark attractions of arcane language, even though a saturation into all possible intertextualities into which the adaptation is embedded may "regress into multimedia cacophony" (Lev 338), and even though our undergraduates may become impatient with the slow reading that serious literature requires, we need to continue to teach those very texts that reveal "the problems of the human heart in conflict with itself" and, in such revelation, nudge the reader along the path of wisdom. Film adaptations, as art in themselves and as interpretations, can illuminate serious literature and make criticism and theory more approachable.

Bibliography

Abrams, M. H. *A Glossary of Literary Terms*. New York: Holt, Rinehart and Winston, 1957.

_____. *A Glossary of Literary Terms*. 6th ed. Fort Worth: Harcourt Brace Jovanovich, 1993.

_____. "How to Do Things with Texts." *Partisan Review* (1979). Rpt. in Adams & Searle 436–49.

_____. *The Mirror and the Lamp: Romantic Theory and the Critical Tradition*. 1953. Oxford: Oxford University Press, 1971.

_____, ed. *The Norton Anthology of English Literature*. 3rd ed. Vol. 2. New York: W.W. Norton, 1974.

Adams, Hazard, and Leroy Searle, eds. *Critical Theory Since 1965*. Tallahassee: Florida State University Press, 1986.

Adler, Thomas P. *A Streetcar Named Desire: The Moth and the Lantern*. New York: Twayne, 1990.

Andrew, Dudley. *Concepts in Film Theory*. Oxford: Oxford University Press, 1984.

Armstrong, Nancy. "A Brief Genealogy of 'Theme.'" Sollors 38–45.

Arnavon, Cyrille. "An American *Madame Bovary*." Introduction. *Edna*. Paris, 1953. Trans. Bjorn Braaten and Emily Toth. *The Kate Chopin Miscellany*. Eds. Per Seyersted and Emily Toth. Natchitoches: Northwestern State, 1979. 168–88. Rpt. in Culley 184–88.

Baker, Carlos. "Sensation and Vision in Wordsworth." Introduction. *William Wordsworth's The Prelude*. New York: Rinehard, 1954. Rpt. in *English Romantic Poets*. Ed. M. H. Abrams. New York: Oxford, 1960. 95–109.

Balizet, Ariane M. "Teen Scenes: Recognizing Shakespeare in Teen Film." *Almost Shakespeare: Reinventing His Works for Cinema and Television*. Ed. James R. Keller and Leslie Stratyner. Jefferson, NC: McFarland, 2004.

Baym, Nina, ed. *The Norton Anthology of American Literature*. 6th ed. Vol. C. New York: W.W. Norton, 2003. Vols. A–E.

_____. *The Norton Anthology of American Literature*. 3rd ed. Vol. 2. New York: W.W. Norton, 1989. 2 vols.

Bazin, André. *What is Cinema?* Trans. Hugh Gray. Vol. 1. Berkeley: University of California Press, 1967.

Becker, Brenda L. "Harold Brodkey's 'Darkness'—journal of dying." *Sun* [Baltimore] 20 Oct. 1996: F5.

Beckett, Samuel. *Film*. New York: Grove, 1969.

Bedient, Calvin. "There are Lives that Desire Does Not Sustain: *A Streetcar Named Desire*." Kolin 45–58.

"Behind the Name: The Etymology and History of First Names." 31 Jan. 2009. <http://www.behindthename.com>.

Beja, Morris. *Film and Literature*. New York: Longman, 1979.

Bergman, Ingmar. "Bergman Discusses Film-Making." *Four Screen Plays of Ingmar Bergman.* New York: Simon & Schuster, 1960. Rpt. in Harrington 224–28.

Birkerts, Sven. *The Gutenberg Elegies: The Fate of Reading in an Electronic Age.* New York: Fawcett Columbine, 1994.

Bizzaro, Patrick. *Responding to Student Poems: Applications of Critical Theory.* Urbana: NCTE, 1993.

Bloom, Harold. *The Anxiety of Influence.* 2nd ed. New York: Oxford University Press, 1997.

_____. Introduction. *Kate Chopin.* New York: Chelsea House, 1987. 1–6.

_____. "Poetry, Revisionism, Repression." *Poetry and Repression: Revisionism from Blake to Stevens.* New Haven: Yale, 1976. Rpt. in Adams & Searle 331–43.

_____, ed. *Tennessee Williams's* A Streetcar Named Desire. New York: Chelsea House, 1988.

_____. *The Visionary Company: A Reading of English Romantic Poetry.* 1961. Ithaca: Cornell University Press, 1983.

Bluestone, George. *Novels into Film: The Metamorphosis of Fiction into Cinema.* 1957. Berkeley: University of California, 1971.

Bobo, Jacqueline. *Black Women as Cultural Readers.* New York: Columbia, 1995.

Bordwell, David, and Kristin Thompson. *Film Art: An Introduction.* 1979. 4th ed. New York: McGraw-Hill, 1993.

Bowra, C. M. *The Romantic Imagination.* 1949. New York: Oxford University Press, 1961.

Boyum, Joy Gould. *Double Exposure: Fiction into Film.* New York: New American Library, 1985.

Brann, Eva. "Can the Reading of Literature Make Us Better?" *Maryland Humanities* (Fall 1992).

Brantley, Ben. "Looks It Not Like the King? Well, More Like Burton." *New York Times* 1 Nov. 2007: E1.

Brightwell, Gerri. "Charting the nebula: gender, language and power in Kate Chopin's 'The Awakening.'" *Women and Language* 18.2 (Fall 1995). 4 Mar. 1998 <http://web2 searchbank.com/infotrac>1–8.

Brinker, Menachim. "Theme and Interpretation." Sollors 21–37.

Brooks, Cleanth. *The Well Wrought Urn: Studies in the Structure of Poetry.* 1942. San Diego: Harcourt Brace, 1975.

Brown, John. "The impossible object: Reflections on *The Shining.*" Orr and Nicholson 104–121.

Brown, Thomas. "*Parole*: From Shakespeare to Tennessee Williams." fearelesse-shakespeare.org. 5 Dec. 2007.

Brummett, Barry. *Rhetorical Dimensions of Popular Culture.* Tuscaloosa: Alabama University Press, 1991.

Buchman, Lorne M. *Still in Movement: Shakespeare on Screen.* New York: Viking, 1971.

Cahir, Linda Costanzo. "The Artful Rerouting of *A Streetcar Named Desire.*" *Literature / Film Quarterly* 22.2 (1994): 72–77.

_____. *Literature into Film: Theory and Practical Approaches.* Jefferson, NC: McFarland, 2006.

Cardullo, Bert. "Birth and Death in *A Streetcar Named Desire.*" Kolin 167–80.

Cardwell, Sarah. *Adaptation Revisited: Television and the Classic Novel.* Manchester: Manchester University Press, 2002.

_____. "Adaptation Studies Revisited: Purposes, Perspectives and Inspiration." Welsh and Lev 51–63.

Cartmell, Deborah, and Imelda Whelehan, eds. *Adaptations: From Text to Screen, Screen to Text.* New York: Routledge, 1999.

_____. Introduction. *The Cambridge Companion to Literature on Screen.* Cambridge: Cambridge University Press, 2007. 1–12.

Cather, Willa. "A Creole Bovary." "Books and Magazines." *Pittsburgh Leader* 8 July 1899: 6. Rpt. in Culley 170–72.

Cavell, Stanley. *The World Viewed: Reflections on the Ontology of Film.* Ithaca: Cornell University Press, 1978.

Champion, Dean J. "Learning from the Stars: Do Motion Pictures in the Classroom Make a Difference in Student Performance?" *Journal of Popular Film and Television* 15.1 (Spring 1987): 43–50.

Chatman, Seymour. *Coming to Terms: The Rhetoric of Narrative in Fiction and Film.* Ithaca: Cornell University Press, 1990.

_____. *Story and Discourse: Narrative Structure in Fiction and Film.* Ithaca: Cornell University Press, 1978.

Chopin, Kate. *The Awakening.* Ed. Margo Culley. Norton Critical Editions. 2nd ed. New York: W.W. Norton, 1994.

Christian, Barbara. "Does Theory Play Well in the Classroom?" *Critical Theory and the Teaching of Literature: Politics, Curriculum, Pedagogy.* Eds. James F. Slevin and Art Young. Urbana: NCTE, 1996. 241–57.

Cirlot, J.E. *A Dictionary of Symbols.* Trans. Jack Sage. New York: Philosophical Library, 1962.

Cohen, Keith. *Film and Fiction / The Dynamics of Exchange.* New Haven: Yale University Press, 1979.

Cohen, Leonard. "Who By Fire." *New Skin for the Old Ceremony.* Columbia, 1974.

Coil. "Who By Fire." *Horse Rotorvator.* World Serp, 1986.

Collins, Robert. "The Dismantling of Edna Pontellier: Garment Imagery in Kate Chopin's *The Awakening.*" *Southern Studies* 23 (Summer 1984): 176–90.

Cramer, Timothy R. "Testing the Waters: Contemplating the sea in ED's poem 520 and Kate Chopin's *The Awakening.*" *Dickinson Studies* 88 (June & December 1992): 51–56.

Crowther, Bosley. "Poor Mom: New Films Defile the Image of Mother." *New York Times* 22 April 1961: sec. 2:1.

_____. "Edna Pontellier: 'A Solitary Soul.'" Rpt. in Culley 247–51.

Dawson, Hugh J. "Kate Chopin's *The Awakening*: A Dissenting Opinion." *American Literary Realism* 26.2: 1–18.

Demanski, Laura. "The Culture Wars divide, but they do not conquer." *Sun* [Baltimore] 1 Nov. 1998: "Arts and Society."

Derrida, Jacques. "Structure, Sign and Play in the Discourse of the Human Sciences." 1967. *Writing and Difference.* 1967. Trans. Alan Bass. 1978. Rpt. in Adams & Searle 83–94.

Desmond, John M., and Peter Hawkes. *Adaptation: Studying Film & Literature.* Boston: McGraw Hill, 2006.

Donaldson, Peter S. *Shakespearean Films / Shakespearean Directors.* Boston: Unwin Wyman, 1990.

Dowling, Ellen. "The Derailment of *A Streetcar Named Desire.*" *Literature / Film Quarterly* 9.4 (1981): 233–40.

Dressler, Mylène. "Edna Under the Sun: Throwing Light on the Subject of *The Awakening.*" *Arizona Quarterly* 48.3 (Autumn 1992): 59–75.

Dylan, Bob. "Things Have Changed." *Wonder Boys.* Paramount Pictures, 1999.

Eco, Umberto. *Six Walks in the Fictional Woods.* Cambridge: Harvard University Press, 1994.

Eidsvik, Charles. "Soft Edges: the Art of Literature, the Medium of Film." *Literature / Film Quarterly* 2.1 (Winter 1974): 16–21.

_____. "Toward a '*Politique des Adaptations.*'" 1975. Rpt. in Harrington 27–37.

Eliot, T. S. "Tradition and the Individual Talent." *The Sacred Wood: Essays on Poetry and Criticism.* 1920. London: Methuen, 1964. 47–59.

_____. "The Waste Land." *The Complete Poems and Plays of T. S. Eliot.* 1969. Rpt. in Baym Vol. D. 1430–43. vols. A-E.

Ellis, John. "The Literary Adaptation: An Introduction." *Screen* 23 (May / June 1982): 3–5.

Emerson, Ralph Waldo. "The Over-Soul." *The Norton Anthology of American Literature.* Ed. Nina Baym. 2nd ed. Vol. 1. New York: W.W. Norton, 1979. 910–23. 2 vols.

Emmitt, Helen V. "'Drowned in a Willing Sea' : Freedom and Drowning in Eliot, Chopin, and Drabble." *Tulsa Studies in Women's Literature* 12.2 (Fall 1993): 315–32.

The End of August. Dir. Bob Graham. With Sally Sharp. Sewanee Productions, 1981.

Esslin, Martin. *The Field of Drama: How the Signs of Drama Create Meaning on Stage and Screen.* New York: Methuen, 1987.

Faulkner, William. "Nobel Prize Speech." *The Faulkner Reader.* New York: Random House, 1954.

Fell, John L. *Film: An Introduction.* New York: Praeger, 1975.

Ferguson, Frances. "The 'Immortality Ode.'" *Wordsworth: Language as Counter-Spirit.* New Haven: Yale University Press, 1977. Rpt. in *William Wordsworth.* Modern Critical Views. Ed. Harold Bloom. New York: Chelsea House, 1985. 137–49.

Ferris Bueller's Day Off. Dir. John Hughes. With Matthew Broderick. Paramount Pictures, 1986.

Film Studies. *Catalogue.* Columbia University Press, 2005.

Fish, Stanley. "Is There a Text in This Class?" *Is There a Text in This Class?* Cambridge: Harvard, 1980. Rpt. in Adams & Searle 525–33.

Foote, Horton. "Writing for Film." *Film and Literature: A Comparative Approach to Adaptation.* Eds. Wendell Aycock and Michael Schoenecke. Lubbock: Texas Tech, 1988. 5–20.

Freeman, Mary E. Wilkins. "The Revolt of 'Mother.'" *"A New England Nun" and Other Stories.* Rpt. in Baym 6th ed. Vol. C. 733–43.

Frost, Robert. "The Oven Bird." *The Poetry of Robert Frost.* 1969. Rpt. in Baym 6th ed. Vol. D. 1188.

Friskin, James, and Irwin Freundlich. *Music for the Piano: A Handbook of Concert and Teaching Material from 1580 to 1952.* New York: Dover, 1954.

Geertz, Clifford. "Blurred Genres: The Refiguration of Social Thought." *The American Scholar* 49 (Spring 1980). Rpt. in Adams & Searle 514–23.

Gibbs, Wolcott. "Two Views of the South." *New Yorker* 25 Feb. 1956: 90+. Rpt. in *The Critical Response to Tennessee Williams.* Ed. George W. Crandell. Westport: Greenwood, 1996. 56–58.

Giddings, Robert, Keith Selby, and Chris Wensley. *Screening the Novel: The Theory and Practice of Literary Dramatization.* New York: Macmillan, 990.

Gilbert, Sandra M. "The Second Coming of Aphrodite: Kate Chopin's Fantasy of Desire." *Kenyon Review* 5 (Summer 1983): 42–66. Rpt. in Culley 271–81.

_____, and Susan Gubar. *Masterpiece Theatre: An Academic Melodrama.* New Brunswick: Rutgers, 1995.

Gill, Stephen. *William Wordsworth: A Life.* Oxford: Clarendon, 1989.

Goldstein, Laurence. *The American Poet at the Movies.* Ann Arbor: Michigan University Press, 1994.

Gossman, Lionel. "History and the Study of Literature." *Profession 94.* New York: MLA, 1994. 26–33.

Grand Isle. Dir. Mary Lambert. With Kelly McGillis and Adrian Pasdar. Turner Pictures, 1992.

Grassian, Esther. "Thinking Critically about World Wide Web Resources." 1997. Last Update 4 Jan. 1999. <http://www.library.ucla.edu>.

Groden, Michael, and Martin Kreiswirth. *The Johns Hopkins Guide to Literary Theory &*

Criticism. Baltimore: Johns Hopkins, 1994.

Hanks, Pamela Anne. "Must We Acknowledge What We Mean? The Viewer's Role in Filmed Versions of *A Streetcar Named Desire.*" *Journal of Popular Film and Television* 14 (Fall 1986): 14–22.

Harrington, John, ed. *Film And / As Literature.* Englewood Cliffs: Prentice-Hall, 1977.

Harrison, Stephanie. *Adaptations: From Short Story to Big Screen.* New York: Three Rivers Press, 2005.

Hartley, Dean Wilson. "'How Do We Teach It?': A Primer for the Basic Literature / Film Course." *Literature / Film Quarterly* 2.1 (Winter 1975): 60–69.

Hartman, Geoffrey H. "The Fate of Reading Once More." *PMLA* III.3 (May 1996): 383–89.

_____. "Literary Commentary as Literature." *Criticism in the Wilderness.* New Haven: Yale University Press, 1981. Rpt. in Adams & Searle 345–58.

_____. *The Unremarkable Wordsworth.* London: Methuen, 1987.

Headley, Robert K. *Motion Picture Exhibition in Baltimore.* Jefferson, NC: McFarland, 2006.

Hirsch, David H. Rev. of *The Emperor Redressed: Critiquing Critical Theory.* Ed. Dwight Eddins. *South Atlantic Review* 61.2 (Spring 1996): 150–54.

Hoder-Salmon, Marilyn. *Kate Chopin's* The Awakening: *Screenplay as Interpretation.* Gainesville: Florida University Press, 1992.

Hodgson, John A. *Wordsworth's Philosophical Poetry, 1797–1814.* Lincoln: Nebraska University Press, 1980.

Holditch, Kenneth W. "The Broken World: Romanticism, Realism, Naturalism in *A Streetcar Named Desire.*" Kolin 147–66.

Holland, Norman N. "Meaning as Defense." *The Dynamics of Literary Response.* Oxford: Oxford University Press, 1968. Rpt. in Harrington 336–49.

Hornaday, Ann. "The Method and the motivations." *Sun* [Baltimore] 13 Mar. 1999: E1+.

Horne, William. "*The Pumpkin Eater*: Novel, Screenplay, Film." *Literature / Film Association Conference.* Towson University. Baltimore, 9 Nov. 1996.

_____. "See Shooting Script: Reflections on the Ontology of the Screenplay." *Literature / Film Quarterly* 20.1 (1992): 48–54.

Hovet, Theodore R. *The Master Narrative: Harriet Beecher Stowe's Subversive Story of Master and Slave in* Uncle Tom's Cabin *and* Dred. Lanham: University Press of America, 1989.

Howells, William Dean. "Novel-Writing and Novel-Reading." 1899. *A Selected Edition of W. D. Howells.* Rpt. in Baym 3rd ed. Vol. 1. 266–82.

Hulley, Kathleen. "The Fate of the Symbolic in *A Streetcar Named Desire.*" *Themes in Drama.* Ed. James Redmond. Cambridge: Cambridge University Press, 1982. Rpt. in Bloom, ed. *Tennessee Williams's* A Streetcar Named Desire 111–22.

Hutcheon, Linda. *A Theory of Adaptation.* New York: Routledge, 2006.

Instrell, Rick. "*Blade Runner*: The economic shaping of a film." Rpt. in Orr and Nicholson 160–69.

Izod, John. "Words selling pictures." Rpt. in Orr and Nicholson 95–103.

Jackson, Esther Merle. "The Synthetic Myth." *The Broken World of Tennessee Williams.* Wisconsin, 1965. Rpt. in *Modern Critical Views: Tennessee Williams.* Ed. Harold Bloom. New York: Chelsea House, 1987. 23–42.

Jackson, Shelley. *Patchwork Girl.* Watertown, MA: Eastgate, 1995.

"Jacques Lacan." Introduction. Adams & Searle 733–56.

Jenkins, Greg. *Stanley Kubrick and the Art of Adaptation: Three Novels, Three Films.* Jefferson, NC: McFarland, 1997.

Johnson, Thomas H., ed. *The Complete Poems of Emily Dickinson.* Boston: Little, Brown, 1960.

Joplin, Janis. "Ball and Chain." *Cheap Thrills.* Columbia, 1968.

Kawin, Bruce F. *Faulkner and Film.* New York: Ungar, 1977.

Kazan, Elia. *Elia Kazan: A Life.* New York: Knopf, 1988.

Kleb, William. "Marginalia: *Streetcar*, Williams, and Foucault." Kolin 27–43.

Kolin, Philip C., ed. *Confronting Tennessee Williams's* A Streetcar Named Desire: *Essays in Critical Pluralism.* Westport: Greenwood Press, 1993.

_____. "Eunice Hubbell and the Feminist Thematics of *A Streetcar Named Desire.*" Kolin 105–120.

Koller, Alice. *Believing in Ourselves: A Calendar.* 28 June 2007.

Kranz, David L. "Trying Harder: Probability, Objectivity, and Rationality in Adaptation Studies." Welsh and Lev 77–102.

Krieger, Murray. "An Apology for Poetics." *American Criticism in the Post-Structuralist Age.* Ed. Ira Konigsberg. Ann Arbor: University of Michigan, 1981. Rpt. in Adams & Searle 535–42.

Kucich, John. "Confessions of a Convert: Strategies for Teaching Theory." *Teaching Contemporary Theory to Undergraduates.* Eds. Dianne F. Sadoff and William E. Cain. New York: MLA, 1994. 45–56.

Landow, George P. "What's a Critic to Do?: Critical Theory in the Age of Hypertext." *Hyper / Text / Theory.* Baltimore: Johns Hopkins University Press, 1994. 1–48.

_____. "Twenty minutes into the future, or how are we moving beyond the book?" *The Future of the Book.* Ed. Geoffrey Nunberg. Berkeley: University Press of California, 1996. 209–37.

Landwehr, Margarete Johanna. "Egoyan's Film Adaptation of Banks's *The Sweet Hereafter.*" *Literature / Film Quarterly* 36 (2008): 215–22.

Lant, Kathleen Margaret. "The Siren of Grand Isle: Adèle's Role in *The Awakening.*" *Southern Studies: An Interdisciplinary Journal of the South* 23.2 (Summer 1984). Rpt. in Bloom. *Kate Chopin* 115–24.

Lawrence, D. H. "Odour of Chrysanthemums." *The Complete Short Stories.* Vol. 2. New York: Penguin, 1976. 283–302. 3 vols.

_____. *Studies in Classic American Literature.* 1923. New York: Penguin, 1977.

Leeson, Richard M. *William Inge: A Research and Production Sourcebook.* Westport: Greenwood Press, 1994.

Leitch, Thomas. *Film Adaptation and Its Discontents: From* Gone with the Wind *to* The Passion of Christ. Baltimore: Johns Hopkins University Press, 2007.

Leslie, F. Andrew, adaptor. *Splendor in the Grass.* From the screenplay by William Inge. Dramatists Play Service, 1966.

Lev, Peter. "The Future of Adaptation Studies." Welsh and Lev 335–38.

Liggera, J. J. "'She Would Have Appreciated One's Esteem': Peter Bogdanovich's *Daisy Miller.*" *Literature / Film Quarterly* 9 (1981): 15–21. Rpt. in *Henry James: A Study of the Short Fiction.* Ed. Richard A. Hocks. Boston: Twayne, 1990. 141–17.

Lilla, Mark. "The Politics of Jacques Derrida." *The New York Review of Books* 45:11 (June 25, 1998): 36–41.

Linden, George W. "The Storied World." *Reflections on the Screen.* Rpt. in *Film and Literature: Contrasts in Media.* Ed. Fred H. Marcus. New York: Chandler, 1971. 157–63.

Lloyd, D. Myrddin. "Ode." *The Princeton Encyclopedia of Poetry and Poetics.* Ed. Alex Preminger. Princeton: Princeton University Press, 1974.

Limsky, Drew. "Academic criticism does have a role in real life." *Sun* [Baltimore] 7 July 1996: 1F+.

Lodge, David. *The Practice of Writing.* New York: Penguin, 1996.

Lotman, Yurij. *Semiotics of Cinema.* Trans. Mark E. Suino. Michigan Slavic Contributions No. 5. Ann Arbor: University of Michigan, 1976.

Lynn, Steven. *Texts and Contexts: Writing about Literature with Critical Theory.* 2nd ed. New York: Longman, 1998.

Macksey, Richard. Foreword. Groden and Kreiswirth. v–viii.

Magnuson, Paul. *Coleridge and Wordsworth: A Lyrical Dialogue.* Princeton: Princeton University Press, 1988.

Marcus, Millicent. *Filmmaking by the Book: Italian Cinema and Literary Adaptation.* Baltimore: Johns Hopkins University Press, 1993.

Mast, Gerald. "Literature and Film." *Interrelations of Literature.* Eds. Jean-Pierre Barricelli and Joseph Gibaldi. New York: MLA, 1982. 278–306.

Mayne, Judith. "Dracula in the twilight: Murnau's *Nosferatu* (1922)." Rentschler 25–39.

McClure, Arthur F. *Memories of Splendor: The Midwestern World of William Inge.* Topeka: Kansas State Historical Society, 1989.

McCraw, Harry W. "Tennessee Williams, film, music, Alex North: an interview with Luigi Zaninelli." *The Mississippi Quarterly* 48.4 (Fall 1995): 763–76. <http://sbweb3.med.iac net.com/infotrac/session/908/606/9168492w3/8!xm_18&bkm_8>.

McFarlane, Brian. *Novel to Film: An Introduction to the Theory of Adaptation.* Oxford: Clarendon, 1996.

McGann, Jerome J. *The Beauty of Inflections: Literary Investigations in Historical Method and Theory.* Oxford: Clarendon, 1985.

McGhee, Richard. *Guilty Pleasures: William Wordsworth's Poetry of Psychoanalysis.* Troy: Whitston, 1993.

Mellard, James M. "Lacan and the New Lacanians: Josephine Hart's *Damage*, Lacanian Tragedy, and the Ethics of *Jouissance*." *PMLA* 113.3 (May 1998): 395–407.

Melville, Herman. *Moby-Dick or, The Whale.* New York: Penguin, 1992.

Merriam Webster's Encyclopedia of Literature. Ed. Kathleen Kuiper. Springfield: Merriam-Webster, 1995.

Metz, Walter. "Signifying Nothing?: Martin Ritt's *The Sound and the Fury* (1959): A Deconstructive Adaptation." *Literature / Film Quarterly* 27.1 (1999): 21–31.

Miller, J. Hillis. "The Critic as Host." *Deconstruction and Criticism.* New York: Seabury Press, 1979. Rpt. in Adams & Searle 452–68.

Miller, Laura. "www.claptrap.com." *New York Times Book Review* 15 Mar. 1998: 43.

Mitchell, Joni. "Marcie." *Song to a Seagull.* Warner, 1968.

Monaco, James. *How to Read a Film.* New York: Oxford University Press, 1977.

Moses, Gavriel. *The Nickel Was for the Movies.* Berkeley: University of California, 1995.

Mulvey, Laura. "Visual Pleasure and Narrative Cinema." *Screen* 16 (1975): 6–18.

Murfin, Ross C. "What Is Psychoanalytic Criticism?" Nancy Walker 218–33.

Murray, Janet H. *Hamlet on the Holodeck: The Future of Narrative in Cyberspace.* New York: Free Press, 1997.

Murray, Simone. "Materializing Adaptation Theory: The Adaptation Industry." *Literature / Film Quarterly* 36.1 (2008): 4–20.

Naremore, James, ed. *Film Adaptation.* London: Athlone Press, 2000.

Newton, K. M. *Interpreting the Text: A Critical Introduction to the Theory and Practice of Literary Interpretation.* New York: St. Martin's, 1990.

_____. *Twentieth-Century Literary Theory: A Reader.* New York: St. Martin's, 1988.

"Origin of the Song ["Who By Fire"]. <http://www.guitaretab.com/c/cohen-leonard/3767. html>. 2 Sept. 2007.

Orr, Christopher. "The Discourse on Adaptation." *Wide Angle* 6.2 (1984): 72–76.

Orr, John. "Introduction: Proust, the movie." Orr and Nicholson 1–9.

_____, and Colin Nicholson, eds. *Cinema and Fiction: New Modes of Adapting, 1950–1990.*
    Edinburgh: Edinburgh University Press, 1992.
The Oxford English Dictionary. Eds. J.A. Simpson and E.S.C. Weiner. 20 vols. Oxford:
    Clarendon Press, 1989.
Pagan, Nicholas O. *Rethinking Literary Biography: A Postmodern Approach to Tennessee
    Williams.* Rutherford: Fairleigh Dickinson University Press, 1993.
Paul, Christiane. *Unreal City: A hypertext guide to T.S. Eliot's "The Waste Land."* Water-
    town, MA: Eastgate, 1995.
Pauly, Thomas H. *An American Odyssey: Elia Kazan and American Culture.* Philadelphia:
    Temple University Press, 1983.
Pease, Donald E. "Bloom, Harold." Groden and Kreiswirth 94–97.
Perkins, David. "Literary Histories and the Themes of Literature." Sollors 109–120.
Phillips, Gene D., S. J. *The Films of Tennessee Williams.* Philadelphia: Art Alliance Press,
    1980.
_____. "*A Streetcar Named Desire*: Play and Film." Kolin 223–39.
Platizky, Roger. "Chopin's 'The Awakening.'" *The Explicator* 53.2 (Winter 1995): 99–102.
Pollard, Percival. "The Unlikely Awakening of a Married Woman." *Their Day in Court.*
    New York: Neale Publishing, 1909. Rpt. in Culley 179–81.
Pound, Ezra. *ABC of Reading.* 1934. New York: New Directions, 1960.
Presley, Elvis. "Hound Dog." *Elvis' Golden Records.* RCA, 1997.
Prince, Gerald. "Narratology." Groden and Kreiswirth 524–28.
Quirino, Leonard. "The Cards Indicate a Voyage on *A Streetcar Named Desire.*" *Tennessee
    Williams: A Tribute.* Ed. Jac Tharpe. Jackson: University Press of Mississippi, 1977.
    Rpt. in Bloom. *Tennessee Williams's* A Streetcar Named Desire. 61–77.
Ramsey, Jonathan. "Context for Teaching the Immortality Ode." *Approaches to Teaching
    Wordsworth's Poetry.* Ed. Spencer Hall. New York: MLA, 1986. 96–99.
Ray, Robert B. "The Field of 'Literature and Film.'" Naremore 38–53.
Rentschler, Eric, ed. *German Film and Literature.* New York: Methuen, 1986.
_____. "Introduction: Theoretical and historical considerations." Rentschler 1–8.
Reynolds, Christopher. "Southern comfort level." *Sun* [Baltimore] 15 Aug. 1999: 1R+.
Richards, I.A. *Principles of Literary Criticism.* New York: Harcourt, Brace, 1925.
Richardson, Robert. *Literature and Film.* Bloomington: Indiana University Press, 1969.
Robertson, Robbie. "The narrative sources of Ridley Scott's *Alien.*" Orr and Nicholson
    171–79.
Rowe, John Carlos. "The Economics of the Body in Kate Chopin's *The Awakening.*" *Per-
    spectives on Kate Chopin: Proceedings from the Kate Chopin International Conference.*
    Natchitoches: Northwestern State University Press, 1990. Rpt. in *Kate Chopin Recon-
    sidered: Beyond the Bayou.* Eds. Lynda S. Boren and Sara de Saussure Davis. Baton Rouge:
    Louisiana State University Press, 1992. 117–42.
Said, Edward W. "The Problem of Textuality: Two Exemplary Positions." *Critical Inquiry*
    4 (1978): 673–714. Rpt. in Newton *Twentieth-Century Literary Theory: A Reader.* 165–
    70.
Salvesen, Christopher. *The Landscape of Memory.* Lincoln: Nebraska University Press, 1965.
Schlueter, June. "Imitating an Icon: John Erman's Remake of Tennessee Williams's *A
    Streetcar Named Desire.*" *Modern Drama* 28 (1985): 139–47.
_____. "'We've had this date with each other from the beginning': Reading toward Clo-
    sure in *A Streetcar Named Desire.*" Kolin 71–81.
Schickel, Richard, dir. *Elia Kazan: A Director's Journey.* Nar. Eli Wallach. Videocassette.
    First Run Features, 1995.
Schvey, Henry I. "Madonna at the Poker Night: Pictorial Elements in Tennessee Williams's
    A Streetcar Named Desire." *Costerus: From Cooper to Philip Roth: Essays on American*

Literature 26. Ed. J. Bakker and D.R.M. Wilkinson. Amsterdam: Editions Rodopi, 1980. Rpt. in Bloom. *Tennessee Williams's* A Streetcar Named Desire. 103–09.

Seger, Linda. *The Art of Adaptation: Turning Fact and Fiction into Film.* New York: Henry Holt, 1992.

Shakespeare, William. "Smilet." *The Sonnets.* New York: Signet, 1999.

Shapiro, Stephanie. "Poets embrace multimedia form." *Sun* [Baltimore] 21 June 1999: 1E+.

Shklovsky, Victor. "Art as Technique." *Russian Formalist Criticism: Four Essays.* Trans. and eds. Lee T. Lemon and Marion J. Reis. Lincoln: University of Nebraska Press, 1965. 5–22. Rpt. in Newton *Twentieth-Century Literary Theory: A Reader.* 23–25.

Showalter, Elaine. *Sister's Choice: Tradition and Change in American Women's Writing.* Oxford: Clarendon, 1991.

Shuman, R. Baird. *William Inge.* New York: Twayne, 1965.

The Simpsons. "*A Streetcar Named Desire*: The Musical." Comedy Channel: Comcast TV.

Sinyard, Neil. *Filming Literature: The Art of Screen Adaptation.* New York: St. Martin's, 1986.

Sitterson, Joseph C., Jr. "The Genre and the Place of the Intimations Ode." *PMLA* 101.1 (Jan. 1986): 24–37.

Skaggs, Peggy. "Three Tragic Figures in Kate Chopin's *The Awakening.*" *Louisiana Studies* (Winter 1974): 345–64.

Skube, Michael. "Ode to hegemony, rearticulation." *Sun* [Baltimore] 21 Mar. 1999: 6C.

Sleeper. Dir. Woody Allen. With Woody Allen and Diane Keaton. United Artists, 1973.

The Snake Pit. Dir. Anatole Litvak. With Olivia de Havilland. Twentieth Century–Fox, 1948.

Sollors, Werner, ed. and intro. *The Return of Thematic Criticism.* Cambridge: Harvard University Press, 1993.

Spaceballs. Dir. Mel Brooks. With Rick Moranis. Brooksfilms, 1987.

Splendor in the Grass. Dir. Elia Kazan. With Natalie Wood and Warren Beatty. Warner Brothers, 1961.

Stam, Robert. "Beyond Fidelity: The Dialogics of Adaptation." Naremore 54–76.

_____. *Literature through Film: Realism, Magic, and the Art of Adaptation.* Malden, MA: Blackwell, 2005.

_____. *Reflexivity in Film and Literature from Don Quixote to Jean-Luc Godard.* New York: Columbia University Press, 1992.

_____, and Alessandra Raengo, eds. *Literature and Film: A Guide to the Theory and Practice of Film Adaptation.* Malden, MA: Blackwell, 2005.

Steiner, George. "Roncevaux." Sollors 299–300.

A Streetcar Named Desire. Dir. Elia Kazan. With Marlon Brando and Vivien Leigh. Warner Brothers, 1951.

Suddenly Last Summer. Dir. Joseph L. Mankiewicz. With Elizabeth Taylor. Columbia, 1959.

Sullivan, Ruth, and Stewart Smith. "Narrative Stance in Kate Chopin's *The Awakening.*" *Studies in American Fiction* 1 (1973): 62–75. Rpt. in Culley 227–30.

The Taming of the Shrew. Dir. Franco Zeffirelli. With Elizabeth Taylor and Richard Burton. Columbia, 1967.

Thomas, Francis-Noel, and Mark Turner. *Clear and Simple as the Truth: Writing Classic Prose.* Princeton: Princeton University Press, 1994.

Thompson, Howard. "Inge's Kansas through a Kazan kaleidoscope." *New York Times* 22 May 1960: sec. 2:7.

Thoreau, Henry David. Walden *and* Civil Disobedience. Ed. Owen Thomas. Norton Critical Editions. New York: Norton, 1966. 1–221.

Thornton, Big Mama. "Ball and Chain." 1977. *Justin Time Records*, 2003.
_____. "Hound Dog." *Peacock*, 1992.
Trilling, Lionel. "The Immortality Ode." *The English Institute Annual, 1941*. New York: Columbia University Press, 1942. Rpt. in Trilling, *The Liberal Imagination: Essays on Literature and Society*. New York: Scribner's, 1950. 129–59.
Truffaut, François. "A Certain Tendency of the French Cinema." *Movies and Methods*, ed. Bill Nichols. Vol. 1. Berkeley: University of California Press, 1976. 224–37.
Tyson, Lois. *Critical Theory Today: A User-Friendly Guide*. 2nd ed. New York: Routledge, 2006.
Vendler, Helen. "Lionel Trilling and the *Immortality Ode*." *Salmagundi* 41 (1978): 66–86.
Vlasopolos, Anca. "Authorizing History: Victimization in *A Streetcar Named Desire*." *Theatre Journal* 38 (October 1986): 322–38.
Voss, Ralph F. *A Life of William Inge: The Strains of Triumph*. Lawrence: Kansas University Press, 1989.
Wagner, Geoffrey. *The Novel and the Cinema*. Rutherford: Fairleigh Dickinson, 1975.
Walker, Alice. "Nineteen Fifty-Five." *Ms.* 9 (March 1981).
Walker, Nancy A., ed. *Kate Chopin, The Awakening*. Boston: Bedford Books, 1993. 19–137.
Wells, Paul. "'Thou Art Translated': Analysing animated adaptation." Cartmell and Whelehan 199–213.
Welsh, James M. "Classic Folly: *The Scarlet Letter*." *Literature / Film Quarterly* 23.4 (1995): 299–300.
_____, and Peter Lev. *The Literature/Film Reader: Issues of Adaptation*. Lanham, MD: Scarecrow Press, 2007.
_____, and John Tibbetts, eds. *The Cinema of Tony Richardson: Essays and Interviews*. Albany: SUNY Press, 1999.
Whitman, Walt. "Out of the Cradle Endlessly Rocking." Baym Vol. C. 102–06.
_____. "When Lilacs Last in the Dooryard Bloom'd." Baym Vol. C. 116–22.
Williams, Tennessee. *Cat on a Hot Tin Roof*. New York: Signet, 1955.
_____. *A Streetcar Named Desire*. 1947. New York: New American Library, 1974.
Wimsatt, W.K., Jr. *The Verbal Icon: Studies in the Meaning of Poetry*. 1954. Lexington: University Press of Kentucky, 1982.
Winchell, Mark Royden. "The Myth Is the Message, or Why *Streetcar* Keeps Running." Kolin 133–45.
Wolff, Cynthia Griffin. "Thanatos and Eros: Kate Chopin's *The Awakening*." *American Quarterly* 25 (October 1973): 449–71. Rpt. in Nancy Walker 233–58.
_____. "Un-utterable Longing: The Discourse of Feminine Sexuality in *The Awakening*." *Studies in American Fiction* 24.1 (Spring 1996): 3–23.
Wordsworth, Jonathan. *The Prelude: 1799, 1805, 1850*. Eds. M.H. Abrams and Stephen Gill. Norton Critical Editions. New York: W.W. Norton, 1979.
Yacowar, Maurice. *Tennessee Williams and Film*. New York: Frederick Ungar, 1977.
Zaehner, R. C. *Mysticism: Sacred and Profane*. 1957. Oxford: Oxford University Press, 1971.
Zettl, Herbert. *Sight Sound Motion: Applied Media Aesthetics*. 2nd ed. Belmont: Wadsworth, 1990.
Zholkovsky, Alexander. "Beyond 'Form vs. Theme.'" Sollors 297–98.

Index